ENVISIONING
CAHOKIA

RINITA A. DALAN

GEORGE R. HOLLEY

WILLIAM I. WOODS

HAROLD W. WATTERS, JR.

JOHN A. KOEPKE

ENVISIONING

CAHOKIA

A LANDSCAPE PERSPECTIVE

NORTHERN

ILLINOIS

UNIVERSITY

PRESS

DEKALB

© 2003 by Northern Illinois University Press

Published by the Northern Illinois University Press,

DeKalb, Illinois   60115

Manufactured in the United States of America

using acid-free paper

Design by Julia Fauci

Dedicated to the memory of

V. Anita Dalan

(1936–1998)

Library of Congress Cataloging-in-Publication Data

Envisioning Cahokia : a landscape perspective /

Rinita A. Dalan ... [et al.].

   p.   cm.

Includes bibliographical references and index.

ISBN 0-87580-302-4 (alk. paper) (cloth)

ISBN 0-87580-594-9 (alk. paper) (pbk.)

1. Cahokia Mounds State Historic Park (Ill.)

2. Mississippian culture. 3. Human

ecology—Illinois—Cahokia Mounds State Historic Park.

I. Dalan, Rinita A.

E99.M6815 E59 2003

977.3'89—dc21

2002026316

Cover images: (top) J. A. Koepke's depiction of Cahokia, courtesy of the Goodhue County Historical Society, Red Wing, Minnesota, (bottom) E. G. Squier's *Great Mound of Cahokia, Illinois* (1860), (back) Birger figurine courtesy of the Illinois Transportation Archaeological Research Program, University of Illinois.

Frontispiece: J. A. Koepke's reconstruction of the building of Monks Mound.

CONTENTS

ILLUSTRATIONS

ACKNOWLEDGMENTS

To the countless individuals—field school students, collaborators, and those who offered funding, administrative, logistical, and personal support—whose efforts made possible our work at Cahokia we are deeply indebted. For inspiration we would like to acknowledge Melvin L. Fowler, who has always stressed that Cahokia should not be interpreted as simply a big Mississippian site. William R. Iseminger of the Cahokia Mounds State Historic Site is living testimony to the knowledge that can accrue in one individual about a place. We also wish to thank Ken Kolson, deputy director, Division of Research Programs, National Endowment for the Humanities (NEH), for his ardent support of our efforts to relate the Cahokia experience in terms that most readers could understand.

Funding for this project was provided by a grant from NEH with additional funds provided by the Southern Illinois University Edwardsville (SIUE), the Cahokia Mounds Museum Society, and an Illinois Board of Higher Education 1999 state matching grant. We would like to express our gratitude to the reviewers of our NEH proposal, Wendy Ashmore, James Stoltman, and William Doolittle, for the positive and encouraging comments that helped to get this project off the ground. The opinions, findings, and conclusions expressed in this book are those of the authors and do not necessarily reflect the views of the National Endowment of the Humanities.

We also wish to acknowledge the support of the National Endowment for the Arts for Professor Koepke's research on "Historic Contributions of Native Americans to the Art of Landscape Architecture," and the Graduate School Fund of the University of Washington for support of his research at the Cahokia site.

Assistance in acquiring photographs and maps was generously provided by Melvin L. Fowler and W. R. Iseminger. We also wish to thank the staff of the Madison County Historical Society for helping us to navigate through their documentary collection relating to Cahokia and for making available the wonderful nineteenth-century painting of the Cahokia Mounds that appears as figure 1 in this book.

Technical support in computer-generated graphics was provided by Andrew Martignoni Jr. and Mary Claire Goodwin of the Office of Contract Archaeology and the Department of Geography at SIUE. Andrew Martignoni Jr. was instrumental in preparing final graphics. Josephine Barnes and Steven Hansen of the Office of Research and Projects, SIUE Graduate School, were helpful in smoothing out the bumps encountered during grant tenure. Dale Schaefer of the Office of Contract Archaeology deserves our sincere thanks for keeping the paperwork flowing. Minnesota State University Moorhead provided a supportive environment from which to effect the publication of this project.

We would like to extend our heartfelt appreciation to our two technical editors, Chris Carlson and Ellen Proctor, who performed their thankless jobs with patience and skill. Our manuscript was greatly improved by their efforts. We would also like to thank Mark Mehrer and an anonymous reviewer for their detailed reading of an earlier version of the manuscript and for their insightful and helpful suggestions. Finally, we would like to thank Martin Johnson and Northern Illinois University Press for their enthusiasm and guidance in providing a forum for our ideas about the fascinating site of Cahokia.

ENVISIONING
CAHOKIA

INTRODUCTION

The American bottom is a tract of rich alluvion [*sic*] land, extending on the Mississippi, from the Kaskaskia to the Cahokia river, about eighty miles in length, and five in breadth; several handsome streams meander through it; the soil of the richest kind, and but little subject to the effects of the Mississippi floods. A number of lakes are interspersed through it, with high and fine banks; these abound in fish, and in the autumn are visited by millions of wild fowl. There is, perhaps, no spot in the western country, capable of being more highly cultivated, or of giving support to a more numerous population than this valley. If any vestige of ancient population were to be found, this would be the place to search for it—accordingly, this tract . . . exhibits proofs of an immense population. If the city of Philadelphia and its environs were deserted, there would not be more numerous traces of human existence. The great number of mounds, and the astonishing quantity of human bones . . . with a thousand other appearances, announce that this valley was at one period, filled with habitations and villages.

Such are the remarks of Henry Marie Brackenridge, writing of his travels in the area in 1811 (Brackenridge 1814, 186). His curiosity aroused by local tales of mounds just across the Mississippi River from St. Louis (Hammes 1981, 146), Brackenridge crossed the American Bottom and proceeded to comment on the "largest assemblage" of mounds within this tract of land— what we now call the Cahokia Mounds State Historic Site. Today we know this to be the largest grouping of man-made earthen mounds in North America. His first observations are of the largest mound at the site, which he estimates to be 90 feet high and at least 800 yards in circumference (Brackenridge 1814, 187–88).

When I reached the foot of the principal mound, I was struck with a degree of astonishment, not unlike that which is experienced in contemplating the Egyptian pyramids. What a stupendous pile of earth! To heap up such a mass must have required years, and the labors of thousands. . . . Were it not for the regularity and design which it manifests, the circumstances of its being on alluvial ground, and the other mounds scattered around it, we could scarcely believe it the work of human hands.

Brackenridge then turns his attention to other mounds surrounding the principal mound and seen on the distant bluff, as well as to ubiquitous "small elevations of earth" and "pieces of flint, and fragments of earthen vessels" (Brackenridge 1814, 188). His conclusions as to the significance of

4

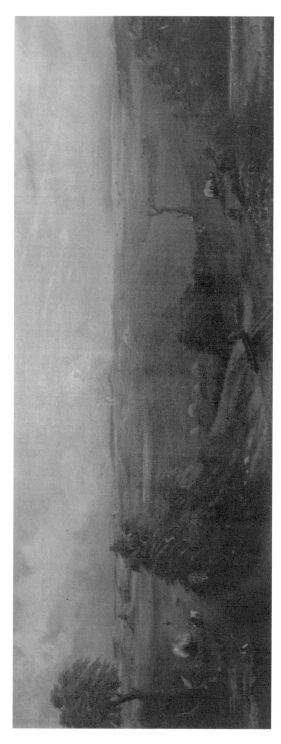

1. The romantic notions of landscape are presented in this idealized panoramic view of the American Bottom and Cahokia. Unsigned oil painting (1846–1850?). Courtesy of the Madison County Historical Society (Illinois).

these remains run to the immensity of the community that produced them, both in terms of population and in terms of the greatness and power of their leaders (Brackenridge 1814, 188).

For the nearly two centuries since Brackenridge penned this first analytical account of Cahokia, this constellation of more than one hundred mounds has inspired comment by those who have visited it (Fowler 1997). During the first half of the nineteenth century, the American interior was the focus of intense international interest, explored by thousands of travelers. Visits to Cahokia by a series of explorers, scientists, authors, and artists resulted in a series of descriptions, sketches, and maps spanning the nineteenth century (e.g., figs. 1 and 2). The most detailed examinations of the landscape ever conducted in North America were produced during this time. In a region that was notably stingy with picturesque sites and exotica, mounds were a compelling feature (Dunlop 1995).

As American settlers penetrated the interior of the continent over the course of the eighteenth and into the nineteenth century, they encountered constructed earthen features at seemingly every turn. Though many of these features were cloaked in vegetation, the process of clearing the land revealed their form and ubiquity. These vestiges of the past were primarily mounds of various types, but also included the low-relief effigies in the north country and large geometric enclosures in Ohio.

Despite sixteenth-century accounts of aboriginal mound construction in the Southeast, many scholars were unable or unwilling to accept the Native American origins of these earthworks. Instead, elaborate tales were concocted of an ancient race of Mound Builders who were exterminated or driven from North America. Speculations as to the geographic origin of this "lost race" abounded: Greece, Rome, Phoenicia, Wales, and Scandinavia, among others, were all considered reasonable candidates, as were connections to the ten lost tribes of Israel and the submerged continent of Atlantis (Silverberg 1968).

Unfortunately, extensive arguments and debates over the origin of the mounds diminished appreciation of this paramount center of the Mississippian period (ca. A.D. 1000–1400). The raging debates over who could have built the mounds at Cahokia included elements common to the Mound Builders myth (Silverberg 1968). Themes of nineteenth-century essays on Monks Mound and others evoked the exotic stone monuments of both the Old and New Worlds, such as the pyramids of Egypt and Central American temples, often presuming cultural links between them and the "Moundbuilders."

The *Twelfth Annual Report* of the Bureau of Ethnology (1891), devoted exclusively to a report on mound explorations written by Cyrus Thomas, seemingly laid to rest the various manifestations of the Mound Builders myth. Yet, as late as 1903, the Reverend Henry Mason Baum (1903, 222) felt compelled to write in relation to mounds in general, and Cahokia in particular: "In considering the great earth-works of North America we must dismiss, as unworthy of consideration, the statement made by some writers, that a certain number of men carrying a certain number of cubic feet of earth each

2. *Trappists Hill opposite St. Louis,* a pencil-and-ink drawing by Karl Bodmer from the 1830s, is a more realistic rendering of the landscape. Courtesy of the Joslyn Art Museum, Omaha, Nebraska; gift of Enron Art Foundation.

day would be able to build one of the great earth-works in a given number of days. Of course they could. But who has ever known or heard of a tribe of Indians who did or ever had the least inclination to do so?"

Whether the earthen mounds at Cahokia could be ascribed a cultural origin at all was the subject of a more fundamental debate (e.g., Peck 1837). This was especially prevalent in discussions of Monks Mound, the principal mound at the site, likely owing to its immensity (there is no other earthen monument in the United States that is comparable in size or stature) and to the lingering effects of the Mound Builders esthetic. For some scholars, particularly geologists, the reality of Monks Mound as a creation of Native Americans continued to nag them. A substantial contingent could not only "scarcely believe," as did Brackenridge, that the mounds were the work of humans; they were not able to believe so at all. From the mid-nineteenth century, several eminent geologists (e.g., Crook 1916; Fenneman 1911; Worthen 1866) took up this argument, maintaining that the mounds were erosional remnants. Worthen writes: "We infer that these mounds were not artificial elevations, raised by the aboriginal inhabitants of the country, as has been assumed by antiquaries generally, but, on the contrary, they are simply outliers of loess and drift, that have remained as originally deposited, while the surrounding contemporaneous strata were swept away by denuding forces" (1866, 314).

An alternate conception, maintained by Fenneman and others (e.g., Snyder 1917, 259) with respect to Monks Mound, was that it was originally an erosional outlier of the bluff formation that had subsequently been molded into its present geometric proportions by human hands. In fact, the summit elevation of this mound at 519 feet is rather close to the average elevation of the nearby bluffs at 550 feet. It was not until the 1920s that the extensive archaeological excavations of Warren K. Moorehead provided unshakable evidence that the mounds were entirely of human origin, which paved the way for an ensuing period of modern archaeological investigations of the Cahokia site and surrounding region.

Taken together with earlier representations and writings, our account will show less about physical changes in the character of the land over the time of observation than about how the perception of Cahokia has changed—how it has been seen and experienced through the years by those who have come into contact with it. Our observations are different from those who have preceded us and from those who will come after, and we are egocentric enough to believe that these observations should be widely shared, not only with those interested in Cahokia, but also with those more generally concerned with landscape studies. Like our predecessors, we are driven to leave a record of what we have observed at Cahokia, to make sense of this grouping of mounds. This is the essence of landscape. Based on over fifty collective years of research at the site, this volume is the result of a maturing of both our work and our viewpoints in tandem with theoretical and methodological progress within our respective disciplines. Landscape is a vehicle through which we can integrate both these developments.

Although our observations and interpretations of the Cahokia site are unique, they are informed by those who have preceded us and, we hope, will be informative to others as well. An important component of our presentation is a dialogue between ourselves and those who saw the site at different times and with different eyes. The early accounts can obviously be used to trace physical changes in the land that have occurred over time; they serve as a source for data that may now be lost or at least not immediately apparent by purely visual inspection. Above all, these varied accounts serve as a source for introspection into how the Cahokia landscape is perceived and the features that are seen to define it. Not only the narrative sections, but also the visual representations, provide clues to changing conceptualizations of the Cahokia landscape.

In a recent book on the prehistory of North America, Kennedy (1994) refers appropriately to Cahokia as a "hidden city." Despite its status as a National Register of Historic Places property and a UNESCO World Heritage Site, the site, amazingly, still largely rests in obscurity. This seems to be a pernicious and long-standing problem. The Cahokia site was largely missed (or ignored) by seventeenth- and eighteenth-century travelers on the Mississippi (Fowler 1997; Skele 1988). By the eighteenth century, the area was well settled, and the mounds were undoubtedly known and understood by locals as a unique place relating to Native American use of the area, but written descriptions are almost nonexistent. The French even had a mission on the principal mound at the site between 1735 and 1752. The first known, albeit brief, written reference concerning the mounds was penned by John

3. This early (1904) photograph, "The Cahokia Temple Mound—Showing its Entire Length, 1080 feet," shows Monks Mound as an undifferentiated part of the rural landscape. Courtesy of the Madison County Historical Society (Illinois).

Messinger, a land surveyor, in the field notes for the U.S. Government Public Lands Survey in 1808 (Messinger 1808, 76). This obscure reference was hardly a source for wide distribution and impact.

Brackenridge's visit to the site in 1811 and the newspaper articles and book recounting his observations (Brackenridge 1814) constitute the first detailed descriptions of Monks Mound and the Cahokia site in general and were the first sources that provided opportunity for a widespread appreciation of the mounds; however, they did not receive the attention that he had anticipated. Two years later, in a letter written to Thomas Jefferson (Brackenridge 1818), he expressed his astonishment that the mounds had gone so long unnoticed and, furthermore, that his published descriptions of them in St. Louis newspapers (including his first published account in the January 9 edition of the *Missouri Gazette*) had failed to arouse much interest.

In view of Dunlop's (1995) comments on the dichotomy between travelers' and settlers' appreciation of and interest in the moundscape, this is understandable. Many of the travelers of the nineteenth century commented on the indifference of locals to these earthworks and to their wholesale destruction. Early settlers certainly knew about Cahokia and other mound groups in the area but, with few notable exceptions (such as the Ramey family), the moundscape was given no more special handling than any other landform (fig. 3). At least one of the mounds at Cahokia was even prospected for oil. In 1838, Edmund Flagg predicted that the St. Louis inhab-

itants were so busy that in a few years the mounds would be gone (Flagg 1838, 155). Greville Chester (quoted in Dunlop 1995, 82–83) observed so much alteration of the mounds in St. Louis that he concluded that American taste was "not yet sufficiently educated to disapprove such vandalism." Interestingly, these travelers differentiated their search for relics from settlers' activities that disturbed prehistoric remains.

From time to time, interest in the Cahokia site reaches a higher pitch. For instance, at the beginning of the twentieth century, both popular and scholarly interest was mounting. A number of proposals were forwarded (Baum 1903, 222; Smith 1902, 203) for the scientific study of the prehistoric remains at Cahokia and elsewhere in the Mississippi Valley in conjunction with the Louisiana Purchase Exposition held in St. Louis in 1904. Though these plans were not realized, the Cahokia site was a regular stop on the Interurban Line that ran out of St. Louis (fig. 4), and scores of visitors to the fair came to see the site, many taking souvenirs of earth or artifacts as mementos. The site was visited by many American archaeologists as well as scholars from various parts of the world. E. O. Randall, secretary of the Ohio State Archaeological Society, and his party made one such trip during the fair. Wm. C. Mills, curator and librarian of the Ohio State Archaeological and Historical Society, became interested in the mounds during the World's Fair and visited the site several times, bringing with him "representatives from various parts of the world" and, on one occasion, "a party of scientists numbering more than forty" (Madison County 1913).

4. Cahokia, particularly Monks Mound, became a regular stop on the Interurban Line. A. Cover of an East St. Louis & Suburban Railway Company excursion booklet. B. Postcard showing Monks Mound and the gate at which the excursionists disembarked. Courtesy of the Madison County Historical Society (Illinois).

Even after the 1904 World's Fair, visitors to the mounds continued to use the interurban electric lines as a convenient way to travel to the mounds. The interurban line ran for several miles along the Madison–St. Clair County line, which cuts through the center of the Cahokia site. Three stops were described within the Cahokia mound group (Pustmueller 1950, 48–54).

Another period of heightened interest in the prehistoric remains at Cahokia arose in the 1920s, when the central area was designated as a state park as a result of extensive archaeological excavations (Moorehead 1929). Over most of its modern history, however, the site can be labeled a well-kept secret at best.

The reason for this is puzzling. Is it just the result of timing—missed as it was by the first explorers, languishing in obscurity until a time when its impact would be ameliorated by commonplace knowledge of North American mound centers and prevailing Mound Builders myths? Perhaps the arguments over the origin of the mounds precluded full appreciation of the significance of these remains. Lacking details of pageantry and gods, sacrifice and gold, were the first glimpses the public had of the site too devoid of interpretive detail? Dunlop (1995, 85) maintains that nineteenth-century travelers wanted portable items of artistic value made not of stone but of gold, silver, and ivory, and that they were only marginally interested in the landscape of the mounds. Is it simply that piles of earth are never as impressive as cut stones of the Mayan ruins or the great pyramids? Certainly, Brackenridge did not think so and neither do we. Yet Brackenridge's lament that no one reacted to his observations rings true today.

Whatever the cause, those of us who have recorded our experiences at and interpretations of the Cahokia site have failed to precipitate a long-standing familiarity with and knowledge of this paramount mound center. We have failed to sustain both public and academic interest with engaging, yet factual, accounts of the workings of Cahokia society. In walking the tightrope between billing Cahokia as something exceptional and even unique versus a place containing the common threads of the broader Native American experience, we have failed to demonstrate either convincingly. We have also been biased in our understanding of Cahokia by documentary sources and archaeological excavations of small-scale towns of the Mississippian period. The eyewitness accounts of Native Americans in the eastern United States were of societies and towns quite different from the Cahokia of the past, and we need to move away from these in our efforts to understand the site.

The Cahokia Mounds Interpretive Center currently promotes the site as the "City of the Sun" in efforts to encapsulate, with a phrase, the greatness of this past civilization. To capture the public's interest and imagination, this is probably as necessary as touting Sheboygan, Wisconsin, as the "Bratwurst Capital of the World" or Taunton, Massachusetts, as the "Largest City for Its Size" (Tuan 1972, 41). Inspiration for this name probably derives from comments made by William McAdams that appeared in an early history of Madison County, Illinois (1882). McAdams believed that Cahokia was "the Mecca, or grand sacred shrine of the mound builder's empire" and that on the summit of Monks Mound were their adoratories, "glittering with barbaric splendor, and from whence could be seen from afar the smoke and flames of the eternal fire, their emblem of the sun" (McAdams 1882, 61).

Communicating Cahokia's importance has always been a challenge. The key to success is building a context for the site, together with its effective interpretation. The number of visitors to the Cahokia Mounds State Historic

5. Oblique aerial photograph from the 1940s of Monks Mound viewed from the south-west. Monks Mound, preserved within the original park, was the site of the first mu-seum, built in the 1930s, which can be seen near the southwestern corner of the base of the mound. Courtesy of the Cahokia Mounds State Historic Site.

Site increased markedly after the grand opening of a 33,000-square-foot inter-pretive museum in 1989. For 1990, records indicate that 358,000 people vis-ited the new Interpretive Center and show a total site attendance of 503,000. At the old (ca. 3,000-square-foot) museum facility, approximately 80,000 vis-ited annually (fig. 5). Total site attendance has currently stabilized at over 336,000. Though most visitors come from Illinois and Missouri, in 1996 visi-tors from seventy-eight foreign countries signed the museum's guest book (statistics provided by Paul Nixon, Cahokia Mounds State Historic Site).

The success of the new Interpretive Center shows that a strong demand exists for interpretation and showcasing of this resource. The impact of the new displays is certainly powerful, and the visitation records indicate that knowledge of the site is growing both regionally and beyond. The number of visitors, however, must be balanced against a continued lack of public knowledge and understanding of the Cahokia site.

Among the local population, monumental Monks Mound, the principal mound at the site, is easily confused with a monument of modern civiliza-tion, the Milan Landfill, a large, mound-shaped feature also located along the U.S. Interstate 70 artery a few miles distant (McGuire 1996). In academic circles the Cahokia site may be better known, but not by much. This may be partially due to its behemoth nature and a perceived uncertainty as to how such a unique site relates either to other Mississippian period centers or to broader perspectives. For the most part, the archaeological community does not have the information that it needs to place the Cahokia site in context. There exists a large collection of "gray literature," detailing many of the most interesting aspects of the site, that is not widely available, and, despite a lengthy history of professional work at the site (Fowler 1997), synthetic studies are lacking. Several recent volumes do exist (e.g., Barker and Pauketat 1992; Emerson 1997; Emerson and Lewis 1991; Pauketat 1994; Pauketat and Emerson 1997; Stoltman 1991); however, these provide either broader perspectives or focus on single issues about the site. There remains a lack of volume-length, holistic considerations of the cultural dynamics at Cahokia. We maintain that a landscape approach can be used to synthesize our knowledge about the Cahokia site and to provide a robust account of how a people interacted with the environment at a critical point in human history.

The aims and goals of the present volume are broader, however, than just providing a current reading of the Cahokia landscape. Our use of the landscape concept as a vehicle to synthesize research at the site has led us on a lengthy exploration of the development and use of this term within western European thought and within various academic traditions including archaeology, geography, history, and landscape architecture. We have been struck by the broad applicability of the landscape concept and its current resurgence in archaeology, geography, and other disciplines. Abstracts of the Society for American Archaeology annual meetings illustrate this trend. In the mid-1980s (1984 annual meeting), when we began to do work at the site, there were two abstracts listed whose titles used the word "landscape." A decade later (1994 annual meeting), the number of abstracts incorporating "landscape" into their titles had increased to seven. In 1996, eighteen titles of papers read at the meeting included the word "landscape," and in 1998 this number had swelled to fifty-one.

Despite the currency of the term in academia, we find that its use, especially in archaeology, is often unexamined. Landscape is more of a buzzword than a concept that is actively debated and placed securely within both an approach (methodology) and a disciplinary framework. Within the discipline of geography, there exists a much deeper literature concerned with the meaning of this concept. As will be discussed in chapter 1, there are myriad definitions of landscape. In archaeology, landscape is variously used to consider and to interpret the physical environment, land use systems or settlement patterns, cultural economies, sacred sites, formation processes, Geographic Information Systems (GIS) data sets, and conceptual systems.

Our exploration of the landscape concept has led us to consider its historical foundations and how these intersect with disciplinary goals. We also consider how this conceptual basis relates to the various definitions and current usages. As archaeologists, we have been especially concerned that our

definition of landscape explicitly recognizes the relationship between landscape and culture, another ambiguous, but critical, concept. We have also
tried to be explicit about how we made the transition from concept to approach. We consider various critical issues that arose in developing our landscape approach for application to the Cahokia data. These concerns resonate
with those being raised in various disciplines and are related not only to
how we interpret our data, using this concept, but how we then convey this
information. Inasmuch as Cahokia provides a context for developing our
landscape approach, we also use it as a basis for evaluating our efforts and
for considering the applicability of our approach for archaeological research
in general.

Examination of the history of the landscape concept illustrates the inter-
relatedness of landscape and representation. It is from the landscape painters
of the Renaissance that the contemporary Western concept of landscape
arose (Cosgrove 1984, 1985; Relph 1981). Close relationships between the
particular way that landscape is conceptualized and represented remain. Historically, these relationships have followed several trends, some of which we
find quite limiting in terms of our conception of the term. Hence, we also
consider new ways of presenting our interpretation to ensure that the visual
segment of our volume effectively captures and conveys the very essence of
our landscape experience.

There has been a proliferation of landscape studies in historic archaeological settings in recent years (Rubertone 1989). In these, the archaeological
data are compared with historical records to substantiate or illuminate social
or symbolic trends noted in these records (e.g., Leone 1984; Mrozowski and
Beaudry 1989). For prehistoric applications, landscape studies have been almost overwhelmingly concerned with physical, rather than cognitive, interpretations (for an exception, see Bender 1992). Cahokia flourished prior to
the written record, but it obviously has inspired people since its inception,
both as an idea that led to its creation and as a physical manifestation. During its heyday, Cahokia was not a hidden city but a burgeoning metropolis
with ties and influence across the Eastern Woodlands of North America. We
wanted to incorporate the impact of this monumental creation into our interpretation and to understand how it was achieved.

To a large extent, inspiration for this book derived from the work of one
of the pioneer interpreters of American cultural landscapes, J. B. Jackson
(Lewis 1983; Meinig 1979b). His influence on us has been not so much for
his definitions or redefinitions of the concept of landscape (Jackson 1984),
but for how he wrote and thought about landscape. His efforts in transcend-
ing the human/environment relationship in the biological sense to look at
various social and sensory relationships have provided many ideas that we
have incorporated into our research at Cahokia. As Ervin Zube (1970) so
aptly says in his foreword to *Landscapes: Selected Writings of J. B. Jackson,* Jackson's focus has been on "the landscape that man is a part of, not apart
from—the humanized landscape."

At the heart of our landscape approach at Cahokia lies a desire to document the relationship that the Mississippians had with the land. Brackenridge grasped the extraordinary richness of the American Bottom and the opportunities it provided. But this is only part of the story. We want to explore more than relationships of settlement and subsistence. To use a term put forth by Bender (1992), we are concerned with the way the Cahokians *engaged* with the physical world.

In his novel *A Way in the World*, V. S. Naipaul (1995), a writer of fiction and nonfiction, comments on the lack of physical sensation, and therefore the lack of landscape, in early Spanish accounts of the Caribbean. His thoughts about this "narrower way of seeing and feeling" spark in us thoughts regarding the sometimes sterile archaeological approach to the past that avoids landscape by positing people interacting in a purely social world. What we are attempting to explore at Cahokia is the interrelationship of society and land in a fuller sense, one that relates more closely to culture in all its richness and glory. This book is concerned with the extent to which we can approach this objective by using the landscape concept.

Our first stop on this journey is a consideration of the term "landscape." In chapter 1, we "unpack" the landscape concept, considering its historical, conceptual, and definitional bases and their implications for archaeological study. We look in particular at landscape representation and, as part of this, at the varied ways in which the Cahokia site has been depicted. This issue is an important one to us because it relates to the ways in which the Cahokia landscape has been perceived, interpreted, and communicated. In chapter 2, we take these dissected threads and weave them into an approach to be used on the Cahokia data. Our interpretation of the Cahokia landscape is presented in parts 2 and 3, chapters 3–11, and an evaluation of our efforts and consideration of implications follows in the conclusion.

PART ONE

LANDSCAPE

AND

CULTURE

CHAPTER ONE

THE
LANDSCAPE
CONCEPT

Landscape is a particularly "slippery" term (Stilgoe 1982) that has eluded any definition by consensus. Within the discipline of geography, where the term is central, definitions have been so diverse that some feel there is a need to define it precisely whenever it is employed (Hart 1995). Others believe the looseness of the term is an asset that renders it relevant to a wide variety of research emphases and perspectives (Rowntree 1996). Despite such ambiguity, landscape remains an attractive and important concept (Meinig 1979a, 1). The following list presents some of the more widely embraced definitions.

- The physical framework within which human societies exist (Roberts 1987)
- Human-made space or collection of space (Jackson 1995)
- Land shaped by humans, land modified for permanent human occupation, such as dwelling, agriculture, manufacturing, government, worship, and pleasure (Stilgoe 1982)
- Landscape = habitat + humans (Fairbrother 1972)
- Nature seen at a certain distance (Lash 1995)
- The segment of earth space that lies between the viewer's eye and his or her horizon (Salter 1978)
- Everything that I see and sense when I am out-of-doors (Relph 1981)
- Landscape not merely as the world we see but as a construction, a composition of that world (Cosgrove 1984)
- A mode of human communication, a medium within which social values are actively debated and symbolically realized (Wagner 1972, 43–61)
- A signifying system through which a social system is communicated, reproduced, experienced, and explored (Duncan 1990, 17)

Note the divergence between subjective and objective definitions. Certain definitions explicitly acknowledge perception and subjectivity. For example, Cosgrove (1984) defines landscape as a way of seeing the world. Other more "pictorial" definitions include Salter's (1978) and Lash's (1995). In contrast, some definitions, such as Roberts's (1987), posit landscape as a more objective phenomenon. In its more "scientific" usage, landscape is a physical phenomenon that can be objectively studied—as either space or a material record of creation and use by humans. According to Stilgoe (1982), landscape is land shaped by humans, not due to chance but to contrivance, premeditation, design.

There are also certain noteworthy commonalities among these definitions of landscape. All of these definitions implicitly allow for a multiscalar nature of landscape. For example, Salter's (1978) definition of landscape (the segment of earth space between the viewer's eye and his or her horizon) implies that the scale of the landscape will change with the visual intent and physical location of the viewer. Many definitions, such as those of Fairbrother and Wagner, include the concept of dynamism. According to Fairbrother (1972), landscape is not a static background that we inhabit, but the interaction of a society with the habitat in which it lives. If either people or the habitat changes, then so, inevitably, must the resulting landscape. Wagner (1972) states that landscape is a medium within which social values are actively debated and symbolically realized. Finally, all definitions of landscape implicate humans—whether humans create landscape through the act of viewing or experiencing (Relph 1981) or consciously shape it (Jackson 1995; Stilgoe 1982); or whether landscape is a setting or framework for humans (Roberts 1987) or an interactive medium within which society is contested (Duncan 1990).

In contrast to geography, significantly less concern with a common, or at least an explicit, definition of landscape exists within archaeological circles. Though "landscape" is an increasingly popular term, diverse uses seem to be accepted. When definitions appear, they run a gamut of meanings similar to those presented above, with perhaps more emphasis on the artifactual nature or the cultural content of landscape. For example, Deetz (1990) defines landscape as the total terrestrial context in which an archaeological study is pursued. He distinguishes a cultural landscape as that part of the terrain that is modified according to a set of cultural plans, the largest and most pervasive artifact with which archaeologists must deal. Savulis (1992) defines landscape as a dynamic cultural artifact. Shapiro and Miller (1990) define landscape as the dynamic record (i.e., artifact) of interactions between people and the environment.

In contrast to geography with its impressive history of landscape studies, archaeology has only recently embraced landscape as a central working concept. However, an interest in what many geographers would recognize as landscape has been a part of the discipline for a long time. Only in recent decades, however, has an explicit articulation of this interest coalesced. The following story illustrates this shift.

As part of my graduate work at the University of Minnesota, I (Rinita Dalan) arranged a directed readings course in geography with Dr. Fred E. Lukermann to explore the concept of landscape and its use in both geography and archaeology. Dr. Lukermann assigned several readings, including Robert J. Braidwood's *Mounds in the Plain of Antioch: An Archaeological Survey* (1937) and Robert J. Braidwood and Linda S. Braidwood's *Excavations in the Plain of Antioch* (1960). At first I was nonplused. Why were these readings assigned? Were we not supposed to be talking about landscape? We discussed particulars of these investigations and then moved on to what I considered more pertinent sources such as William Norton's *Explorations in the Under-*

standing of Landscape (1989) and *Landscape and Culture,* edited by J. M. Wagstaff (1987). It was only much later, after reading and discussing many other sources, that the light turned on. What was obvious to the geographer but not to me, the archaeologist, was that the Braidwoods *were* studying the landscape, at least in a sense commonly recognized in geography. They were recording the distribution of a diverse range of features over a broad area of the land and attempting to understand these remains in terms of time, environmental change, and other factors affecting the choice of townsites.

Landscape traditions in archaeology are closely tied to those in geography. The first explicit landscape approach in archaeology appeared in the cultural ecology school developed by Karl W. Butzer in the late 1970s and early 1980s (Butzer 1978, 1982). Butzer, a geographer, was concerned with the dynamic interplay between culture and environment. Landscape was the term he used to encompass the interaction (or by-product) of humans with habitat. He applied a systems approach to analyze the dynamic interactions between societies and their environments (divided into multivariate phenomena such as flora, fauna, geomorphology, climatology, and others). This cultural ecology paradigm was very much in line with the traditional morphologic approach derived from Sauer (1925). Like Sauer (Rowntree 1996), Butzer defined the relationship between culture and the environment narrowly as one of land use, that is, settlement and subsistence.

Butzer's paradigm resonated within archaeological circles and has carried forward to the present. A recent example is the work of Rossignol, Wandsnider, and others (Rossignol and Wandsnider 1992). Their approach maintains a regional focus and emphasizes explicit considerations of geology and ecology in interpreting spatial aspects of human land use strategies.

Rossignol and Wandsnider contrast their landscape approach with that of "landscape archaeology," a school they characterize as having an explicitly historical and contextual emphasis that does not incorporate ecological and geological system variables. They cite Deetz (1990), Roberts, a geographer (1987), and Crumley and Marquardt (1990) as representatives of this school.

There is a current polarization in archaeology between those that use a concept of landscape with an explicit environmental emphasis focused mainly on questions of settlement and subsistence, and those that focus on social and symbolic aspects of landscape, that is, those that conceptualize landscape solely as physical entity and those that recognize the role of human perception in the creation of landscape. These latter studies necessarily incorporate different concepts of how landscapes are defined, perceived, and studied. Returning again to our barometer of the Society for American Archaeology annual meeting abstracts, we see not only a growing representation of landscape studies in the papers presented, but also a growing proportion of those that focus on culture and landscape. In 1985, the two landscape papers were both concerned with questions of land use. In 1994, four of the seven landscape papers emphasized land use. The remaining three were concerned with sacred and symbolic aspects of landscapes. In

1996, nine out of eighteen landscape papers focused on aspects other than those of subsistence and settlement relationship. In 1998, two entire symposia were explicitly focused on the role of culture and perception in relation to landscape.

Both landscape camps give at least a partial nod to geographers for their developmental roots. Landscape studies in geography have experienced similar polarizations. One of the most famous examples of this division is Hartshorne's questioning (1939) of Sauer's landscape agenda (*Morphology of Landscape* [1925]) because of its subjective implications. Postwar developments in North American geography resurrected and further solidified these tensions by giving birth to two distinct epistemological approaches to landscape. One focused on data quantification within the framework of logical positivism (landscape as material culture), the other applied more historical and interpretive methods (Rowntree 1996). It is to this more humanistic connotation of landscape that the recent resurgence of interest in the term is ascribed.

LANDSCAPE AS REPRESENTATION

The elusiveness of the definition of landscape and the perceived contrast between various landscape camps have been ascribed to dichotomous roots and to the ambiguity of meaning inherent in them (Butlin 1993; Rowntree 1996). These roots can be traced to Anglo-Saxon and German terms denoting an identifiable tract of land *(landschaft),* and to a pictorial concept of landscape derived from western European landscape painters.

How a landscape is represented is linked to how it is conceptualized. This holds not only for the development of the landscape concept, but also for archaeological depictions of Cahokia. How a landscape is conceptualized affects what aspects of the physical world are considered important. This is the cultural filtering of the world meant by "landscape as text" (Walton 1996). For us, a historical perspective of landscape representation opened our eyes to various ways of looking and allowed us to rethink the relationship between landscape and people in a more explicit way as we applied the landscape concept at Cahokia. A historical examination of landscape art also provided a framework for us to analyze representations of Cahokia. We summarize here developments both in western European landscape art and in landscape representation at Cahokia and follow up with conclusions that we have drawn about the need for a more humanistic interpretation and depiction of the landscape at Cahokia.

From the fifteenth to the late nineteenth century throughout western Europe, the concept of landscape denoted the artistic and literary representation of the visible world—the scenery as viewed by a spectator (Cosgrove 1984, 1985; Relph 1981). Cosgrove (1984, 1985) discusses at length the material foundations of this concept and how a particular way of seeing and representing developed in conjunction with the transition from feudalism to capitalism. Howett (1990), King (1990), and others provide information on scientific, social, economic, and technical developments during this period that is useful in an understanding of the evolution of the landscape concept.

Landscape painting first emerged in Flanders and northern Italy in the fifteenth century. It flourished in the Dutch and Italian schools of the seventeenth century and in the French and English schools of the eighteenth and nineteenth centuries. In the early sixteenth century, the term "landscape" was first used to refer to specific painted scenes (Cosgrove 1985). Use of the term successively broadened to include the pictorial representation of the scene, the painting, and the view itself. By the middle of the eighteenth century the term had gained wide currency and was used by artists, poets, gardeners, and gentlemen to refer to landscape in general as well as to a particular landscape scene (Relph 1981).

This shift accompanied a more general trend throughout western Europe toward increasingly accurate, formal, and detached representation in landscape painting. The development of linear perspective during the Italian Renaissance was a particularly critical component in this evolution (Richardson 1980). Presaged by both the medieval study of optics and by the increasing realism *(il vero)* demonstrated by artists like Cimabue and Giotto, linear perspective revolutionized spatial perceptions throughout the West. It was regarded as the discovery of the inherent properties of space itself. Founded on Euclidean geometry, the orderliness of the system, with its completely unified space, had as much, or perhaps more, appeal than its realistic effects (Richardson 1980, 151).

In Renaissance developments also lie the roots of the "privileging of vision" apparent in contemporary Western culture (Howett 1990; King 1990). The sensibility implied by landscape representation, that is, a particular way of experiencing the external world, was closely connected to a growing dependency on sight as the medium through which truth was obtained. From the late thirteenth to the late fifteenth century, the word "vision" became used not only in a mystical or mental sense (e.g., "a vision") but to refer to the act of seeing with the bodily eye (King 1990). Linear perspective (and, by implication, geometry) was regarded as a system that revealed visual truth. Vision and perspective made geometry a fundamental tool in the realist representation of space and the external world (Cosgrove 1985).

Prior to the development of linear perspective, views (or prospects) were generally symbolic and often served as imaginary backgrounds to religious pictures. By the first half of the sixteenth century, however, subject matter became secular rather than mythical or religious—what was once "background" scenery became the dominant feature of a picture. In these representations, a particular scene was not conveyed completely or accurately. Nor was landscape detached from the events taking place. Landscape was the setting or context for events and thus provided a fusion of human activities with the natural world (Relph 1981, 24).

Preperspective urban landscapes also did not convey accurate scenes of towns. The impression gathered by a pedestrian walking down the streets and seeing buildings from many different sides was the goal of the representation—a sensory, rather than an intellectual, measure. How it felt to be in them was the focus (Rees 1980). However, over time landscape art moved away from human content to more detached accurate representation.

These trends in landscape art—the role of landscape as setting and the lessening of the observer's sensory experience—mirror a broader shift in Western thought during this time. Subjective, rational man was becoming separated from objective, material nature. Nature was to be observed, studied, and classified through a "methodical, but scrupulously disinterested, process of human inquiry" (Howett 1990). Clarence Glacken (1967) outlines this shift in attitude toward environment and of the Europeans' place in it. He calls attention to the increased emphasis on the individual in the modern period, first as microcosm of the natural order and increasingly as its controller; the decline of theology as the source of explanation of the features of the natural world; and a developing assurance among Europeans of their ability to transform and improve a nature that could be manipulated.

Landscapes manifesting this detachment first appeared in early-seventeenth-century Dutch paintings. (Cosgrove [1985] points out the ties between Dutch expertise in optics at this time and this great school of landscape art.) These paintings were not "filled with mythological or imaginary trimmings" (Relph 1981, 25–26), nor were they merely generalized settings. "They were topographically accurate, depicting typical and often recognizable scenes in which people and events had become incidental" (Relph 1981, 26).

Other significant developments in the concept of landscape occur in eighteenth-century England (Barrell 1972). By this time the word "landscape" had achieved wide currency and was generally used to mean inland rural scenery. In contrast, the Dutch landscape painters initially used linear perspective to represent the spaces of the city (Cosgrove 1985). Eighteenth-century British landscape art also stressed the visual composition and formal qualities of a view. Being a careful and accurate observer of the landscape was still important, but the landscape could also be reconfigured to achieve a more pleasing composition (Relph 1981, 29–35).

During the nineteenth century this pictorial concept of landscape was questioned on a number of fronts. The detached, mechanical idea of landscape was challenged by the romantic notion that landscapes had a spiritual force that could be understood by those who were sensitive to it (Relph 1981, 35–41). Landscape representation based on linear perspective was also challenged by painters who believed that the abstract, impersonal character of scientific perspective was too mechanical and too confining (Richardson 1980). Consequently, they explored new ways of representing the complexities of vision. Today there is renewed interest by radical contemporary artists to find new ways of representing the landscape (Cutts et al. 1987).

It is against the backdrop of this evolution in art and the heyday of travel writing about the American interior (Dunlop 1995) that the first representations

6. The central area of Cahokia viewed from the east through the perspective of the romantic landscape tradition. Drawing by J. C. Wild (1841).

7. Monks Mound, serving as the sole attraction for most artists, is ornamented with the sign of the times, in this case the emphasis on industrial technology as expressed in the train and trailing smoke. Drawing entitled *Great Mound of Cahokia, Illinois* by E. G. Squier (1860).

of Cahokia appear. The J. C. Wild drawing of 1841 (fig. 6), a view of the central area of Cahokia that includes Monks Mound as well as several other prominent mounds, is typical of the English romantic landscape tradition. It is a formal pastoral scene of ancient ruins contemplated by Wild and a companion (the human figures who appear in the drawing). Their view looks to the west across the site, yet Wild bends the rules of perspective to show more mounds than would actually have been observable from this viewpoint. The scene is also vertically exaggerated. Trees and even some buildings are added to enhance reality. Finally, two cows complete the idyllic, bucolic scene. The addition of cultural details, however, did not extend to showing the site as it might have been during the prehistoric occupation. This is partly due to stylistic dictates, but can also be ascribed to the confusion reigning at the time over who built the mounds. Such confusion may have curtailed the reconstruction of the past. Several other nineteenth-century drawings appear stylistically quite similar to the Wild drawing (Fowler 1997; Skele 1988). One, printed in a late-nineteenth-century *Harper's Weekly* (fig. 7), even included a passing train to emphasize commerce and industry over the pastoral character of the rural scene.

Drawings of Cahokia by the artist Karl Bodmer (fig. 8; see also fig. 2) likewise date from this period. They were completed as part of an expedition led by Prince Maximilian de Wied to the upper Missouri River area. Though they still emphasize the rural, pastoral character of the scene (one of the views includes a cow), they are quite different from Wild's and other early drawings. They clearly presage the changes to come in representations of Cahokia in the late nineteenth and twentieth centuries. All the Bodmer drawings are perspectives, but they are more faithfully and precisely executed. All are bare, almost photographic, in tone. Even modern cultural detail is sparse and muted. However, they represent the area much more accurately in what its vegetation and land use would have been when seen from a single perspective. Like Wild's and the drawings of others, they provide enough detail to inform, yet leave out much of the detail provided in written descriptions. Overall, the early-nineteenth-century drawings of Cahokia are stylistically and conceptually quite similar to the landscape art of this period. Within the general trends noted in the evolution of landscape representation, they appear during the transformation from more romantic, pastoral views to those in which the viewer is removed, both emotionally and physically, from the scene.

The challenges to landscape representation that occurred in the nineteenth century coincided with an intellectual division of the arts and sciences. The landscape tradition did not maintain a prominent position in the arts. Rather, the concept was adopted by academia, and it became an important area of concern to geographers, historians, landscape architects, and others. The emergence of geography as a distinct intellectual discipline that used the concept of landscape extensively and the development of landscape architecture as a distinct profession coincides with the decline of landscape as a preeminent concept in art (Cosgrove, 1984, 26).

8. Karl Bodmer's drawing, showing unidentified mounds at the Cahokia site, is representative of a more realistic portrayal. *Prehistoric Indian Mounds opposite St. Louis,* pencil-and-
ink drawing from the 1830s. Courtesy of the Joslyn Art Museum, Omaha, Nebraska; gift
of Enron Art Foundation.

This shift in interest can be seen clearly in representations of Cahokia
from this time. There is a move away from "artistic" views of the site to the
more "scientific" views presaged by Bodmer. Documentation of real space
and scale becomes more and more important, and bird's-eye perspectives replace single-perspective views in order to capture the immensity of the remains, to illustrate interrelationships among site features, and to document
geometric patterns.

In the 1870s, Dr. J. J. R. Patrick commissioned the first detailed map of the
locations and forms of the mounds (fig. 9). The survey, known as the Patrick
Map, was done by the county surveyor F. G. Hilgard and serves as the first in
a long line of cartographic representations of Cahokia (Fowler 1997). It is
also the first bird's-eye representation of the site.

Maps and sketches were later augmented by aerial photographs. The first
aerial photographs made of an archaeological site in North America were
taken at Cahokia in 1922 by U.S. Army Air Service pilots. The poor quality of
these initial photos (Rowe 1953, 907–8) was addressed quickly by a series of
very clear low obliques taken at the site by Lieutenants G. W. Goddard and
H. K. Ramey of the Army Air Service the same year (Crook 1922) (fig. 10).

In 1933 the first vertical aerial photographs were taken by Colonel Dache
Reeves of the Army Air Service (Fowler 1977, 68; Reeves 1936). The Cahokia
photos were received with great interest as early examples of aerial photography used in archaeology. They extended the use of the bird's-eye perspective

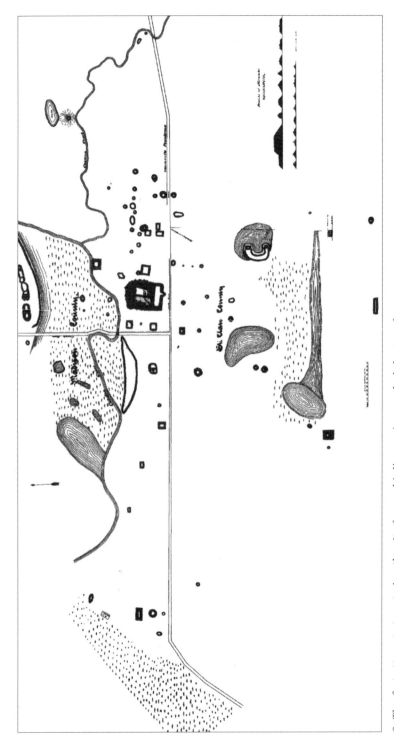

9. The first attempt at capturing the site from a bird's-eye view marked the transformation from an impressionistic to an analytical perspective. Reconstruction of the 1876 Patrick Map. Photographic negatives supplied by Melvin Fowler and the University of Wisconsin-Milwaukee Archaeological Research Laboratory

10. Advances in archaeological techniques continued to cement the notion that the view from above was the "enlightened" perspective. Oblique aerial photograph taken from the east of the Cahokia Mounds site in 1922 by Lt. George W. Goddard. Courtesy of the Illinois State Museum. Photographic negative supplied by Melvin Fowler and the University of Wisconsin-Milwaukee Archaeological Research Laboratory.

initiated by Patrick and cemented the idea that landscape features and site organization should be viewed and evaluated from above rather than from ground level.

Modern archaeological investigations at Cahokia began in the 1920s with the work of Warren King Moorehead (Moorehead 1929) as part of efforts to promote the preservation of the area as a state park. His maps, drawings, and photographs constitute the first representations by a professional archaeologist who had a working knowledge of the site. Moorehead, however, did not put a lot of effort into mapping and relied heavily on sketches of the Patrick Map. Representations in Moorehead's reports focus more on depicting archaeological study and involvement. They include a series of photos showing work in progress—from horse-drawn cuts through mounds to workers involved in various situations (fig. 11). Photographs of artifacts as well as sketch maps of excavation results are also common.

Although there has been a gradual move away from using work photos in archaeological reports to emphasize plans, profile maps, artifact drawings,

11. The first systematic archaeological investigations at the site focused on the mounds. A work photograph from Moorehead's 1927 investigations at Mound 66 (Harding Mound, now known as Rattlesnake Mound), looking east, shows a horse-drawn cut and profile. Courtesy of the Cahokia Mounds State Historic Site.

interpretational maps, and the like, most archaeological representation maintains Moorehead's tradition. A detailed map of the entire Cahokia site was prepared in the mid-1960s by using photogrammetry (Fowler 1997). This map established the Cahokia master grid on the landscape (a grid system set up by James Porter in the early 1960s, which has been used to integrate all subsequent archaeological research at the site) and continued the trend toward increased precision and accuracy by using applied technology. Since then, smaller areas within the site have been mapped and detailed. A logical next step in the use of such technology will be to apply GIS (Geographic Information Systems) to the whole site and its surroundings.

Another innovation in twentieth-century representation is the schematic map (e.g., Morgan 1980). These maps use a generalized bird's-eye perspective that shows only the horizontal location and form of the various mounds. Though they give the appearance of distilling a site down to its very essence, these maps are often marred by glaring errors and lack the detail and complexity that is in a very real sense the essence of a site. Schematic maps are often used as the basis for another form of representation that also has its roots in the twentieth century—the reconstructive drawing. A reconstructive drawing tries to illustrate a site as it was at a specific period in time. Its purpose is to inform, rather than to clothe a site in the splendor of the past. Use of the bird's-eye perspective is often the primary graphic technique used to capture the scale or breadth of the remains and to convey an impression of a burgeoning civilization. Reconstructive drawings are largely generated by trained artists who use previously generated maps and take advantage of previously accumulated knowledge. The interpretive museum at Cahokia currently houses a series of reconstructive paintings as a central feature of its exhibit. The drawings provide a visual interpretation of what the site may have been like, in order to evoke a public response and to augment the archaeological maps that have become prevalent. In keeping with this tradition, a reconstructive drawing of Cahokia was prepared by John Koepke that is now on display at the Goodhue County Museum in Red Wing, Minnesota (fig. 12).

Many positive and helpful consequences have come from archaeological representations of Cahokia over the nineteenth century. For example, the numbering system for the mounds provided by Patrick in the 1870s remains in use. Aerial photographs taken early in the twentieth century provide excellent evidence of soil patterns that indicate important subsurface features such as a palisade that once enclosed the central portion of the site (Fowler 1977). Along with the early maps, the representations also provide critical detail about features now lost to modern development.

Yet, we can also recognize a trend toward the representation of increasingly precise, but impersonal and culturally sterile, views of the Cahokia landscape that perhaps is not entirely beneficial. As an extension of the *pianta prospettiva* (bird's-eye view) of cities, which was popular at the turn of the sixteenth century, aerial photography (remote sensing) has become the primary technique in archaeology and geography for capturing visual truth. It is now the principal way in which we represent Cahokia. Even the terminology, *remote* sensing, captures the essence of this detachment. Subsequently, it has removed the landscape from ground level and a human perspective, where people actually move through, feel, and experience the landscape.

A notably minor component of twentieth-century representations of Cahokia is ground-level depictions or photographs of the site. For the most part, they do not provide views that relate to people actually using space. Not only has such detachment led us further away from a more human view of Cahokia, but also the claim to precision in such representations has not led to an actual increase in accuracy. Schematic maps, for instance, lack detail. On the Patrick Map, large areas distant from Monks Mound were not surveyed with the same care as areas within the Central Precinct and are almost sketches. The reconstructive drawings magnify errors made in base materials (maps) and filter out critical details, such as the time dimension.

Even though the aerial perspective appears to capture the site in its entirety and to clarify spatial alignments and patterns, it is notoriously bare of details. The overall focus, as in nineteenth-century representations, is usually the mounds. The largest of these, Monks Mound, continues to serve as a constant frame of reference. In essence, twentieth-century views of Cahokia are "visual tables," recording the location and estimated heights of mounds and only cursorily noting environmental context and other cultural features. Thus, mounds have become surveying points, synonymous with monuments. We continue to recognize and record them, yet, although informed by recent scholarship, we fail to include other features such as large open

12. Attempts to capture the essence of Cahokia combine the current state of knowledge with a bird's-eye view. Pen-and-ink and watercolor depiction entitled *Cahokia, Ancient North American City, ca. A.D. 800–1200* by J. A. Koepke. Courtesy of the Goodhue County Historical Society, Red Wing, Minnesota.

borrow pits (pits from which earth was "borrowed" to build the mounds) or causeways that appear to link mounds at the site. Only one causeway was recorded on the Patrick Map. Yet, we know from work at the site that these shared features—causeways and platforms (Fowler 1997; Holley et al. 1990, 1992, 1995, 1996)—as well as shallow depressions indicating refilled borrows adjacent to mounds are common and found extensively (Holley et al. 1992, 1993, 1996; Dalan 1993b). There are also numerous small mounds, noted as undulations of the surface in nineteenth-century textual accounts, that are perhaps now largely lost due to centuries of plowing and modern cultural activities. All of these unrecorded features point to a complexity of the record that is missing from modern representations.

Twentieth-century representations of Cahokia also deliberately exclude modern cultural features. Only major roads or channelized canals are included to orient the viewer. The intention here may be related to a struggle within the factual school between showing the site as it existed at the time of depiction and showing the site as it may have existed before the "contamination" of the historic record and the "decay" of time.

One is faced with a further conundrum in the reconstructive drawings. Even though there has clearly been an effort to exclude modern-day cultural features, there is every intent to show everything else as it exists today. This, together with detail gained from scholarly knowledge, is conflated into one time period. For example, the drawings always show all the mounds, despite the knowledge that they were not all built at one time. And we know that even at the time of Cahokia's florescence, the decline in mound construction and maintenance had already begun; yet this knowledge is not reflected in these reconstructions. In other words, the reconstructive drawings minimize the ontogeny of the site as a place that has an accumulated history of varied use and weathering. They present the Cahokian world as unchanging.

Finally, the purpose of the reconstructive drawings is to give people a feel for what Cahokia would have looked like during occupation and to, perhaps, provide a necessary first step in this visualization process. However, they do not convey the perspective nor the details one would have experienced had one been present on site at the time. The remote bird's-eye view also minimizes cultural content. Its purpose is to illustrate the layout of the landscape. People are employed largely as scalars, owners, or referents, in much the same way that cows were inserted into early-nineteenth-century representations.

Representations of Cahokia eradicate emotions, passions, and feelings in order to focus on accuracy and detail. A marked decline in the inclusion of work photos in archeological reports removed from the scene the very professionals who interpreted and viewed it. The trend has been to minimize our personal and archaeological involvement, not presenting our view gained from on-the-ground efforts, and often not employing information gained from our work below the surface of the ground. The focus of our work is cultural dynamics, and yet we continue to produce static, conflating views of Cahokia.

As useful as topographic maps, aerial photographs, plan views, and the like are as part of a landscape package in providing an overall picture of and possible insights into systematic and geometric patterns in the spatial ordering of an area, one should always keep in mind that map space is quite different from ground space. Maps by definition employ a number of conventions in portraying three-dimensional space on a two-dimensional plane, i.e., they are scaled, generalized representations (Monmonier 1991), abstractions wherein geographic data are processed via operations such as classification and simplification in order to make them more comprehensible (Robinson et al. 1984). At a site as large as Cahokia, what may be perceived on maps or other aerial views as apparently planned relationships may prove to be less reasonable on the ground. For example, ground-level obstructions such as trees and mounds can be symbolized on maps or delineated on aerial photos, but their impact on those who move through the land can easily be overlooked. Similarly, a person's position in relation to the landscape also changes the character of the observation; around the base of Monks Mound its sheer mass blocks the view of virtually anything on any side of it, whereas, conversely, the breathtaking view from the top terrace appears limitless. These maps also filter out aspects of life that must have been important to the Cahokians, aspects such as movement, color, smell, and seasonal changes. Additionally, the necessary reduction in scale that enables a comprehensive view of a large area, one of the many useful functions of plan views, may lull the map reader into forgetting just how large a site Cahokia actually is and the effort and time it takes for a person to move from one part of the site to another. Given such limitations, it is important that bird's-eye views not be used exclusively but be supplemented by narrative and other representations or techniques that rectify these deficiencies.

A MORE HUMAN CONCEPT OF LANDSCAPE AT CAHOKIA

We have discussed the historical trend at Cahokia and, more broadly, in western European landscape art toward increasingly removed and detached views of the landscape. Earlier in this chapter, we considered differences in the concept of landscape. We contrasted landscape as representation of the visible world, as scenery, with landscape as an object of scientific study, an interaction of natural and human phenomena capable of being empirically verified and analyzed. These two views of landscape, as maintained by Cosgrove (1984), Relph (1981), and others, are connected historically and conceptually through the faculty of sight, the predominant way of appropriating the world. Let us look more closely at this connection.

What does a pictorial concept presuppose? First, it presupposes that the external world is framed (bounded) and isolated from an observer, who is located outside of that space. The observer is physically removed and thus a nonparticipant. The connection between the external world and the observer is strictly visual. Developments in landscape art resulted in humans and land being separated not only spatially but also emotionally.

In privileging vision (seeing with the bodily eye), experience is narrowly defined. Content other than that seen with the eye is deleted, and this narrowing of content reduces landscape to a superficial concept—superficial in the sense of being restricted to the surface of the earth and superficial emotionally. The intellectual and the visual are emphasized over the sensual, i.e., sound, touch, smell, taste, and even consciousness of space. Observation, organization, and control are emphasized over experience. The symbolic sense of landscape is diminished.

According to Cosgrove (1984, 1985), the concept of landscape in painting and garden design was about the visual and ideological control of space as an objective entity. This control was achieved through the use of linear perspective, based on Euclidean geometry. Instead of intuition, a number of abstract rules were now employed in order to achieve a "truthful" representation of vision. Over time, this order was embraced over affective response. Perspective views removed the viewer from the landscape and arrested the flow of time. Thus, landscape was composed, regulated, and made static.

Positivist use of the concept of landscape is completely in line with these pictorial roots. Positivist use is ultimately an extension of the disinterested, objective view, the perspective way of seeing the world (Cosgrove 1984, 32–33). It was the scientific revolution during the Renaissance that reinforced the visual and formalist characteristics of linear perspective forwarded by the landscape artists. Linear perspective was even alternately referred to as scientific perspective (Richardson 1980). Its technical name, "central projection" (Richardson 1980, 144), reflected the centrality of the viewer in the composition of the scene.

As the concept of landscape was transferred from the arts to the sciences, this visual and formalist emphasis remained intact. For example, the term "landscape architect," first coined in 1863 for the landscape gardeners and artists of Georgian England (Relph 1981, 41–47), signified a relationship with the landscape similar to that of an architect with a building. The landscape was (and still is) an object of professional and technical concern capable of manipulation. This relationship implied detachment from and authority over the land.

The concept of landscape appropriated by geography as its special area of scientific concern was also a visual and formalist notion, linked historically to science through Renaissance developments. The separation of subject and object, culture and nature, and insider and outsider already apparent within the arts was incorporated into it. "Indeed in some respects geography's concept of landscape may be regarded as the formalizing of a view of the world first developed in painting and the arts into a systematic body of knowledge claiming the general validity of a science" (Cosgrove 1984, 27).

Archaeological use of the concept of landscape also involves a detached observer—a subjective, rational person who methodically observes, analyzes, and classifies an objective, material nature. Thus, it is not surprising that academic representations of Cahokia in the twentieth century continue many of the trends noted in landscape art of earlier times. And it is understandable if one recognizes that the evolution of cartography as a technique for representing spatial relationships is closely related to that of landscape painting (Harvey 1980; Rees 1980). Each reinforces visual and formalist influences. Each shares, together with the sciences, a common structure in which the world is defined in visual terms by a detached observer/reader from a fixed point of view (Howett 1990; King 1990).

Positivist landscape approaches stress the outsider's view and concentrate on the morphology of external forms. They ignore "the symbolic and cultural meaning invested in these forms" (Cosgrove 1984, 18) by those who produce, use, and come into contact with them. Objective identification, classification, measurement, and a rigorous exclusion of subjectivity are the focus. In contrast, geographical humanism emphasizes the identity and experience of the insider and considers affective qualities of landscape (Relph 1981). "Science strives to remove the possibility of multiple readings" (Tuan 1972, 185). A humanistic approach implies multiple viewpoints and perceptions.

Though proponents of such an approach have been praised for advocating a richer sense of the landscape, they have also been criticized as unscholarly. Criticisms center around the narrowing distance between observer and landscape. Though humanistic geographers aim to explore the subjective implications of landscape, it has been said that they have not yet developed a clear methodology for doing so (Cosgrove 1984, 33–38).

An interest in more humanistic concepts of landscape is also being voiced within landscape architecture, especially in recent writings about prehistoric Native American landscapes (Melnick 1981, 1983; Motloch 1991; Pregill and Volkman 1993; Scott 1979). In archaeology, challenges to a positivist research paradigm are also being heard, though these have not yet been clearly voiced. Most landscape studies still arise from the cultural ecology school. However, there has been a noticeable increase in landscape studies that attempt to incorporate cultural variables more broadly.

At the outset of this chapter, we noted the centrality of people in definitions of landscape. Perhaps a key to unlocking a richer, more "cultural" concept of landscape is to revisit the relationship between landscape and culture emphasized by archaeological definitions and to consider more carefully the articulation of these two concepts.

The articulation of the concepts of landscape and culture is made explicit through the linking term of "artifact." In archaeology, landscape is an artifact of culture, an artifact that is imbued with cultural information. Landscape is culturally produced and can be studied to tell us about culture. Other definitions (e.g., Savulis 1992) further distinguish landscape as a dynamic artifact, implying that it can be studied to understand culture change.

Until recently the relationship between landscape and culture was not given a great deal of attention in archaeology and in geography (Duncan 1980; Johnston 1986, 91–92). In many respects, the history of culture within anthropology and archaeology parallels that of landscape within geography. Each is a critical concept within its discipline. Each has proven to be complex and hard to define. Each concept has also been largely disregarded by the other disciplines. Thus, to explore landscape and culture together is doubly challenging.

Within geography, the term "cultural landscape" is distinct from a "natural landscape" that has not been affected by humans. In *The Dictionary of Human Geography* (Johnston 1986), cultural landscape is defined as "a concrete and characteristic product of the complicated interplay between a given human community, embodying certain cultural preferences and potentials, and a particular set of natural circumstances" (Wagner and Mikesell 1962). This distinction between a cultural and natural landscape is now falling out of favor within geography because of a growing understanding about the pervasive effects of humans on the landscape (Conzen 1990; Roberts 1987; Martin 1996, and others) and also because of an increasing recognition of cultural constraints on perception.

A geographer's cultural landscape is a by-product (or artifact, in its broadest sense) of human habitation (Rowntree 1996). In *The Morphology of Landscape* (1925), Sauer stated that "culture is the agent, the natural area is the medium, the cultural landscape is the result." It is this "result" outlined by Sauer that cultural geography has traditionally focused upon (Johnston 1986); understanding *material* culture, as opposed to culture, has been the ultimate object of understanding (Duncan 1990, 3). Understanding the process by which material culture has been achieved (the dynamic interaction between culture and the environment) has been largely restricted to the study of humanity's immediate subsistence and habitation needs. Though definitions of landscape universally recognize a human factor, inserted variously into creating, using, perceiving, or experiencing the landscape, they seldom focus on the role of cultural beings in these activities.

Archaeological landscape studies emphasize a similar perspective. Butzer's systems paradigm melded together a number of positive directions for archaeological landscape research, including investigations of site formation, the dynamics of archaeological terrains, multiple regional scales, and often neglected archaeological features such as fields. Yet, an impressive depth and breadth of coverage for environmental systems contrasts markedly with the slight coverage of the cultural system. Although the ultimate goal of his "cultural paradigm" is to determine the interrelationship between culture and the environment, the relationship is conceived of very narrowly. Humans are relegated largely to their role as biological entities, not as cultured members of society.

An emphasis on the morphology of land as opposed to culture and its workings makes it easy to sidestep the role of culture in producing landscape. Yet, if an understanding of the interaction between humans and environment is to include subjectivity, scenery, and interactions between people and their environment, then the issue of people as cultural entities and the issue of culture and its intersection with the environment must be considered. If one accepts that landscape encompasses the human/environment interaction on some level, and if one also accepts that people are cultural beings, then it follows that landscapes are culturally produced, either physically or mentally, and thus we must situate landscape analysis with respect to our conception of culture. It also becomes critical to explore the intersection of landscape and culture if landscape is viewed as an artifact and if the goal of studying the landscape is to say something about culture or society. Especially for archaeologists, culture must necessarily be a critical end product of research.

New concepts of culture perhaps make it easier to articulate the relationship between landscape and culture within a program of research. During the first quarter of the twentieth century, the "superorganic" theory of culture as a powerful autonomous force was forwarded by the anthropologists Alfred Kroeber and Robert Lowie. It was this concept of culture, refined by Leslie White, that Sauer passed into geography and that dominated cultural geography for much of the twentieth century (Duncan 1980). Yet, viewing culture as something separate from humans, but somehow mysteriously guiding them, makes it difficult to conceptualize how culture is involved in shaping or perceiving the landscape or how we can study landscape to arrive at a fuller understanding of societies and culture. As Duncan states (1990), this concept of culture is not only unconvincing as an explanatory variable but impedes explanation.

More recent considerations in both geography and archaeology view culture as an active and interactive process. Groth speaks of a culture of everyday actions and structures that humans consciously and unconsciously mold (1990, vii). Duncan (1990) defines landscape as a cultural production integral to both the reproduction and contestation of political power. Definitions such as these hold promise for less materialistic studies of landscapes that say something about the society that produced them. They allow us to understand not only the result but also the agency and process, i.e., the intersection of culture with the material world. Definitions of landscape that emphasize its dynamic and communicative aspects also fit such concepts of culture.

A strong aspect of recent archaeological and anthropological literature is the concept of an interactive relationship between constructed space and culture. In such studies, human practices create built form, and built form then structures and transforms human practices (e.g., Donley-Reid 1990; Hodder 1990; Lawrence 1986). Bourdieu (1973, 1977) emphasizes that constructed space bears certain meanings and significances that are "read" by people in the process of their day-to-day lives. A wonderful example of such a reading is Winston Churchill's response (quoted in Brand 1994, 3) to the cramped, oblong chamber of the House of Commons. He saw it as an essential feature that this building was too small to seat all members. Great occasions, therefore, provided standing room only. The building's shape also forced members to sit on one side or the other and thus choose unambiguously one party or the other. Churchill did not doubt the influence of architecture and structure upon human character and action. During an awards ceremony for the Architectural Association in 1924, he said, "We make our buildings, and afterwards they make us. They regulate the course of our lives."

Other studies (Donley-Reid 1990; Moore 1986) discuss the importance of movement through space and ritual as one means by which the visibility of a landscape or structure may be enhanced. Giddens (1979) describes the concept of a "structuring structure" that is both the medium for and the outcome of social practices. This concept offers great promise for landscape studies in that it allows us to go beyond landscape as an artifact of culture (i.e., as a passive reflection of cultural variables) and move toward landscape and its transformation in culture change. This is the connection between landscape as experience and cultural processes. A brief look at monument building illustrates this connection.

The act of monument building creates a large social group and it is this "process of unification," the creation of unity out of many elements, that is exemplified most dramatically in monumental architecture (Wilson 1988, 12). Wilson discusses how death is overcome through the construction of permanent monuments, and how, through this association with permanence and ancestors, a group can achieve legitimacy and substance (1988, 129).

Hodder (1990) touches upon some of these same ideas in relation to the European Neolithic. He elaborates on how long houses, linear tombs, long mounds, and enclosures were symbols of group definition used to create, expand, or tighten social relationships and dependencies. Renfrew (1983) comments on the role of western European henge monuments in the processes of centralization and social cohesion. Sherratt (1990) argues that the construction of megalithic monuments in an arc around the central European loess belt was an essential part of the transformation of indigenous foragers and hunters into farmers. Cereal cultivation required permanent and cooperative labor pools formed from several household groups. Like the longhouse villages of central Europe, tombs of these peripheral regions were marks of continuity and common descent. They served as the basis for the symbolic construction of the community and as a way to create and perpetuate social relations. They crosscut families and assured a commitment to place and to the social and ecological transformation of the landscape. Other examples of how communal undertakings expressed in a landscape can unite communities and make them explicit include Mapuche monuments (Dillehay 1990), the Betsileo of Madagascar (Kus and Raharijaona 1990), and Southwestern Great Kivas (Adler and Wilshusen 1990).

Cherry (1978) asserts that monument building serves as one way to integrate different parts of society and that peaks in monument building characterize periods of drastic change in a society. He maintains that energy inputs to ideology in the form of monumental architecture may be used to legitimate authority, especially in cases where political relations with explicit power relations are not well established. In essence, he suggests that the need for monument construction is greatest when the social order is the most fragile or is being reformed.

At Cahokia, it seems reasonable to consider those social integrative functions that relate to the construction, use, and maintenance of monumental

constructions. We will examine how monument construction and modifications to the landscape may relate to the development of intensive maize
agriculture, population movement and reorganization within the American
Bottom region, and the creation and sustenance of social relations necessary
for the production of this important Mississippian center. We will also explore aspects of visual display and movement through space that would
have been part of the Cahokian experience.

The concept of landscape as it has developed from artistic and academic
traditions is a restrictive way of seeing the world that has failed to capture a
broader experience of life and the affective bonds between humans and their
landscapes (Cosgrove 1984, 269–70). Given this, how do we include dynamic, contextual, and cultural aspects in our archaeological landscape studies and, more specifically, in our work at Cahokia? How do we, as outsiders,
begin to understand the engagement of past societies with the land? We
know that the use of the current, limited suite of maps and representations to
interpret and represent archaeological landscapes precludes consideration of
alternative points of view. Certainly they do so in relation to Cahokia. Something more than the traditional bird's-eye view should be used as the basis for
an interpretation of spatial order. We suggest that an explicit consideration of
cultural meaning and experience enrich our interpretation of this spatial order. And what about the role of the other senses, beside vision? How do we
arrive at an understanding of the richness of social experience without them?

Riley (1990) contrasts a figural composition of the landscape, a picture,
with the experience of the landscape as a social phenomenon. The latter is
precisely what we, as archaeologists, want to understand at Cahokia. We also
want to include an ecological consideration of the landscape, for both are
important if we are to arrive at a more complete and in-depth understanding
of the Cahokia experience.

Can we use the concept of landscape to provide a less static interpretation
of the past? Can the concept of landscape be broadened so that an ecological and economic characterization of the human/environment relationship
includes a characterization of past societies and their engagement with the
land? If we are truly interested in landscape and culture and seriously com-
mitted to understanding the dynamic relationship between people and their
physical world on a human scale, we must subscribe to this richer concept of
landscape.

CHAPTER TWO

A
LANDSCAPE
APPROACH

We have attempted to come to an understanding of what has led to our, and perhaps others', dissatisfaction with the conceptions and uses of the term "landscape." Others (Butlin 1993; Howett 1990; Relph 1981) have cited a number of recent directions that serve as possible, partial explanations. Among these are new developments in physics (e.g., the chaos theory) that challenge the separation between an observer and a measurable, knowable, predictable world; an increasingly vigorous debate between scientism and humanism; and a softening of barriers between the arts and sciences. Multimedia developments such as virtual tours on the Internet also contribute to dissatisfaction with static visual landscapes.

A number of developments within the field of archaeology can also be cited. These changes are more theoretical than methodological in nature and are particularly apparent within historical archaeological studies (Gleason 1994; Rubertone 1989). They include changes in orientation in the conception of space, artifacts, and boundaries. The discipline of archaeology has until recently tended to focus on architecture and settlement plans rather than on the space between houses and communities. The realization that this space forms "the very connective tissue that gives houses and communities their proper context" has been an important change in orientation (Deetz 1990, 1). As developed, the concept of landscape has often served as a vehicle to incorporate studies of architecture and surrounding space. A shift from land as a contextual setting to landscape as the subject of investigation has been an important aspect of the study of historic fields and gardens (Gleason 1994).

Equally important developments have included a broadening of the term "built environment" within the field of anthropology to include any physical alteration of the natural environment (Lawrence and Low 1990) and the recognition of the role of perception in our interaction with this natural environment (Duncan 1990; Kaplan and Kaplan 1989; Ruggles 1994; Ruggles and Kryder-Reid 1994; Walton 1996). A number of theoretical advances in cultural and social approaches to the study of built form are also relevant (Lawrence and Low 1990). Types of studies include interactions of the built environment with social organization and spatial behavior; symbolic approaches concerned with the meaning of built form; psychological treatments of human interactions with the built environment; and concern with the social processes that produce built form. More and more, social theorists are being tapped in order to arrive at an understanding of the interplay between societies and their environments. This expansion of theoretical perspectives is rooted in more recent conceptualizations of culture, which treat culture as an active and interactive process that can be played out on the land.

In addition to these broader changes, we have been influenced by our experiences at Cahokia, by the data we have collected, and by those who have preceded us over the last two hundred years at the site. Much of the work at Cahokia during the twentieth century, including our own, has been conducted in a piecemeal fashion, and much of this has been accomplished as part of CRM (Cultural Resource Management) work. Yet, after completing reports on individual projects, there is a need to combine and interpret this information. The landscape concept is a vehicle for synthesizing archaeological work at the site and for offering new insights into Cahokian culture.

Our work at the site has also emphasized the importance of understanding the transformation of the physical world. In 1988, during the first of a series of annual research field schools we conducted at the site (Holley et al. 1989), we realized that beyond surface manifestations of earthmoving activities, such as the mounds and open borrows, additional large areas of the site had been modified by the Cahokians. We began to concentrate on investigating the more diffuse subsurface evidence of earthmoving and impact. Subsequent research within the Grand Plaza at the site (Holley et al. 1993; Dalan 1993b) reinforced our belief in the importance of understanding the processes of borrowing and reclamation manifest in subsurface deposits. Below the level surface of the plaza, evidence was found of borrowing of diverse fills to various depths, evidence suggestive of a variety of activities and purposes. Reclamation of this area to create the Grand Plaza early in the sequence indicates that the transformation of Cahokia into a paramount Mississippian center was far from a humble beginning.

The picture of the landscape gained from the subsurface is equally, or perhaps even more, important in understanding this transformation process. Not only did the Cahokians construct mounds, but they borrowed various types of earth to build these mounds. They also reworked the landscape by filling and leveling large expanses of ground between the mounds. Considering not only the mounds, but this other evidence of reworking the landscape, provides a new appreciation of the nature, scale, and dynamics of landscape change at Cahokia. Roberts (1987, 83) draws a parallel between visible landscapes and icebergs; at Cahokia, surface manifestations are indeed only the tip of the transformation story.

These transformations are, not coincidentally, happening at critical times at Cahokia. Spurts in the earthmoving process are recognizable. For example, the construction of a principal mound and the Grand Plaza, both on a scale previously unrealized across the Eastern Woodlands, occurred very early in the Mississippian sequence. This consideration can be expanded beyond "planned" construction activities to include other alterations of the land.

13. In spite of the "ideal season" perspective of landscape artists, Cahokia today, as in the past, experiences extremes of weather. A. Winter at Cahokia: Monks Mound covered in snow, as viewed from the southern end of the Grand Plaza. B. Bailing rainwater from archaeological test excavations during early summer prior to the construction of the Interpretive Center.

For example, near the end of the Mississippian occupation, there is a marked increase in the erosion of loessial sediments from the adjacent bluffs and a choking of the creeks that drain into the bottoms (Lopinot and Woods 1993; Woods and Holley 1991). Both types of transformations are critical to understanding Cahokia and will be outlined in parts 2 and 3.

The basis of our knowledge of the site is not solely visual. Our contact with Cahokia is not limited to maps, photos, or text (fig. 13). Over the years and seasons, we have experienced Cahokia with all our senses. We have sweated through sticky, hot summer days rampant with mosquitoes, chiggers, and other wildlife. We have been awed by the beauty of snow-mantled mounds. We have chipped through frozen or dried "gumbo" clay (a term applied locally to a clay-rich bottomland soil) and slogged through flooded borrows in order to collect data. And we know firsthand how long it takes to walk across the site and how one's heart pounds when climbing the 30-meter-high Monks Mound. The Cahokians must have had similar experiences. Although these visual and textual details are not part of the standard archaeological report, they are important information to use in our archaeological interpretations.

The geographic landscape has traditionally been a generalization derived from the observation of individual scenes (Relph 1981, 48–49). This process of generalization occurs spatially and temporally. Local variations are deemphasized in favor of the regional landscape. Seasonal variations are de-emphasized in favor of an average landscape. In contrast, the characterization of the landscape at Cahokia presented here will be quite specific. This contrast is illustrated by comparing the map of a site with the experience gained during the process of mapping. Walking the rod and deciding where to place shots provides a "feeling" for the land because one is forced to not only closely observe but to move through it while simultaneously thinking about it. It is this sort of sensual experience of landscape that will be integrated into the interpretation presented in parts 2 and 3.

Walton (1996) comments on the cultural filtering of the world that is meant by the analogy of landscape as text. Conceptualizing landscapes as text derives from developments in linguistics and semiotics and carries with it the notion that landscapes are read in much the same way as literary texts (Cosgrove and Jackson 1987; Duncan and Duncan 1988; Ley 1985). Despite a physical world existing apart from our senses, we can only come to know this physical world through our perception or "reading" of it. Thus, whether landscape is a "natural" or a cultural phenomenon, it is made cultural through the filter of perception.

We concur with the basic premise of the "landscape as text" conceptualization, that is, that our knowledge of the physical world comes only through our perception of it. A textual analogy has also been cited as valuable for preserving a sense of human action, creativity, and layering of meaning in contrast to geographical analogies such as system, organism, and structure (Cosgrove and Jackson 1987). Yet, analyzing landscapes using such terms as "authored," "read," "discourse," and "text," seems also to reinforce the quality of separateness that is inherent in the role of the detached observer of the landscape. As pointed out by Peet (1993), the notion "reading the landscape . . . makes the world sound like one big library inhabited by bookish intellectuals" who have minimal connection with the material realm of social practices. Landscape is not a text in that it is read like a book; it is read in a sensual manner. Landscape is not only seen, it is experienced. Past experiences and attitudes are necessarily implicated in perception as well.

Defining landscape as a totality of material and cultural phenomena, as dynamic and ever changing, renders it impossible to capture in its entirety. Selection must be involved in perceiving and in characterizing any landscape, much in the same way that map makers choose how to represent an area and what to include in that representation. Hart (1995) criticizes those who have treated a single facet of the landscape as though it were the whole. He provides examples of geomorphologists who have written about landscape evolution when they were dealing only with rocks and the features of the land surface, botanists and ecologists who used the term when dealing with plants and vegetation, and architects concerned only with buildings or even certain types of buildings. Yet, there is multiplicity to landscape because of perception. It is always filtered, not fixed, always some chosen part of a whole. The observer, through selection as well as through interpretation, is clearly present in the process of creating a landscape. Thus, a landscape approach, through the choice of various phenomena, can accommodate individual goals, databases, and theoretical and methodological stances. It necessarily allows for individuality and creativity in interpreting archaeological remains.

A cultural focus is a necessary and critical component of the landscape approach in an archaeological application. In our landscape approach at Cahokia, we also want to insert ourselves into the process, and we want to consider and interpret the engagement of the Cahokians with their physical world during their lifetimes. Although it is impossible to know the Cahokians' mindset, there are certain commonalities of human experience and human behavior that can be employed to place them in their landscape and to help understand the intertwining of setting and event. The engagement of the Cahokians with their landscape can also be approached through the vehicle of culture. The interpretation and presentation (representations) of landscape in parts 2 and 3 attempt to convey this social experience.

We have all been impressed by certain qualities of landscape and nature writing. In general these works tend to be interesting, evocative, and eminently readable. They contrast markedly with the often dry tables of stones and bones presented in archaeological reports. Yet archaeology is considered by many to be intrinsically fascinating. What have we left out of our presentation of archaeological information? How can we better characterize the prehistoric landscape and landscape experience?

The history of landscape representation provides some important clues. It suggests that over time the landscape concept developed into one that was largely visual and static, and increasingly removed and detached. Cultural content became incidental at best. Culture and nature were separated, and it is only recently that the affective response of humans and the role of perception have been seriously considered.

Representations of archaeological landscapes have largely followed these dictates. In chapter 1, we discussed dissatisfaction with the totality of representations of the Cahokia landscape. Clearly, new ways of interpreting the landscape relationship must be formulated—ways that use culture to incorporate new theoretical insights and ways that change thoughts, metaphors, representation, and text.

We do not always have to place ourselves outside of the landscape. To do so may be one component of archaeological analysis, but it does not have to be the only one. The western European concept is not the only way of understanding landscape, and it is not likely to have been the common Cahokian's view. Alternative conceptions of landscape offer an approach that may be more emotive and less detached. Put in terms of representation, we should perhaps consider breaking some of the rules of linear perspective. Shifting points of view or shifting scales, as in medieval drawings, to emphasize the critical importance of certain features (Richardson 1980) may be one effective way. Modern progressive landscape artists using new procedures for an art of landscape (e.g., Cutts et al. 1987) are also challenging a mechanical, constricting vision of landscape that has developed from painted landscape art.

A pictorial conception of landscape is spatially static. It denies process. It is not a landscape through which a person moves, or one that changes. Rather, it is isolated from the observer and attempts to isolate nature from culture. It is a superficial phenomenon that does not recognize the subsurface changes that are the very essence of archaeology.

Softening the barriers between the pictorial and the experienced can facilitate a sense of dynamics and social content in landscape study. Spatial and temporal scales should be flexible, not fixed. Human activity should be central, not incidental, and the other senses beyond vision should be included. Even our physical and sensual experiences at Cahokia, to the extent that they can be used to inform us about the prehistoric situation, should be integrated into our interpretation of the Cahokians and their making and experience of the landscape that we now study.

Only a portion of our interpretation is focused on regular geometrical relationships identified from aerial views. Interestingly enough, though mounds have been the focus of landscape characterizations at Cahokia, they are particularly poorly represented by an aerial perspective. Such bird's-eye views (unless one uses stereo pairs) distort the scale of the vertical which is the essence of the mounds' monumentality.

The Cahokia landscape presented in parts 2 and 3 is "lived in" as well as "looked at." Smells, sounds, movement, and people are inserted in the interpretation to provide a richer, more robust sense of the past. Krogstad (1989) discusses the significance of smell and its absence in anthropological literature. Relying on spatial apprehensions linked to linear perspective tends to prevent these other interpretations. Drawings, as well as text, can be used to impart a sense of movement and to activate sensual keys. And both can be employed to situate the data on a human scale in terms of time and space and to consider the practicalities of daily life. Bender (1992) employs a multilevel, multiaxial approach in dealing with the landscape of prehistoric Stonehenge. Rather than confining herself to a sequence-oriented narrative, she reworks the archaeological evidence along a number of different axes. This is an attractive alternative because it allows for a more dynamic characterization in space and time.

Landscape is always conceptualized. Our interpretation of the prehistoric landscape experience does not explore individual relationships with the land but adopts the larger perspective of society or of certain social groups. The purpose of the interpretation presented here is not to understand the Cahokians' mindset, for that is as difficult to do as it is to remove ourselves from the interpretive process. Rather, it is to present a broader conception of landscape informed by our experiences and by data from the archaeological context. This text contributes to the Cahokia literature by providing both a broad visual array and a humanistic perspective, aspects that are lacking in traditional discourse on the site. Through the application of a landscape approach, we offer a synthetic interpretation of Cahokia that we hope will be of interest to a diverse audience and bring this remarkable site some measure of the popular and professional attention that it deserves.

Landscape studies in archaeological contexts, especially prehistoric contexts, are limited. Archaeological applications guided by a landscape approach are in their infancy. Yet, archaeologists are the scholars with the most potential for peeling back the layers of time and placing lost visions and ancient landscapes in the discourse of human achievements. In this volume we offer an approach that is an amalgam of our respective disciplines (archaeology, geography, and landscape architecture). This approach considers culture, landform, and design in a dynamic context, providing a look at the Cahokia landscape that is both material and cultural.

When dealing with prehistoric settlements, geographers have tended to focus on land use and thus consider all economically used lands. Archaeologists, on the other hand, have traditionally concentrated on the site, the place of habitation, and the activities that go on there. This study of landscape and landscape change at Cahokia goes beyond the investigation of a single community's occupancy to consider the dynamic functioning of a continuous succession of living settlements and their economically utilized lands through time. Our landscape study at Cahokia offers geographers a unique application of the landscape concept in that it considers not only what is happening to the landscape but also the cultural component of the human/environment interaction (the who and the why), and it does so in a prehistoric setting. In addition, our focus is on a very specific cultural landscape, as opposed to the more generalized treatment of landscapes prevalent in geographical literature.

We also expand on the dialogue prevalent in geography regarding the conceptual basis of the term "landscape" within landscape art to consider the interplay between archaeological interpretation and representation.

Another distinctive aspect of our study is the incorporation of the viewpoint of a landscape architect in the physical evaluation of the Cahokia landscape. In this designer's point of view, the medium of land is comprehended in terms of making physical and cultural space. A landscape architect questions how a culture organized the landscape spatially and how the evolving form and function of that space accommodated practical needs, promoted cultural activities, and expressed an ever evolving view of the world. Analyzing space by using traditional archaeological techniques combined with a landscape architecture approach based on the application of fundamental design principles provides another avenue to explore the Cahokians' understanding and manipulation of the physical space of their community and a more holistic perspective of Cahokia. This combined approach has also allowed us to build three-dimensional representations of plausible lived-in landscape space and the character of the landscape over time. Our perspective differs from traditional archaeological investigations in that we have an eye to the lay of the land and a consideration of the extent to which the land was consciously manipulated. These components, as well as a focus on the human dimension of landscape elements, a consideration of cross-cultural elements of design and landscape use, attention to topics such as construction and maintenance of landscapes, and an unashamed incorporation of personal experience into our interpretation enrich current archaeological viewpoints.

APPLYING A LANDSCAPE APPROACH AT CAHOKIA

The landscape approach proposed here is not a recipe that details the needed data and the methods to be applied in order to arrive at a standardized understanding of an archaeological landscape. For one thing, our research was not conducted in this manner. The desire to provide a synthetic understanding of the Cahokia landscape arose much later and only after more than a decade of work at the site. Our work at Cahokia has been driven by different goals, most of which have been project- or contract-related (e.g., locating sections of the Central Palisade, or conducting mitigation-based excavations in conjunction with the construction of the new Interpretive Center at the site).

We also draw on data collected at the site by other scholars (appendix). Various archaeologists have worked at the site since the first systematic research was conducted by Moorehead in the 1920s. Highway construction projects prompted a flurry of archaeological work at Cahokia during the 1960s, and it is from this period that we have the most extensive exposures, with large areas of the site machine-bladed and the exposed subsurface features excavated. A reasonable estimate is that less than 1 percent of the site has been opened by shovel or machinery as a result of all projects, however, nearly all of the cultivated ground has been inspected either through survey or by controlled surface collection. Although the data from Cahokia were not collected with the intention of optimizing an understanding of the Cahokia landscape, much can still be said about landscape, even using data from these disparate sources. The melding of archaeological and geographical perspectives used in the collection and interpretation of our data has produced information most amenable to a humanistic landscape study.

A list of data or methods couched in a procedural recipe is also inappropriate because a landscape approach is necessarily fluid, incorporating not only disparate data sets, but different observers. As part of our research, however, we have developed methods both for data collection and for the analysis and interpretation of data that are potentially useful for those seeking to explore past landscapes. It is these methodological contributions that we wish to highlight here. We first discuss a package of methods, involving geophysical techniques, fine-scale topographic studies, and soil analyses. We then turn to interpretive approaches used to reevaluate and recombine data gathered from various projects, including the use of design principles derived from architectural and landscape architectural studies.

A Geophysical Approach

"There is no such thing as an 'archaeological divining rod.'" One of our old workmen in the State of Maine, who served on many expeditions between 1910 and 1920, in his simple way uttered a great truth: "Nobody can look into the ground." We think this rather commonplace expression covers the Cahokia situation.

Such are the remarks of Warren K. Moorehead (1929, 33) following the first professional archaeological investigations of the Cahokia site in the 1920s. At this time, and up until recently, archaeological excavation was the primary means of providing an understanding of subsurface conditions. Today, however, geophysical surveys, which "look" below the surface to measure changes in subsurface properties, are readily available to help the archaeologist interpret archaeological landscapes. These nondestructive methods were used extensively during much of our research at Cahokia (fig. 14).

Geophysical surveys are part of a package of methods applied at Cahokia that also includes fine-scale topographic mapping, soil morphological and soil chemical studies, environmental magnetic techniques, and test excavations. Electromagnetic conductivity surveys and electrical resistivity surveys (Grant and West 1965; Keller and Frischknecht 1966; Parasnis 1986; Telford et al. 1990; Ward 1967) work well at Cahokia due to the varied and contrasting electrical properties of the building blocks of sand, silt, and clay that form the Cahokia landscape. Environmental magnetic, or soil magnetic, techniques (Dalan and Banerjee 1996) in effect extend the application of surface geophysical techniques to the "microgeophysical" scale (Dalan 1993a). They may be used to address questions about anthropogenic earthmoving activities that can only be answered by investigations on this

14. Electromagnetic-conductivity surveying in the Grand Plaza. Monks Mound is in the background. These surveys changed perspectives about the scale of earthmoving activities within the Grand Plaza.

smaller scale, especially in conjunction with other geoarchaeological methods, such as chemical analyses or sedimentological analysis.

Though the methods in this package have been developed and used in diverse fields, when employed as a package, they become even more powerful than when used singly. Their use in an integrated study of archaeological landscapes and culturally modified terrain is particularly appropriate because in combination they (1) are relatively nondestructive; (2) are cost-effective; (3) are equally effective in the study of large and small tracts of land; (4) provide subsurface, as well as surface, information; (5) provide evidence of diffuse, in addition to discrete, human impact; and (6) supply corroborative as well as complementary information.

These qualities are illustrated in work performed in the Cahokia Grand Plaza (fig. 15). Fine-scale topographic mapping was used not only to detail the mounds within this area, but also to delimit refilled borrows located next to these mounds. Slight topographic lows (i.e., as shallow as 10 centimeters), a result of the slumping of the prehistoric fills, indicate the limits of these borrows (Holley et al. 1990). In some cases topographic lows were not the result of prehistoric human activities; hence the topographic results were used only to suggest areas for further testing and exploration, not as a definitive method to locate subsurface features. Electromagnetic conductivity surveys were used to verify borrow locations within the Grand Plaza (Dalan 1991, 1993b; Dalan and Banerjee 1996). Test excavations supplied further detail on how the borrows were filled and on special precautions

15. Schematic of the central portion of the Cahokia Mounds site, showing the location of Monks Mound, the Grand Plaza, and the estimated limits of the palisade.

taken during the reclamation procedure (Holley et al. 1993). Magnetic and other physical and chemical properties of the soils from the mounds and the area surrounding the mounds (into which the borrows were excavated) were used to establish that mound fills tend to be characteristic of the locally available soils and thus that a pattern of local fill procurement was followed at the site, with the earth for a mound obtained from the area next to the mound (Dalan 1993b; Dalan et al. 1994).

An electromagnetic survey of the Grand Plaza also helped delineate the natural ridge and swale topography that the Cahokians had to work with in creating their great mound center (Dalan 1991; Dalan and Banerjee 1996) (fig. 16a and b). With this information, we began to unravel how this topography had been modified. For example, borrows located next to mounds

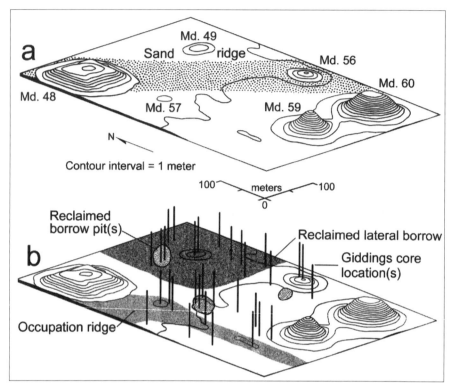

16. Interpretation of the Grand Plaza. A. Interpretation of the natural topography of the Grand Plaza. A buried sand ridge runs diagonally through the study area. Swales are to the northeast and southwest of this ridge. B. Modifications of this area during the Emergent Mississippian and Mississippian periods. The large borrow across the northeast section of the study area provided fill for the construction of Monks Mound, whereas the smaller borrows provided fill for the construction of adjacent mounds. As part of efforts to create a level plaza surface, all of these borrows, including the large lateral borrow, were refilled. Both interpretations are presented upon a current topographic map base. Vertical lines indicate the locations of cores.

that had been filled in with contrasting sediments were identified. Topographic and geophysical surveys, however, did not reveal the presence of a large lateral borrow in the northern section of the plaza. There was no obvious topographic low over this feature, nor was there any discernable electrical anomaly (because the borrow was filled with material very similar to the natural soils in this area). This extensive refilled borrow was revealed only through a combination of test excavations and environmental magnetic and other soil studies. Soil development over the century since the borrow was filled, together with the relative "cleanliness" (i.e., sterility) of the filling sediments, made it difficult, even with excavation and detailed studies of soil morphology, to show that this area had been disturbed (Holley et al. 1993).

It was only through the application of environmental magnetic techniques that the critical evidence for cultural modification and reclamation was supplied, even identifying the various sources of fill used and estimates of the relative quantity of each (Dalan and Banerjee 1996, 1998).

In summary, this package of methods was applied within the Grand Plaza to provide information on the landform as it existed prior to the Mississippian emergence and then to indicate how this landform had been transformed, in both nature and extent. Information on mound building and on larger-scale earthmoving operations that included borrowing as well as land reclamation was also obtained. In addition, the package of methods was used to locate and study smaller-scale features that related to the Mississippians' partitioning of and use of the land. An example of this is the location of prehistoric trenches (Dalan 1989b) that form the remains of palisades that once encircled the Central Precinct. Coring and soil magnetic studies were used to provide detail on the form and structure of individual mounds and information on the preparation of surfaces prior to mound construction (Dalan 1993b). Historic excavation trenches from Moorehead's work at the site in the 1920s were also identified using these methods (Dalan et al. 1993).

During many of the research field schools that we have taught at Cahokia, we have also used "surface units" to provide areal sampling of the site with minimal disturbance. This methodology was designed to replace a planned surface collection at one of the mound groups at the site (Holley et al. 1992). The collection was not possible because it would have been necessary to plow very deeply, rather than disk, the surface, in order to rid the surface of planted hay and weeds. To avoid disturbing intact subsurface deposits and to provide an alternative means of assessing the relative density of prehistoric debris within the plow zone, an alternative strategy was adopted.

With this method, 1-by-1-meter units are excavated to a depth of only 20 centimeters below the surface. Plowing, vegetation growth, and pedogenesis (soil formation) have already combined to disturb this uppermost surface. The recovered soils are then screened through a quarter-inch hardware cloth. Observations of the floor of the unit (at the 20-centimeter depth), an analysis of the materials recovered (types and densities), and sometimes even subsurface probing contribute to an assessment of the nature of the subsurface deposits and the potential for subsurface features. Screening these surface soils through a relatively fine mesh provides a greater volume of materials for analysis than other types of surface collection, and a very reliable glimpse into the timing and intensity of occupation and functional variability.

Application of Design Principles

Several spatial organizing and design principles derived from architectural and landscape architectural literature have been used to enhance our understanding of Cahokia. They include the use of monumental scale to create a spirit or sense of place; design of a central focus and the use of verticality to establish domain; the use of cultural symbols in built forms to communicate social and political structure; the placement of key features in the landscape to establish visual recognition; the repetition of similar forms and elements to reinforce cultural messages; the use of proportion and alignment to establish order and hierarchy; and the creation of site symmetry based on directionality. These principles have been employed to frame new questions about the data and to recombine them in different ways. They have also provided a means of approaching some of the social aspects of landscape.

In his book *The Image of the City* (1960), Kevin Lynch set forth some ideas (based on interviews) about the image of the city and how people react to and perceive the city based on its physical elements (i.e., paths, edges, districts, nodes, landmarks) and their interactions with them. In the 1970s and 1980s, a number of people (e.g., Rapoport 1982; Appleyard et al. 1976; Zube 1970) produced studies that confirmed Lynch's early ideas about people's perceptions and understanding of built city form. Though his analysis limited itself to the effects of physical, perceptible objects, Lynch clearly recognized other influences such as social meaning, function, and history of an area.

The design principles used to analyze Cahokia's landscape are set on a human scale with a human focus. In other words, the sensed quality of a place is not viewed as merely decorative but as an indispensable component of everyday life (Lynch and Hack 1984, 153). Sensing is part of the dialogue between the perceiver (human) and object and is central to peoples' interaction with their environment. According to Lynch and Hack (1984, 154), the sensuous experience of place is first a spatial one. Fairbrother (1972) also mentions the importance of the consciousness of space in the experience of a landscape. Temporal aspects of perception are likewise part of the experience, including dynamic aspects introduced by movement and rhythmic landscape change (Motloch 1991, 116–25). Beyond the direct perception or consciousness of space, the literature also identifies landscape as a medium of symbolic communication (Lynch and Hack 1984, 173), whether by means of explicit signs or by the implicit meanings of shapes and motions. Thus, the perceptual organization of landscape is based on the experience and purposes of the observers and on the stimuli reaching their senses (Lynch and Hack 1984, 189). These ideas facilitated the development of notions about the landscape at Cahokia as an expressive environment (Rubertone 1989; Duncan 1980).

Typical design thinking focuses on process including, for example, what the design is meant to achieve and the nature of the material that one has to work with (e.g., natural or existing habitat, existing man-made changes, and forces of change) (Fairbrother 1972). In contrast, typical archaeological and geographical studies focus on final form, describing and understanding it in relation to preexisting habitat(s) and forces of change (morphologic approach). However, it may be beneficial to integrate design process, i.e., design thinking, in an archaeological situation.

In doing so, one can first study how the landscape is structured or ordered by exploring whether there is evidence for design and the meaning or purpose of the design or, at least, the effects of the final design form. According to Simmonds (1961, 7), the designer's lament is that conscious design is not the rule and that growth occurs largely in a piecemeal, haphazard, and illogical manner. Does the notion of a designed, harmonious development versus an unplanned, disjointed, even ill-conceived, development apply to Cahokia? Is there, or can there be, evidence of both? Or, are we predisposed to see only the former as we look for a symmetrical, geometrical, and tidy archaeological landscape?

Meaning and effect of landscape can be approached to some extent by applying some recognized universals (such as the distance that can be seen by the naked eye), by using the ethnographic literature, and by analyzing organizational order within the context of the archaeological data (i.e., within the context of what we know about a particular society and culture). Concepts from the design literature also provide details about the daily life of the Cahokians that may be absent from more descriptive and morphologic landscape approaches, details about, for example, the creation and experience of place and information about the constraints and potential of this creation. According to Lynch and Hack (1984, 189), perceiving an environment is creating a hypothesis, that is, building an organized mental image of space and time. This organization is based upon the expression of aesthetic principles related to the form and composition of a landscape (symmetry, order, repetition, continuity and closure, dominance, rhythm, and common scale or similarity of form or material) in both harmonious and contrasting ways. Four elements of spatial composition in landscapes presented by Higuchi (1983) organize space. They include boundary, focus-center-goal, directionality, and domain (the total space that is brought together and given order by the conditions of the first three). These two sets of principles—one that gives form and composition to a landscape and one that gives structural identity to a landscape—characterize the spatial order of Cahokia. Many archaeological and geographical descriptions of space use similar elements, e.g., core/periphery, bounded/unbounded, focused/unfocused (e.g., Gleason 1994; Renfrew and Cherry 1986; Sack 1980). As part of an investigation of landscape elements, it is important to consider not only their locations and relations, but differences in their character. For instance, Higuchi (1983) mentions streams as boundaries that separate, but do not cut off, the opposite side from view. Natural or preexisting features serving as boundaries or direction elements could also be distinguished from culturally constructed ones.

Patterns of activity, patterns of circulation, and patterns of sensible form that support them (Lynch and Hack 1984, 127–28) reveal conscious motives for organizing space. Pattern of activity is the arrangement of behavior settings, their character, linkage, density, and grain. Pattern of circulation is the layout of movement channels and their relations to the activity locations. Pattern of sensible form centers on the human experience of place: what we see, hear, smell, and feel, and what this means to us. This last type of pattern includes our experience of Cahokia today and how this may be similar to or differ from an experience of it in the past.

Proportion and scale are paramount design tools at Cahokia and fundamental to its success as a designed place (Lynch and Hack 1984, 157). Proportion is the internal relation of parts. Scale is the relation of size to the size
of other objects. In relation to the latter, there are some general quantities
that can be used for humans. These are what seems comfortable to us due to
the characteristics of the human eye and to the size of our bodies. For example, we can detect human beings at about 1,200 meters (4,000 feet), recognize them at 25 meters (80 feet), see their facial expressions at 14 meters (45
feet), and feel them in direct relation to us—pleasant or intrusive—at 1 to 3
meters (3 to 10 feet). Outdoor spaces that correspond to this last dimension
seem intolerably small. Dimensions on the order of 12 meters (40 feet) are
intimate. Up to 25 meters (80 feet) is still an easy human scale. Quantities
such as these cut across cultural systems and can be used to approach landscape meaning, including general social prescriptions for the use of space.
For example, the smaller a space, the greater the sense of security and the
more prone an individual is to interact socially (Motloch 1991, 180).

Studies of visual perception that describe how people influence, guide,
and direct each other by means of sensory signals embedded in the material
environment (e.g., Joiner 1971; Ruesch and Kees 1956) suggest that there is a
highly structured or formal framework underlying nearly all kinds of social
interaction and that the ways in which people use spaces, or expect to be
able to use them, are formalized (Joiner 1971). The arrangement of objects,
and variations in their material, shape, and surface, may be used to indicate
the type of social interaction to be expected, as could associations bearing
on past experience and symbolic decoration.

Landscape symbolism may be more difficult to evaluate than human perception and use of space. However, landscape and other studies suggest that
symbolic meanings of certain landscape features may be cross-cultural. Motloch (1991, 5–8) comments on landform as line—straight lines are structured
and symbolize energy and power, whereas rounded lines are naturalistic.
Ethnographic data and repeated associations in an archaeological context
may also provide information on symbols that may apply to the prehistoric
case. Finally, site development topics, including environmental quality, technical expertise in building, questions of maintainability, and the degree of
adaptability to a site's inherent physical characteristics (Lynch and Hack
1984, 107, 113), are evaluated with respect to what the Cahokians were able
to achieve.

PART TWO

CAHOKIAN

LANDSCAPES

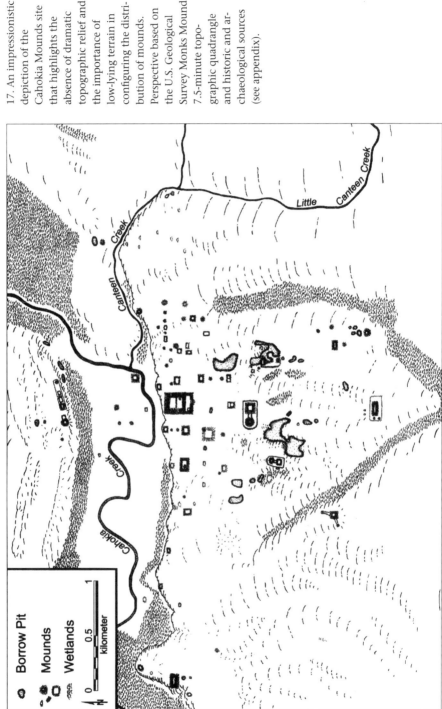

17. An impressionistic depiction of the Cahokia Mounds site that highlights the absence of dramatic topographic relief and the importance of low-lying terrain in configuring the distribution of mounds. Perspective based on the U.S. Geological Survey Monks Mound 7.5-minute topographic quadrangle and historic and archaeological sources (see appendix).

Little Canteen Creek

Canteen Creek

Cahokia Creek

Borrow Pit

Mounds

Wetlands

0   0.5   1
kilometer

N

CHAPTER THREE

THE
CAHOKIA
LANDSCAPE

We begin with a brief description of the Cahokia landscape. This description is unequivocally based on our experiences—gained from walking, working, observing, discussing, all on site. But it is also dynamic, generically human in the scale of what is described, and more than visual—factors equally important during Mississippian times. This description is written in explicit recognition of our perception, selection, and filtering of the physical evidence, but it has also been influenced by what we think was significant so long ago to the Mississippians.

The preparation of this lead landscape description was a useful analytical exercise. Although it has been impossible to separate ourselves completely from detached map and aerial views, an important part of this exercise was walking through the site while keeping in constant focus our broader interests and goals. Describing Cahokia in this brief, textual version helped us focus on which aspects of the landscape were important and to structure our data. According to Relph, "it is apparent that describing landscapes, whether by drawing or writing about them, is a way of improving one's ability to see and sense them clearly" (1989, 159). Raymond Williams agrees, writing that "we learn to see a thing by learning to describe it" (1965, 39).

The landscape description is paired with a map (fig. 17), which serves as an important focusing device. The map is a hybrid in technique and function, a combination of both qualitative and quantitative aspects of cartographic representation. It is meant to provide an impressionistic overview of the entire Cahokia landscape that readers may refer to as they progress through parts 2 and 3. Based in large part on a U.S. Geological Survey 7.5-minute topographic quadrangle (entitled Monks Mound), the mounds and other cultural features are located accurately but depicted with hachure and stippling, graphic techniques that impart a qualitatively suggestive depiction of form and topology. Just as the brief landscape description introduces aspects of the landscape that will be considered in more detail in the chapters that follow, this introductory figure is subsequently enriched with other types of representation.

The organization of part 2 and 3 is analogous to how we think people view landscapes: that is, the cues that serve to attract and focus vision and meaning—including both seeing with the eye and vision of the mind—form the structure of these sections (Berger 1980, 192–98). It is these clues that we have highlighted in the landscape description and in figure 17. This

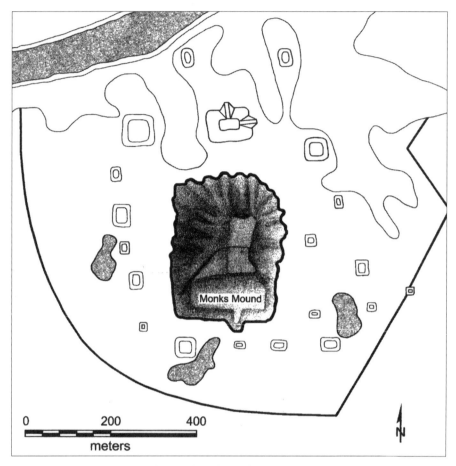

18. Plopping Monks Mound into the plaza of the next largest Mississippian-period mound site, Moundville in Alabama, provides a visual symbol indicating that Cahokia was unequaled in the eastern United States.

approach is more appropriate, both temporally and spatially, than a chrono-logical sequence, which presupposes development and predetermines con-clusions. It explores the multiple interactions between people and the land over time and space and provides a more dynamic and synthetic under-standing of Cahokia as a place and community.

Many of the historic accounts of Cahokia begin with observations about Monks Mound. Other Mississippian sites are perceived first as a concert of vi-sual images; this is not the case at Cahokia. Indeed, no matter from what di-rection you approach Cahokia or from what perspective (ground versus air), the first thing that you see is Monks Mound. Nothing else competes, and nothing else distracts your attention: Monks Mound is wildly out of propor-tion to all surrounding mounds and features.

19. Viewed from atop Monks Mound, Mounds 59 and 60 (the Twin Mounds) are the most visible mounds in this vista. Photograph by William Iseminger. Courtesy of the Cahokia Mounds State Historic Site.

The sheer mass of Monks Mound is its most impressive characteristic. The areal extent of the mound, at approximately 17 acres (7 hectares), is greater than the area of most other Mississippian sites. A favorite slide of ours is one used by John Richards of the University of Wisconsin-Milwaukee that shows Monks Mound descending upon and obliterating the entire Aztalan site. Other Mississippian towns like Toqua, Little Egypt, or the Adams site could also easily fit within the area encompassed by Monks Mound. Our version, in which Monks Mound is projected onto the Moundville site (the second largest Mississippian center) (fig. 18), does not have quite the same visual impact, however, it too emphasizes the imposing stature of Monks Mound. This perspective also serves as a flag, warning us about the possible critical nature of archaeological deposits underneath the mound, which could represent an entire, functioning Emergent Mississippian center.

At over 30 meters (nearly 100 feet) in height, Monks Mound dominates the skyline, and, if one ventures the steep climb up the south edge of the mound to its summit, provides a commanding view of the American Bottom, of the bluffs to the east, and of St. Louis to the west. Yet despite its gargantuan size, there is a human scale in the integration of this great mound with the rest of the site. For example, the limits of the central area, containing the largest concentration of mounds, seem to be tied to the distance from which it is still possible to detect a person standing on Monks Mound. From the Grand Plaza, the meeting grounds for the community, a human voice, echoing off the south wall of the Second and Third Terraces of the mound, can easily be heard.

Wresting one's attention away from Monks Mound, one is overwhelmed by the number and spread of other mounds. Variability in mound height, size, shape, and placement become apparent. The overall impression of amorphous and rounded mound forms, the result of centuries of weathering and erosion, presents a striking contrast with the conceptualized platform, conical, and ridgetop forms that are typically used to model these constructions. At even greater contrast stands our knowledge, gained from detailed topographic maps and excavations, of the variability in slope gradients, terraces, ramps, and other features, and in internal structure, found even among mounds of similar forms.

Wandering about the site, one is awed by the effort that must have gone into the construction of other mounds. At approximately 12.5 meters, Fox and Round Top (Mounds 60 and 59) (fig. 19) are the next tallest mounds. Though about half the height of Monks Mound, these mounds are still on the scale of the largest mounds found at other sizable Mississippian sites. At Cahokia there are at least six mounds found within this 10- to 20-meter category.

The steepness of these mounds is not fully realized without circling on foot around their bases or climbing to their summits. Very different perspectives are gained from the summit and the base. Also, standing atop the summits of sizable platform mounds located near Monks Mound affords a commanding view of the surrounding lower terrain, in contrast to the less imposing vistas afforded from those mounds further from the core or of lesser height. The pairing of platform and conical mounds (fig. 19) in tandem draws attention as well, as do series of mounds forming lines or other geometric shapes. One also starts to perceive the detail of smaller mounds.

The size of the area over which the mounds extend becomes most impressive when one traverses the site. It takes approximately one hour to walk across at a normal pace. This, however, seems much longer in the heat of the summer, or when carrying heavy geophysical gear or excavation equipment, or when fighting bugs while wading through uncut grass (fig. 14). Without the mounds as guideposts, it is easy to lose one's way on the level terrain, especially in areas of high grass.

Yet, as one begins to look past the mounds, the complexity of the terrain becomes apparent; one's perspective varies greatly depending on the location within the site. Sandy ridge and swale topography north of Cahokia Creek contrasts with the flat central and southern landform against which the mounds stand out in sharp relief. But even here, there are subtle indications regarding important topographic variations. Although large, open borrows at the site are typically water-filled year round, seasonal changes in these borrows are apparent, and flooding reveals low areas next to mounds that represent reclaimed borrow pits. Slumping of the fill in these reclaimed borrows has produced slight topographic lows. Large tracts of land in the south and south central portions of the site also become flooded, providing yet another area for birds to gather and an opportunity to see a bit of Cahokia by canoe.

A walk, or perhaps more realistically, a stumbling traverse, through wooded tracts scattered amid the mowed and manicured sections of Cahokia also provides a window to the past. The bumpy and undulating terrain in these clusters of woods indicates that even though the central and southern portions of the site are presently low in relief, the effects of cultivation have been significant. This portion of Cahokia was certainly not as flat during Mississippian times as it is now.

Alterations in the site that have occurred during a time that seems relevant to our lives, i.e., the inception of the central area of the site as a park in the 1920s, and more recent activities that have concentrated on transforming the area from a recreational park to an archaeological interpretive preserve also provide insights. Changing boundaries between public and private spheres have not been limited to the Mississippian past. The state has slowly acquired more and more land, spreading out from the center. Remains relating to historic habitation and, more recently, to historic park use have been eradicated (sometimes posing problems for unwary archaeologists). A drive-in theater has been eliminated, roads have been allowed to grass over, neighborhoods have been removed, and basements have been filled. Mounds have been repaired, groomed, and reconstructed. We are also aware of the efforts necessary to maintain the site, including the control of vegetation, traffic, and erosion. Parallels with prehistoric reclamation, mound construction, and maintenance activities are unmistakable. Thus, just as traces from the prehistoric past remain, a residue of modern history lingers, and sometimes, as in the case of imprints of our knowledge on the landscape, even dominates. Such imprints include the Interpretive Center, rebuilt mounds, cultivated plots of prairie vegetation, segments of the palisade that have been reconstructed, and various markers and interpretive trails.

Our sense of time is reinforced by the nature of our work; the strata observed in our excavations document the complex buildup of occupation involving numerous additions and removals, indicating the varied uses that this land witnessed even prehistorically. One never expects that an excavation unit opened at the site will be clear-cut, obvious, or easy to interpret.

Even shorter-term seasonal dynamics have become reinforced during our tenure at the site. Visitation of the park varies greatly with the seasons. Annual totals exceed three hundred thousand visitors, though the size of the site diminishes the sense that large numbers of people visit the park. When conducting field work away from the Interpretive Center, the impression gained is not that over three hundred thousand people pass through the site each year; rather, it seems as though the number of visitors were much less. Winters tend to be quiet, and the visitors that do come to the museum are kept away from our field work by the cold and wet and mud. November through February tend to be slow, with the smallest number of people coming to the site during

January and February. Although numbers begin to pick up in March, school groups and tourists concentrate their visits on the period from May through October. Visitors are more willing to brave the summer elements to track us down at the site. The height of the tourist season runs from June through August.

During the winter there is no mowing, less activity by park personnel, and more animals come out, especially large groups of deer. Off-season work can be particularly enjoyable, if one is dressed warmly and if the ground is not frozen. At these times it is soft and easy to dig, though the gumbo clay, true to its name, seems to stick to everything. It is easier to make our way through the woods, and subtle variations in the landscape that are obscured by vegetation at other times of the year become visible. In the summer the heat, the bugs, the thick vegetation, and the dry, hard gumbo clay combine to make digging at the site difficult, to say the least.

For us the site is too big to cover easily on a daily basis. One's sense that Cahokia represents a coherent whole is also obscured by natural and cultural elements, which tend to segment rather than unify. Mowed, manicured, trailed segments contrast with pockets of woods, cultivated plots, and surrounding modern neighborhoods. Near the Interpretive Center prairie plots show the visitor what the prehistoric vegetation might have been. An interstate highway (I-55/70) to the north of Monks Mound isolates mounds such as the Kunnemann group from the remainder of the site. A major east-west, four-lane highway bisects the central portion of the site, dividing Monks Mound from the Grand Plaza and other southern regions. This road system also provides a strong orthogonal element, which is mirrored in Cahokia Creek and the string of mounds located along its southern margins and in mound strings forming lines perpendicular to this direction. Cahokia Creek presents an insurmountable boundary for us when walking the site, and we have to ask whether it did for the Cahokians too.

We can also divide the site into a park center, which presents a facade of timelessness, and a surrounding landscape that can be seen as evolving, as evidenced by a fluidity of construction in residential neighborhoods and degradation of the prehistoric remains at the more dynamic edges of the site where public protection is not ensured. The visitor's impression of the site, gained from a trip to the park, is therefore that this area has been frozen in time, that it represents a preserved, pristine slice of the past. Yet this is largely the result of changes directed toward returning the area to what it may have looked like in the past, not a preservation of what once was.

THE MUSEUM LANDSCAPE

How does the landscape of the Cahokia Mounds State Historic Site, encountered by a visitor today, differ from that of Mississippian times? Certainly, this area is of diminished relief; mounds have been lowered and rounded, and certain sections of the terrain have been homogenized. And there have been a number of historic transformations occurring over the course of historic settlement and park tenure. Because many of the historic features have now been removed, and due to the number of mounds that remain, the central portion of the site can be viewed as approximating, or at least providing a glimpse of, the lay of the land as it was during Mississippian times. It can thus impart a sense of the scale, organization, and immensity of Mississippian achievements.

What is perhaps the greatest misconception about the landscape of the Cahokia Mounds site is that it approximates that of the Mississippian cultural florescence, what Cahokia would have been at its peak, although during this period not all of the mounds had been constructed. As the result of changes made over the entire course of the Mississippians' tenure, the landform viewed today, replete with vestiges of many of the major mounds, is actually closer to that of the period of cultural decline, when population was dwindling.

Over the course of the Mississippian occupation, a quite varied landscape would have emerged, transformed through the addition and rebuilding of mounds and through other terrain modifications. For the Mississippians not only built mounds, they also significantly reworked the terrain, especially in the central portion of the site. Here they excavated and reclaimed large tracts of land. So we must add the volumes of earth moved in this fashion to the already impressive amounts manifest in the mounds.

At the Interpretive Center, reconstructive drawings, a slide show, a diorama, and exhibits add detail to this terrain in the form of people, houses and other constructions, activities, and myriad aspects of material life. However, this view of the past often fails to recognize and incorporate the changing nature of the terrain and the accompanying movements of people and reorganization of communities through time. What did the site look like during Emergent Mississippian times? How was the land transformed and what mounds would have been present during the greatest spread of occupation? When virtually all mounds were complete, what was the nature of the occupation and what was the state of repair and use of these mounds? How did people respond to a changing landscape?

Missing from the vision presented at the Interpretive Center are characteristics that capture this sense of change—features that are lacking now but would have been present during the construction of this great center. Absent is the sense of disarray and incompleteness that was most certainly present during late Emergent Mississippian and early Mississippian periods of earthmoving, such as vast tracts of muddy terrain, open borrows, and those in the process of being reclaimed. One salient feature of the site is its substrate of gumbo clay: it certainly figured prominently in the lives of the Mississippians, yet it never appears in reconstructive views.

Reconstructive views of Cahokia tend to be groomed and manicured, just as the site is today. They show a site covered with carefully mowed, Bermuda short grass that covers mounds and connecting terrain alike. Obviously, Cahokia would have looked very different during prehistoric times, and this imported ground cover would not have been there. General Land Office and other historic records (Messenger 1808, Brackenridge 1811) suggest that the area was once covered by prairie vegetation. Construction as well as foot traffic would have denuded much of the site, exposing the underlying gumbo clay. During much of the year, the surface would have been mud. Elsewhere perhaps a scattering of bunch grass would have been present. It is unlikely that these grasses would have covered the mounds during Mississippian times. For one thing, they would have presented quite a fire hazard. Thus, the Cahokians would have fought a constant battle to maintain these largely unvegetated mounds. This battle against erosion and slumping continues today, though it never figures in reconstructive views. In contrast to today, the site would have been treeless for the most part, although there was doubtless a scattering of trees, especially in wet areas next to watercourses. In our excavations in the Grand Plaza area, for example, we have found evidence of prehistoric removal of these isolated trees.

Garbage and other debris are also notably absent from reconstructive exhibits and drawings. Invariably, when discussing Cahokia with others, we are asked about garbage: "Wasn't there garbage everywhere, wasn't the smell terrible?" Although we certainly are not the Rathjes of Cahokia (William Rathje heads the Garbage Project, a systematic look at modern garbage, using archaeological methodology [Rathje 1974]), we can make a few comments about this issue. It is important to remember that the Cahokians were not conspicuous consumers. They did not have, and they did not need, a weekly trash service. The composition of their trash was much different from ours, and they dumped it in subsurface receptacles of any kind—pits, abandoned houses, borrow pits, and over edges of the creek. So, at Cahokia we do not see ring middens, but, through the superpositioning of occupation through time, we see the buildup or concentration of midden in certain occupation areas. This midden is fully mixed with the soil, and typically it is this mixture that is found in the open borrows.

The major component of midden, or garbage, soils at Cahokia is wood ash, introduced from wood used daily as fuel. There would have also been a huge demand for wood for use in construction. Iseminger et al. (1990) have estimated the phenomenal amount of timber needed for the construction and rebuilding of the Central Palisade, nearly twenty thousand timbers per stage. In addition, wood would have been necessary for the construction and maintenance of other palisades and screens, for houses, and for larger structures. Timber would have been largely obtained from the bluffs to the east of the site. Although wood for domestic fuel use was probably obtained during daily foraging expeditions, scrap wood obtained in this manner would obviously not have sufficed for the larger building projects. For such projects, wood was probably brought into the site and stockpiled. In addition, Bareis (1975b, 13) has argued that soils of different compositions were stockpiled during the construction of Monks Mound. At the nearby Mitchell site, evidence of such stockpiling activity in Mississippian mound construction was documented in two small mounds that were interpreted as stock-piles of pure clay and silt (Porter 1974, 336–39). Therefore, in addition to muddy terrain and open borrows, mounds of building materials as well as mounds of earth should figure in our reconstructive views.

In keeping with archaeological perceptions of the past across the eastern United States, pictures of the site tend to be composed of a limited palette of natural greens and browns. Yet a wealth of ethnohistorical observations (Swanton 1946) suggest that the site was probably rife with color and deco-ration. These observations indicate that among historic tribes of the South-east, the human body was often enhanced by the addition of colors, includ-ing red, black, yellow, blue, and white (Swanton 1946, 529). For the most part, it was men that were painted as signifiers of different official and semi-official statuses and roles. Body painting was augmented by a variety of hair-styles, tattoos, feathers, and other decorations. Tattooing was apparently used by women and men alike, though again these were keyed to status, roles, and gender (Swanton 1946, 541).

Just as color was important in transforming and decorating the human body, it was also an important component of manufactured items. Here color was even more varied (Swanton 1946, 608–10). Color on houses is recorded. Red or white plastered houses have been mentioned (Swanton 1946, 389, 394). Though painted designs on dwellings are not mentioned, the use of mats woven of splints of differently colored (dyed) canes to adorn the exteriors of houses is noted (Swanton 1946, 396, 406). Ornamentation of certain types of structures was also present. For example, it was customary to place a carved image (in particular a bird such as an eagle, turkey, or dove) on the roof of the temple/charnel house. Pillars of open-air buildings were also carved and painted (Swanton 1946, 613). Flags, e.g., standards of animal skins with designs, were often flown, as observed by the Spanish entrada (Swanton 1946, 431).

Reconstructive views and exhibits, despite a concentration on seasonal ac-tivities, tend to present the landscape of the site as aseasonal. This viewpoint disassociates the Cahokians from their landscape and tends to make us for-get the conditions with which they had to contend. The harsh winter weather, the wet and muddy terrain, even the round of seasonal activities of-ten slip into the background.

As mentioned earlier in this chapter, a masking of historic impact in the form of the interpretive removal of historic features, both in exhibits and on site, has produced the facade of a timeless terrain. Yet both prehistoric and historic changes are important to consider: despite the removal of obvious features, historic use has left an overlay.

To some extent we can work backward to understand the prehistoric situ-ation. We know that historic cultivation has significantly muted the relief of the area and that features of the landscape with initial low relief are no longer visible. Brackenridge (1868, 255) alludes to small elevations marking the entire plain, which he interprets as former dwellings "whose perishable materials had crumbled down." Today, remains of former prehistoric house locations appear as recognizable circular depressions only in some uncultivated areas. Many mounds were certainly more angular, yet we do know that mound erosion was also a problem during prehistoric times. Only hints of causeways, ramps, shared platforms, and other distinctive elevated features remain. We also know that missing from the record are a number of mounds purposefully removed during historic times and that our picture has been slanted toward the larger landforms; the existence of small mounds, extant most commonly in uncultivated settings, hint at the numerous small mounds that were probably once present. Early aerial photographs indicate the presence of several of these.

On the other hand, historic changes can also inform us about the prehistoric setting. For example, settling of sediments within reclaimed borrows since Mississippian times allows us to identify and define these features through fine-scale topographic surveys. Patterns of historic settlement sometimes mirror the prehistoric situations and suggest common reasons for choosing this land for occupation. In other cases, the historic patterns differ markedly from the prehistoric ones, helping us to understand better what is unique about Mississippian Cahokia. Current problems with mound erosion and slumping, most notably those associated with Monks Mound (Emerson and Woods 1990), direct us to look for evidence of such in the prehistoric situation. The placement of new steps up Monks Mound alerts us to maintenance activities that surely would have been necessary during the hundreds of years that Cahokia was occupied. Historic neighborhood relocation and removal and the transformation of land from private use to public use call forth the dynamism not only of the Cahokia landform but also of the often rapid and drastic fluctuations in land use during Mississippian times. It is enlightening to consider these historic changes not only for their physical impacts but also as a source for a dialogue with the past. Did the Cahokians face similar situations, and, if so, how did they respond? Time depth is the essence of our archaeological contribution, allowing us to modify the static reconstructive conception. Our aim in the following chapters is to do just that by asking a number of new questions of our archaeological data.

We begin with a general sequence of archaeological phases, illustrated with traditional maps showing the distribution of occupation at the site at various times and enriched with a series of landscape drawings that provide a great deal of detail on both cultural and environmental variations. This general sequence is followed by a series of vignettes that provide a picture of the evolving organization and form of the Cahokia landscape during the Mississippian period. We have avoided, in the following work, embedding a string of citations in the text every time data from a particular site area are mentioned. References from which the data were drawn can be easily accessed by looking up the appropriate site area, mound, or mound group in the table in the appendix.

CHAPTER FOUR

SETTLING

CAHOKIA

The Cahokia sequence has been divided into two periods: Emergent Mississippian, which has been dated from A.D. 800–1000 (calibrated A.D. 925–1050), and the Mississippian period, spanning A.D. 1000–1400 (calibrated A.D. 1050–1350). Each period is divided into phases. For our purposes, we speak of an early and late Emergent Mississippian, a division not grounded on the radiocarbon sequence. The Mississippian period is more reliably subdivided into four phases: Lohmann (A.D. 1000–1050; calibrated 1050–1100), Stirling (A.D. 1050–1150; calibrated A.D. 1100–1200), Moorehead (A.D. 1150–1250; calibrated A.D. 1200–1275), and Sand Prairie (A.D. 1250–1400; calibrated 1275–1350). In turn, each of the phases have been subdivided. These are also lacking a radiocarbon-based grounding. Calibrated dates are provided by Hall (1991).

Cahokia was a Mississippian period mound center. The roots for what Cahokia was to become, however, can be traced to the Emergent Mississippian period, so named for obvious reasons. Although there are scattered remains dating to earlier time spans, it is in the Emergent Mississippian period that we first recognize an occupation that has clear continuity with the succeeding Mississippian center.

Beginning slowly, but accelerating rapidly, occupation grew during the Emergent Mississippian period to a nearly continuous spread of houses stretching for some 3.5 kilometers along Helms Ridge, a point bar meander of the Edelhardt paleomeander (fig. 20). Single houses or clusters were displaced to the north and south from this aggregation and varied from two to even larger conglomerations. Population densities were not of a magnitude sufficient to compel house siting in low-lying terrain. During the Mississippian period (A.D. 1000–1400) population pressure and, perhaps more significantly, societal pressure instituted this practice. The occupation at Cahokia can be considered part of a larger spread of Emergent Mississippian settlements within the American Bottom, including those on the bluffs and next to the creeks coursing from the bluffs to the Bottom.

Emergent Mississippian houses were rectangular and small (most 2 to 4 meters on a side). In contrast to the keyhole structures and less substantial houses of the Late Woodland period (A.D. 300–800), they were constructed by excavating a foundation, then using a series of single posts set into the excavated foundation for walls. Though these houses appear small by today's and even Mississippian standards, they were larger than preceding types and their semisubterranean foundation helped ameliorate temperature extremes.

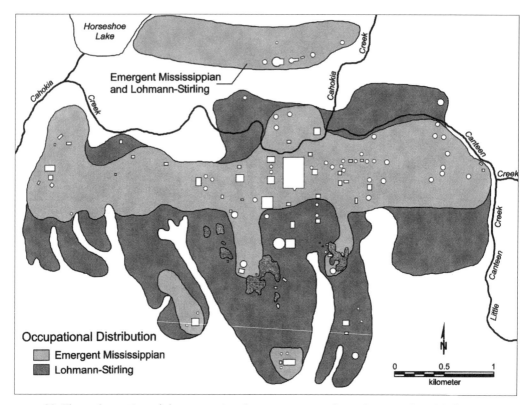

20. The early portion of the occupational sequence arose along the most desirable land, which subsequently became the locus for mound construction, forcing domestic households to spread to less desirable landforms. The Lohmann-Stirling occupational distribution includes that of the preceding Emergent Mississippian period.

Their arrangement bespeaks organizational differences as well. For the most part, multiple houses were organized in a courtyard pattern (fig. 21). A central focus of the courtyard groups was a series of pits, usually large, and now and then central posts. This pattern sometimes took the form of four square-orifice pits arranged in a square (J. E. Kelly 1990b). Such redundancy served to reinforce symbolic communication and is an especially prominent feature of rituality (Rapoport 1982). The pits, which were used as storage and earth ovens, were of a capacity to serve large groups of people. Their presence signifies an unparalleled focus on centrality and symbolic concepts (e.g., four-corner notion of directionality) that continued to resonate throughout the Mississippian period.

A bewildering ceramic sequence has been offered for the Emergent Mississippian period, and it is likely that this will be significantly revised in the future. Over this period, it appears that there was a population increase from early to late such that, by late Emergent Mississippian times, the sprawling village would not at first glance admit to differentiation. Yet, when studied across time, we can see that the area that was to become the core of the site witnessed greater time depth and residence rebuilding, implying a continuity in land tenure and residential stability. In contrast, on the margins we witness fluctuating land tenure, manifest in single-stage residences. The houses in the center were not much larger than those on the margins, although their basins were slightly deeper.

Both mound and plaza ceremonialism at Cahokia arose during this period, yet the transformation from village to mound center is murky in detail. What evidence we do have lends credence to a "big bang" theory (Pauketat 1997a) as opposed to one indicating more humble origins. Sometime late within the Emergent Mississippian period, construction on at least Monks Mound and the Grand Plaza began. Although evidence of earthen construction during the Emergent Mississippian period can be found elsewhere within the American Bottom region (Griffin 1977; Pauketat 1997a), the scale of earthen construction evinced at Cahokia is clearly unprecedented. Once established, it quickly eclipsed that at other fledgling mound centers. For the next four hundred years, indeed, even to the present, the site evolved around Monks Mound and the Grand Plaza.

Monks Mound, the Grand Plaza, and the large tracts of land borrowed from within the central village to supply the earth for their construction subsumed large portions of the Emergent Mississippian central village. The transformation of this residential center into a sacred, largely unoccupied precinct provides the first of many instances of planned domestic resettlement at the site. Scores of families residing in this area were moved out from this center to surrounding areas. Excavations into Mound 72, a small, early Mississippian ridgetop mound located south of Monks Mound and the Grand Plaza, have documented burial pits and deposits indicating that an individual of great importance was buried within, along with an astounding number of grave goods and retainers. The construction of this mound suggests the power that would have been necessary to orchestrate these resettlement efforts.

What separates the Emergent Mississippian period from the succeeding Mississippian period amounts to only a few traits in the archaeological record: the replacement of single-post foundations with wall trenches and select ceramic traits. Nearly all Mississippian houses were constructed with a foundation (i.e., they were semisubterranean) and wall-trench walls. These wall trenches were slit trenches ca. 15 to 30 centimeters wide and 15 to 60 centimeters deep that were excavated into the floor of the foundation basin. The trenches rarely meet, and seldom do we find evidence of an opening. Posts were then set into the trenches. One interesting theory is that the walls could have been prefabricated and placed into the trench as a unit. Presumably they were formed by weaving grass and other materials between the wall posts. Mats may have been used as well. Daub was not common; even well-burned houses lack evidence of daubing. Three types of roofs were possible, including the standard gable form, the dome, and the cone.

21. Artist's reconstruction of an Emergent Mississippian courtyard in autumn. The vantage point is in the vicinity of Mound 42, looking toward Monks Mound as it is being constructed.

In this scene it is fall harvest time. Cahokia is beginning to take shape. A man carries his tools toward Monks Mound, where he will join others as they work to complete the first stages. After the recent rains, which have softened the soil, and a successful harvest, it is time again to work on Monks Mound to help bring to fruition the shared vision of the great town of Cahokia. At the entrance to the courtyard we notice a small garden plot planted with corn and squash. This food will be used to supplement the allotment of the communal harvest given to each family. Farther along the path we notice a man and some boys hanging game to clean and butcher. A pair of neighborhood dogs have also come to wait patiently for scraps. One takes a drink from the puddle near the path before she joins her mate. To the right we see the women of this group gathered to do their work. Some grind freshly dried corn for flour, others weave baskets, learning new techniques and sharing design ideas with one another. A young mother tends to her child as she helps to prepare the midday meal. Nearest the house on the right, the matriarch of the family makes a pot from clay, using the coiled-rope technique. At her side we see freshwater clam shells that are crushed and added to the clay to help harden the pot when it is fired. Her granddaughter is assisting, learning the fine art of pottery design passed down from generation to generation. In the foreground, just to the right of the path, we see four pits dug in the earth. These feasting/ceremonial pits have been formed in the shape of squares and circles. The square, which represents culture, is adjacent to the circle, which represents the order of the natural world. These pits also mark the four directions, east, south, west, and north, reminding the Cahokians of the cycles of the seasons and the marking of time. We will see this combination, the square adjacent to the circle, repeated again in the building of platform mounds and conical burial mounds as the form of Cahokia continues to develop.

For the most part the houses were rectangular during early Mississippian times, changing to square late during the period. Early Mississippian houses were around 10 meters square, middle Mississippian houses were around 15 meters square, and later houses ranged from 20 to 40 meters square. Large structures, 100 meters square, were also present, as were L-shaped (early) and T-shaped (late) buildings and circular structures, which presumably represented sweat baths.

During the Emergent Mississippian period, mounds, which previously functioned as multicommunity burial sites and were located away from the village, were first brought into a community setting. The manipulation of the land through earthmoving activities started during Emergent Mississippian times and gathered steam during the Mississippian period. Mound construction became more prolific and, hence, more visible. During the beginning of the period, the majority of earthen construction was focused on the community center as established during the Emergent Mississippian period, yet a number of large mounds were also built at community margins. Patterning in alignments, locations, and differentiation now became obvious at the site. Thus, we can begin to describe internal boundaries, subcommunities, functional areas, and planning and design concepts with mounds and even borrows for these mounds figuring into these discussions in important ways.

22. Artist's reconstruction of a new neighborhood in summer during Lohmann-Stirling times. The vantage point is southeast of the Interpretive Center, near the Tippetts mound group, looking toward Monks Mound.

Cahokia is a thriving town during Lohmann-Stirling times. In this illustration we see a new neighborhood with houses arranged in an orthogonal fashion—reorganized from the courtyards we saw during Emergent Mississippian times. This new alignment is the result of the development of Cahokia's civic core: Monks Mound, the Grand Plaza, and the numerous platform/conical mound combinations that bound the Plaza. With summer rains, the borrow pits, which were dug to supply soil for mound building, have filled. In the foreground, cattails *(Typha spp.)* and other aquatic plants have started to colonize the older pits. In the distance we see Monks Mound. The ruling family inhabits the larger structure that sits atop the mound. The women have gathered to talk before going out to cultivate the cornfields. They have come together just after the morning meal—notice the smoke that still lingers on the horizon—before the heat of the day makes it too uncomfortable to work. We also see some young boys returning from spearing fish at nearby Cahokia Creek. One boy stops to show his father and his uncle his catch.

The Mississippian period is divided into four phases (Lohmann, A.D. 1000–1050; Stirling, A.D. 1050–1150; Moorehead, A.D. 1150–1250; and Sand Prairie, A.D. 1250–1400). Using an estimate of thirty years as a generation, each phase represents two to five generations. In general, the early Mississippian phases (Lohmann and Stirling [A.D. 1000–1150]) represent a time of cultural florescence, enlargement, and internal differentiation (Holley et al. 1989), whereas Moorehead and Sand Prairie (A.D. 1150–1400), the late Mississippian phases, correspond to a time of decline.

During the Lohmann phase, we see the by-products of the center's shift from profane to sacred. New communities were established in widespread patches throughout the area that we identify as the Cahokia site (fig. 20). The once continuous Emergent Mississippian occupation on Helms Ridge was displaced, but strands of homestead groupings radiating out from this area were consolidated and reformed. Cahokia was no longer a compact village and was clearly on its way to becoming a dominant regional center. Population increased drastically during this time, not because of any changes in birthrates, but due to a rapid influx of people from surrounding regions.

Wall-trench houses of the Lohmann phase are notably larger than their earlier, single-post counterparts. Seemingly symptomatic of this newfound style in house construction are multiroom wall-trench buildings, which proliferated during this phase. In fact, the use of adjoined rooms was seldom seen again in the region. A strong orthogonal organization is evident, attuned to site-wide planning (fig. 22). The paucity of rebuilding within many areas of the site during this phase is indicative of the volatility of the times. Displacement of a community could not have been a pleasant prospect, except for those who profited from the replacement of a domestic setting by an elite setting with restricted access, of which we presume much and know very little.

The Stirling phase (A.D. 1050–1150) constitutes the high point of occupation in all measurable barometers, except in volume of earth moved. During this phase, population reached its zenith and occupation spread reached the limits of what we identify as the site today. External contacts, expressed in trade items, reached their fullest extent, and earthen construction, measured by the number of mounds constructed, was at a maximum.

23. Artist's reconstruction of a housing cluster in winter during the Moorehead phase. The vantage point is south of Mound 48 inside the Central Palisade, looking toward Monks Mound.

Here we see a winter scene during Moorehead-Sand Prairie times. Many of the people have moved inside the palisade. Houses are again grouped close together, reminiscent of the courtyards of the Emergent Mississippian period. The men are clothed in heavier winter garments: having just returned from a hunting trip, they now share stories of the difficulties of the hunt. Several hundred years of continuous occupation have taken their toll on the surrounding ecosystems. The landscape has changed dramatically. Local forests have been cut down for fuel and home building; intensive agriculture has caused erosion and silted in local streams; the local environment no longer provides the abundant resources it once did. With the cold weather, many of Cahokia's remaining citizens stay indoors, waiting out the winter by working on projects and teaching the children their history and culture through storytelling. In the distance, Monks Mound reaches to touch the sky. All terraces have been completed, and a large building sits atop the summit. Just to the west of the structure we see that a large portion of the summit has given way and soil has slumped all the way to the foot of the mound. Erosion has been a continuous problem for the people of Cahokia, and now, with fewer people and dwindling resources, repair of the mounds has become less of a priority than it once was.

The Stirling phase is divided into early and late facets based on ceramic traits. Around the Lohmann/Stirling interface, numerous areas spreading outward from Monks Mound continued to be cleared of residences and began to take on public functions centered around circular woodhenges and large structures and enclosures. This was a time of hurly-burly construction. House construction was sometimes shoddy, basins were not as deep; it appears that the Cahokians were not investing as much in housing as in other construction. Rebuilding was rampant, most likely due to the need for repairs. The geometric orientation of the community also softened. In contrast to the communal nature of Lohmann times, Stirling communities were inward-looking, though on a much larger scale than the courtyards of the Emergent Mississippian period. At the end of the phase, the site looked very different from its appearance at the end of the Lohmann phase. Great changes had occurred, population had decreased, and cultural decline or reformulation was evident. A large, encircling palisade was also begun, which truncated the

Central Precinct, leaving a number of important mortuary mounds, including Mound 72 as well as residential areas, outside the enclosure.

The reductions that emerged during this terminal span of the Stirling phase were fully in place by the Moorehead phase (A.D. 1150–1250) (figs. 23 and 24). Subcommunities had broken down, and the overall organization of the site had disintegrated. An increasing inward focus, hinted at during the Stirling phase, continued. Present again were small courtyard groupings, though the houses were bigger, and fewer were found in a cluster than those in Emergent Mississippian courtyards. Population continued to decline, and the remaining residents moved back, in the main, to occupy the core of the site (although we do see a strong Moorehead presence in a few isolated areas outside of this core, e.g., at the Powell, Kunnemann, and West Borrow Pit groups). Though mound construction had all but stopped by the end of the period, at least in terms of the initiation of new construction, palisade rebuilding continued unabated until the end of this phase. There is

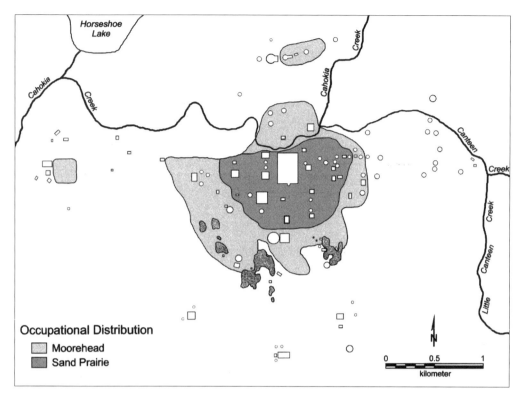

24. Contraction of the area occupied is but one of many characteristics of the decline of Cahokia. Although the Moorehead phase occupation remains substantial, the final Sand Prairie phase was literally confined to the flanks of Monks Mound. The areal coverage of the Moorehead phase includes that of the subsequent Sand Prairie phase.

an impression of an overall wealthier resident population with regard to exotic goods, yet there are also hints that this population may not have been eating as well or have had the ability to utilize choice wood. A greater volume of exotics may also signify times of stress wherein these items were being used to ameliorate tensions between people, an interpretation that may be more consistent with our understanding of other changes taking place during this phase.

What happens next is poorly understood. The resident population during the Sand Prairie phase (A.D. 1250–1400) was at best a "rump" occupation and reused the ruins of previous generations (fig. 24). We have no evidence of construction of either mounds or large features such as the Central Palisade. The Sand Prairie population lived in a landscape that was the result of generations of occupation, one that we now call Cahokia. By the end of the phase, Cahokia was completely abandoned by its Mississippian inhabitants, opening the door for succeeding occupations of the area by Illini and other historic tribes, and by the French and other Euro-American settlers.

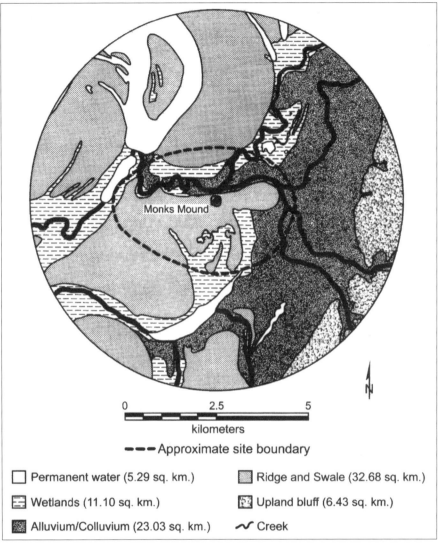

25. Environmental catchment, 5-kilometer radius, centered on Monks Mound. Cahokia's environs were a mosaic of submerged and elevated landforms. Water was a dominant feature, especially seasonally.

SITE SELECTION

Why is Cahokia where it is? To understand why the site was settled, we can point to a number of physical characteristics that made this location desirable to the Emergent Mississippians. In common with other Mississippian sites in the American Bottom, this area provided an expanse of high ground to accommodate habitation; periodically enriched, well-drained

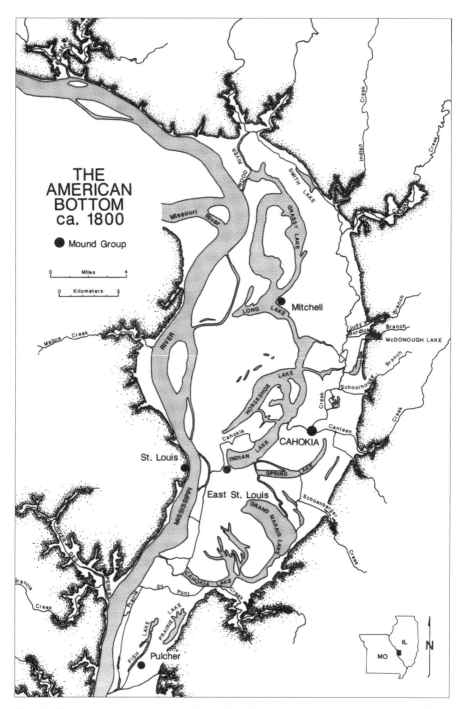

THE
AMERICAN
BOTTOM
ca. 1800

● Mound Group

26. Cahokia was but one concentration of a string of mounds occupying the northern American Bottom, which even included centers in what is now St. Louis and East St. Louis. These centers are connected by waterways, forming an artery parallel to the Mississippi River. Courtesy of Southern Illinois University Edwardsville Office of Contract Archaeology.

soils suitable for cultivation; proximity to water in various forms; access to the uplands via waterways; and a diversity of habitats (fig. 25).

The Cahokia site is located in the center of the widest portion of the American Bottom, a large flood plain found immediately below the confluence of the Illinois, Missouri, and Mississippi Rivers. This flood plain extends between the present Illinois communities of Alton and Chester, with the widest portion located between Alton and Dupo. We surmise, based on early historic data, that during prehistoric times the American Bottom consisted of a series of water-filled channels (fig. 26). William Oliver, who visited the area in 1842, provided the following comments on the environment of the American Bottom (Oliver 1924 [1843], 169–70):

> Immediately opposite of St. Louis, the American Bottom is twelve miles wide, in some places densely wooded and intersected with ponds and back-waters, and in others consisting of prairie, interrupted by groves of pinoak (laurel oak), hiccory, persimmon, paw-paw, etc. The plain, in many places, abounds with those ancient mounds which are so frequently met with in many parts of the States, and which here in some instances run in a continuous line for a considerable distance.

We can conceptualize the Bottom during the Mississippian occupation not as a vast expanse of dry land punctuated by occasional low-lying and water-filled areas, but as an area dissected by a number of interconnected waterways. Similarly, we can conceptualize the main part of Cahokia as an island—a large expanse of habitable ground surrounded by water—bounded by Cahokia Creek along the north and west and the low-lying Spring Lake meander scar and associated cut-off chute along the southeast and southwest (figs. 17, 25, and 26). The General Land Office notes of 1810 (Illinois General Land Office Field Notes, 57:704) describe the land in the vicinity of mound groups located at the southern and southwestern and southeastern perimeters of the site (prairie and Mississippi Bottom) as "wet" (fig. 27).

The sense that Cahokia was intimately connected to a series of waterways is certainly absent from the site today. Yet these bodies of water were extremely important to the Cahokians, providing a diversity of resources and avenues of transport. Cahokia afforded the ideal setting for a Mississippian town in terms of commerce and networks. It was connected to the Mississippi River via sloughs and creeks, although it is true that many spots in the American Bottom are so situated. We know that by A.D. 1000 the Mississippi River had essentially reached its current channel along the western limits of the Bottom, ca. 13.5 kilometers (8.5 miles) distant. Contemporary Cahokia is astride the convergence of two primary creeks, Cahokia and Canteen, which merge to the immediate northwest of Monks Mound, within the Edelhardt meander scar (fig. 28). These creeks were vital networks to the uplands to the east, home of oak-hickory forest and circumscribed zones of woodland, savanna, and prairie vegetation. In the Bottom, ecological zones would have included annually submerged river-edge woodlands, perennially inundated

27. Wet prairie at the Cahokia site, perhaps representative of the environment at the time of the Mississippian occupation.

sloughs and other low areas, flood-plain woodlands, extensive bottom-land prairies, and oak-hickory forests on high, well-drained areas in the north-eastern portion of the Bottom. In the immediate vicinity of Cahokia we can point to large aquatic, semiaquatic, and prairie habitats. Paleomeanders to the north (i.e., Horseshoe Lake) and to the south (marshlands of the older Spring Lake meander) (fig. 28) were habitats harboring rich food sources. Wooded flood-plain habitats would have been a minor component. Since we know that the soils that the Mississippians were farming developed under woodland vegetation and not wet prairie, it is apparent that field clearance would have eradicated wooded flood-plain habitats except for perennially inundated swamps.

The number and variety of microhabitats in the region would have sustained a great diversity of exploitable plant and animal populations, fuel that allowed the Cahokians to rework their landscape and to build their great community. Faunal and floral resources were tapped in a shifting manner throughout the Cahokian occupation. The Mississippians made extensive use of fish, amphibians and reptiles, mussels, birds, and mammals, with reliance placed upon small fish, deer, and aquatic birds. A variety of nuts, seeds, fruits, greens, and tubers were gathered, and a number of plants

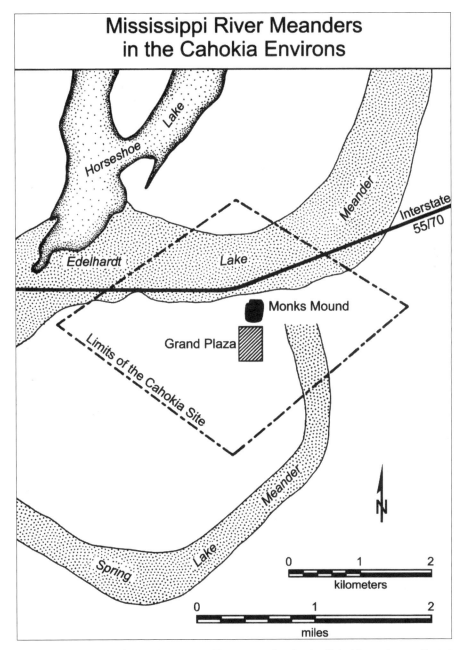

Mississippi River Meanders in the Cahokia Environs

28. Each of the three known Mississippi River meanders in the Cahokia environs affected the growth and development of the site. The oldest, the Spring Lake meander, served as natural boundary of the downtown area. The Edelhardt meander contained Cahokia Creek, a primary artery for the northern American Bottom. Horseshoe Lake, the most recent meander, which likely held water during the Mississippian period, would have been an important resource base.

producing masses of small, starchy seeds (chenopod, erect knotweed, may grass, and little barley) and oily seeds (marsh elder, sunflower) were cultivated, but their use appears to decrease dramatically as the Mississippian period progresses. Squash, gourds, and tobacco were also cultivated (Lopinot 1991). Throughout the Bottom, there is clear evidence for the intensification of the multicropping system from Late Woodland through early Mississippian times (Johannessen 1993; Lopinot 1992, 1997; Rindos and Johannessen 1991; Scarry 1993). Maize, however, was the predominantly produced food and major dietary staple.

Even during the Mississippian period, one cannot speak of a truly "natural" American Bottom landscape. The effects of many millennia of human occupation had resulted in marked changes through the extirpation of local animal species; introduction of exotic plants (including domesticates); forest clearance for fuel, construction materials, and agricultural fields with attendant accelerated erosion and downslope deposition; localized enrichment of soils in habitation areas; the maintenance and extension of prairies and removal of forest undergrowth through burning; and, possibly, managed groves of nut-bearing trees on the bluffs. The widespread acceptance of maize during the Emergent Mississippian period probably also increased some animal populations, such as deer, raccoon, and opossum, by providing additional forage in the maize outfields.

Maize places restrictions on its growers, especially those whose technology includes tillage with hand implements and no fertilization. A thorough knowledge of the characteristics and the distribution of soils would have been critical. Throughout the southeastern United States, the evidence demonstrates that aboriginal cultivators understood the importance of such knowledge and placed their settlements proximal to areas of readily tilled, fertile, nonacid soils whose fertility was periodically renewed by additions of alluvium, but whose flood regimes did not extend into the growing season (Woods 1987, 1993b).

It is probable that Mississippian food production involved an infield-outfield system where gardens were located near structures, and large communal fields were located around settlements (Adair 1930, 435–37; Swanton 1931, 46; 1946, 309). The large maize outfields would have been located in bottom and alluvial fan settings, whereas the multicrop infields and house gardens would have been placed within the habitation zone. These infields and house gardens, situated on productive soils that had often been culturally enriched by prior occupation, formed a major food source. At the Cahokia site, structures were sufficiently scattered to allow for substantial gardening. For example, at the site of the current Interpretive Center, which contained fairly densely packed structures during the Lohmann and early Stirling phases, the built environment, which includes structures and all associated facilities, covers only 10 percent or less of the available area. Therefore, at least 90 percent of this area was available for other uses, including gardening. During the Moorehead phase, this number increases to approximately 97 percent.

At first glance, Cahokia seems to be poorly situated for such an agricultural strategy. The immediate site area consists of texturally mixed soils on ridge and swale topography surrounded by permanently or seasonally flooded zones. There is much clayey gumbo, which is almost impossible to till by hand when either dry or wet. Native vegetation at the site consisted of grasses with scattered woodlands and forest found only as galleries along the watercourses. However, to the east, Cahokia's 5-kilometer catchment radius (fig. 25) contained the largest zone in the American Bottom of soils characterized as optimal for prehistoric hoe cultivation. Maize fields would have extended from the bottom to the lower and midslopes of the bluff. Unfortunately, despite efforts to recover traces of prehistoric agriculture in these areas, no local ridged fields similar to those dramatic examples found in the upper Midwest (Gallagher 1992), have been identified. Ridged fields are easily disturbed by modern cultivation. However, recent excavations indicate that buried examples may exist in the Cahokia area (Holden 1996; Riley and Said 1993).

The interconnected network of waterways would have served as one means of transporting people and produce to and from the fields. Most commonly, however, people would probably have traveled on foot along the high ground bordering the creeks, and this would have been a daily occurrence during certain seasons. Small groups of people would follow this route to the fields for hoeing, weeding, pest control, and so forth. These trips would probably be multipurpose in that fish, small animals, and other resources would be collected, as well as bundles of scrap wood, all in constant demand. During times of tillage (late spring) and harvest (summer and fall), larger groups would be traveling out to the fields. It is likely that field houses would also have been located in the outfields.

Mississippian food production and procurement strategies appear to have been focused on the place of habitation; a strategy made possible by the diversity of microhabitats within the flood plain and nearby upland settings. As successful as this strategy might have been for dispersed populations in such a plentiful environment, the nucleation of large numbers of people at Cahokia, and to an extent at other centers, provided a different adaptive context that ultimately led to ruinous consequences. But before we even begin to think about consequences, let us first return to our initial question regarding the beginnings of Cahokia and the reasons why Cahokia is located where it is. We have described a number of physical characteristics to explain why the Cahokia location, like other Mississippian settings, was chosen. Yet why did this setting spawn Cahokia, the paramount Mississippian site, and not simply another average-sized Mississippian center? Why did this site diverge from other early mound centers in the American Bottom?

Cahokia had physical characteristics common to other Mississippian sites, but in larger proportions. It was located in the center of the widest expanse of the American Bottom and provided the largest continuous block of land above water (with the exception of the Wood River Terrace, though this is sandy and not nearly as suitable for maize agriculture). Its 5-kilometer radius catchment provided the largest zone of optimal soils for hoe cultivation within the Bottom. Surrounded by water, and within striking distance of the uplands, it was a setting capable of drawing in and supporting an astoundingly large population. The area available for settlement, its central location, and rich surrounding resources provided great potential for expansion. In addition, some individual or group of individuals had the inspiration and means to utilize these resources in implementing a vision of what Cahokia could and would become. How these resources were tapped to make that vision a reality is the question to which we will turn shortly.

LIMITS AND BOUNDARIES

Before we continue with an exploration of how this potential was manipulated by the Cahokians over the course of the Mississippian period, we should first discuss what constitutes the Cahokia site. Definitions of the site have been presented for a number of purposes and have resulted in myriad and confusing boundaries. For example, today, the Illinois Archaeological Survey defines Cahokia as two sites (11-Ms-2 and 11-S-34) because the monuments (i.e., mounds) that are documented are found in both Madison and St. Clair counties. The National Register of Historic Places designation provides the most inclusive limits for the site. The National Register boundaries coincide approximately with the area bounded in figure 29. The Cahokia Mounds State Historic Site, as delimited by park boundaries, includes a series of noncontiguous parcels of varying size located within the limits of the National Register site. This configuration of the site is also the most fluid set of boundaries, expanding as park land acquisition progresses.

As pointed out by Dunnell (1992), a site is an archaeological construct whose limits or boundaries are determined by archaeologists. These boundaries are administrative and do not correspond to the limits of settlement. The fact that the limits of the Cahokia site are a contemporary notion is punctuated by historic accounts that indicate a more expansive concept of the settlement. These tend to describe all the mounds in the area stretching from the bluffs to St. Louis. Brackenridge describes a "chain of mounds" located along the southern edge of Cahokia Creek stretching from the East St. Louis group of mounds to the Cahokia mound group (which he called the Cantine mounds) (Hammes 1981, 149). The Bushnell map of 1904 depicts this continuous distribution of mounds. The complete Cahokia map made for Patrick in 1876 also includes the series of mounds between the East St. Louis group and what we now know as the Cahokia site.

Nineteenth- and early twentieth-century observers, while recognizing a clustering of mounds centered around Monks Mound, clearly saw no means—or at least did not see it as their goal—to demarcate or separate this group of mounds from those tailing both up and down Cahokia Creek. The single exception is Lindesay Brine (1894), who attempted to delimit the

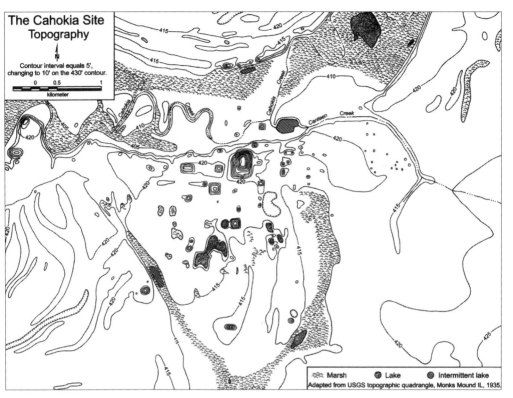

29. A topographic map of the Cahokia Mounds site reveals meanders, creeks, borrows, and mounds. The area covered by the map corresponds roughly to the boundaries of the site and park.

space enclosed by the group of "greatest archaeological importance," but adds that "so many of the mounds had been leveled, that it was difficult to form definite conclusions with regard to its shape or extent." Others of his time obviously conceived of a more continuous prehistoric settlement where the Cahokia group was an integrated part of an occupation that extended across a much broader area.

Unquestionably, the sociopolitical influence of Cahokia extended beyond any of the contemporary boundaries drawn. At the height of the Mississippian development, the entire American Bottom region may have been integrated by Cahokia (Emerson 1997; Milner 1991; Pauketat 1997a; Woods and Holley 1991). Moreover, the people that lived within the area now designated as the Cahokia site traveled beyond these boundaries, probably on a daily basis, to access resources in the uplands and surrounding Bottom.

We will not elaborate further on why the various site boundaries were drawn or how they differ. Nor will we concern ourselves with delimiting a Cahokian entity with exact boundaries, an exercise more relevant to issues concerning the management of the site as a cultural resource. Instead, we use the word "site" only in a general sense according to its meaning as "the place of" or "location of" (Dunnell 1992). As mentioned previously, definitions of the term "landscape" invariably allow for its multiscalar nature. By focusing on the Cahokia landscape, we avoid fixing site boundaries, emphasize dynamic interactions between humans and land, and consider the possible significance of relationships between features of the landscape at and around this place.

For instance, archaeologists, using information on traces of mounds once present as well as extant, have bounded an area of mound distribution that is variously shaped as a diamond or ellipse (Fowler 1997; Gregg 1975) (fig. 28). What were the prehistoric relationships suggested by the proximity, form, and organization of these mounds as they were constructed over the periods of prehistoric occupation? What does the distribution of features and artifacts, as it relates to land use both inside and outside of the area, lend to this discussion?

Archaeologists have also referred to a community core variously defined as downtown Cahokia, the Central Precinct, or central Cahokia. To what extent might such an entity have had prehistoric significance? How might the form, size, and character of such a center have changed through time? How might landscape features outside of this center have articulated with it?

CHAPTER FIVE

LANDSCAPE STRUCTURE

In formal social contexts, presentation and welcoming within highly structured social centers are at the heart of how a group defines itself. Countless observations concerning Native American greetings from the 1500s to the early 1800s within the area now defined as the southeastern United States involve a village or town center to which visitors were brought to meet the chief or council (e.g., Bartram 1955 [1792], 167; Varner and Varner 1951, 354). The center was set apart by the spatial concentration or massing of important public and "chiefly" architecture. Depending upon the time period and region, these centers were described as having a variety of buildings and formally defined areas including a council house, a chief's compound, a plaza, and a "chunkey" yard (a cleared, level playing ground). According to these accounts, the center functioned internally as a theater for presentation and play.

Our archaeological understanding of Mississippian sites corresponds with these ethnographic observations. In Mississippian towns, social life appeared to have a physical component, a recognized *axis mundi* of a center and corresponding noncenter. Thus, the question of what constituted the center of Cahokia is germane. The center would have contained all the elements detailed in the ethnographic record plus additional features, housing all that was important economically, socially, and politically. Much like towns throughout the world before the advent of modern transportation, the center was the setting for both the public and the elite; in essence, spatial positioning reflected a social ordering writ large.

We know that Cahokia had a central focus and that it began at Monks Mound. The limits of this focus, however, are not as obvious. Traditionally, the definition of a center at Cahokia has been overly influenced by the Cahokians' decision to erect a large "central" palisade as a bounding device (fig. 15). Varied functions of this palisade have been posited, including use as a defensive stockade whose purpose was to protect the central area from external threat and as an enclosing fence to inhibit access to the downtown. Excavations along various sections of this palisade, however, have documented that it was erected relatively late within the history of the occupation (i.e., after A.D. 1100–1150), and thus its proposed role to demarcate a community core cannot apply to the first centuries of occupation. Notably, the Central Palisade cuts through what appear to be earlier alignments and relationships established by a series of paired-mound groupings. Available evidence for these groups, although admittedly scant, does not conflict with an interpretation that they were constructed before the palisade. These paired mounds can be thought of as forming a district, one whose design and integrity was interrupted by the palisade. The palisade also isolated Mound 72, an early and significant burial mound, from the central area of the site.

For the pre-Central Palisade time span, there are physical features, such as topographic ridges, waterways, and borrows that can be used to generate a working definition of a community core. Helms Ridge is the name given to the raised levee on the southern edge of the Edelhardt meander (figs. 28 and 29). This prominent landform is visible even today. It is elevated more than 3 meters above the flood plain to the north and formed the backbone for the Cahokia site. During the Emergent Mississippian period, it was the location of the heaviest occupation and, most certainly, the location of a community core or center. From A.D. 900 to 1400, it remained a locus of continuous activity, although not always domestic in nature. Thus, any definition of a center must be focused on this feature. It is not a coincidence that Monks Mound is located on Helms Ridge. Although it is a fairly easy task to define the northern and southern margins of the ridge, eastern and western boundaries are more difficult to draw. Helms Ridge elongates valuable occupation space. This is the landform along which Brackenridge traveled to Cahokia, noting mounds at intervals all the way from the East St. Louis group (Brackenridge 1868, 254).

Helms Ridge can also be characterized as the land of greatest flux—the land where domestic resettlement efforts were concentrated. Through the first part of the Mississippian sequence, the Emergent Mississippian village, evident today as a blanket of structures in all areas around Monks Mound, was over time variously converted from domestic to elite or public use. Later, we find a reversion to domestic use in the same areas. We will return to this topic of domestic resettlement later. The point here is that the location of these resettlement projects and their spread outward from Monks Mound may help us define the boundaries of a center that shifts through time.

As Cahokia grew, occupation spread southward from Helms Ridge into more low-lying areas (fig. 20). Both natural and culturally constructed bodies of water, including creeks, water-filled meander scars, and water-filled borrows, may have served to bound this occupation and also a community core. Though water may have inhibited access, it did not cut off the opposite side from view. Thus, a community core defined in this manner would still be linked visually to peripheral areas of the site.

North of Helms Ridge, Cahokia Creek separates mounds located within its flood plain and the Kunnemann group (fig. 30) from Monks Mound and the rest of the site. Early historic data indicate that in premodern times Cahokia Creek was not a minor body of water. In fact, it was called a river. In 1808, General Land Office surveyors recorded its width at a substantial 100–150 links, or about 66–99 feet (ca. 20 to 30 meters) (Tucker 1942, 46). Not only was it wide, Brackenridge (1868, 254) noted that it was also fairly deep. During this same period, Canteen Creek's width is given as 30 links or approximately 20 feet. Apparently the flood plain occupied by Cahokia and Canteen Creeks was suitable for occupation, because mounds were built there, although the present land is covered by nearly 1 meter of alluvial deposits.

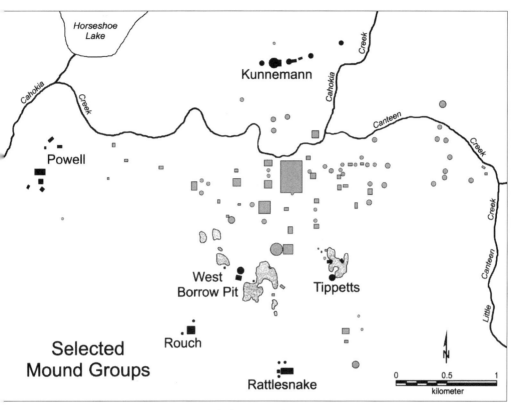

30. Selected mound groups at the Cahokia Mounds site.

South of Helms Ridge, a series of water boundaries is observed, forming a twofold subdivision of the site (figs. 17 and 29). The largest area is enclosed by the Spring Lake paleomeander. This meander scar forms an eastern boundary that arcs around to the south. Combined with a cut-off chute on the western side of the site, a roughly triangular section of ground is enclosed. Travel within this area would for the most part have been unimpeded. A culturally created series of water bodies in the form of open, water-filled borrow pits mirrors the shape of these natural water bodies, forming, in essence, a second or inner ring bounded by water. In between these two rings lies an expanse of largely unoccupied, low-lying ground. Neither of these water boundaries extended far enough north to impede traffic along Helms Ridge.

If we consider the placement of mounds relative to this double ring of water boundaries, a sense of orchestration is apparent. The outer ring of water encircles nearly all the major mounds at the site. Exceptions include the Powell mound group on the west, the Rouch mound group on the southwest, a small group of mounds to the east, and, of course, mounds north of Cahokia Creek (fig. 30). This area corresponds roughly to that described by Brine (1894) as containing what he viewed as the most important mounds at the

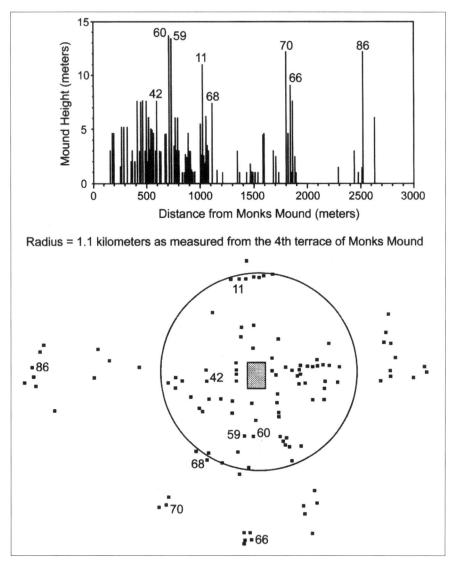

31. Mound height around Monks Mound was on the small side, taking no risk at competing with the largest monument at the site. Moving away from the center, however, the tall mounds sprout in seemingly regular intervals.

site. Brine (1894, 107) describes this area as "an irregular parallelogram, about fifteen hundred yards in length, having at each end a large earthwork or mound, with a wide and well levelled platform on the top. In the centre, there were two conical mounds, which must have been raised in that position for some important purpose. They were each about forty feet high, and appeared to have been so placed as to dominate the mounds forming the sides of the inclosure." The two large mounds are Monks Mound and Rattlesnake Mound. The two mounds in the center are Mounds 59 and 60, the central element of the paired-mound complex.

With Monks Mound as the center, a cluster of mounds is apparent within a distance of 1.1 kilometers, corresponding roughly to the area enclosed by the inner ring of borrows. This cluster also includes mounds located across the creek up to the Kunnemann mound group (fig. 31). This distance corresponds to the distance at which one can detect a human being (Lynch and Hack 1984). At this spacing, one can see an individual on Monks Mound, verified by our personal experience at the site. Of course, closer spacing is required to recognize features, costumes, and other details of an individual. Beyond this distance from Monks Mound, or beyond the inner ring of borrows, there is both a marked drop in the number or density of mounds, as well as a drop in the number of mid-size mounds. Dominant beyond this 1.1 kilometer distance are the small mounds (under 3 meters in height) and the large mounds (over 9 meters in height).

The inner ring of borrows, containing more desirable land as well as focal community features, may define a community core for the expanding Lohmann and early Stirling occupations. This ring expands the more linear focus of the center apparent in Emergent Mississippian times and physically bounds an area containing the principal community features constructed during this time, including Monks Mound, the Grand Plaza, and nearly all paired-mound groupings. These borrows were surely excavated during the heyday of mound construction in the early Mississippian sequence. In contrast to the Central Palisade, this ring does not interrupt the alignments suggested by the paired mounds, nor does it separate Mound 72, another early mound, from other central features.

MOUNDS AT THE MARGINS

As described above (fig. 31), the mounds at Cahokia tend to cluster within a distance of roughly 1 kilometer from Monks Mound. At a distance between approximately 1 and 2 kilometers from Monks Mound a disparate mix of large and small mounds has been documented. The large, or, more correctly, the tall mounds, excluding Monks Mound, are found overwhelmingly at the margins. The only exception is the preeminent paired-mound complex, Mounds 59 and 60.

The Kunnemann Mound (Mound 11), Rouch Mound (Mound 70), Rattlesnake Mound (Mound 66), and Powell Mound (Mound 86) (fig. 30) are all located at this 1- to 2-kilometer distance. All are over 9 meters high, and all have a number of smaller mounds clustered around them. Some regularity is noted in the spacing of these clusters: they average ca. 1 kilometer in distance from the next major mound (moving back toward the core of the site). Although single mounds continue in nearly all directions outward from these mound clusters, the next important clusterings of earthen mounds are the East St. Louis mound group, 5 miles (8 kilometers) southwest of the site along the same landform as the Cahokia site, and the Mitchell group, 7 miles (11.3

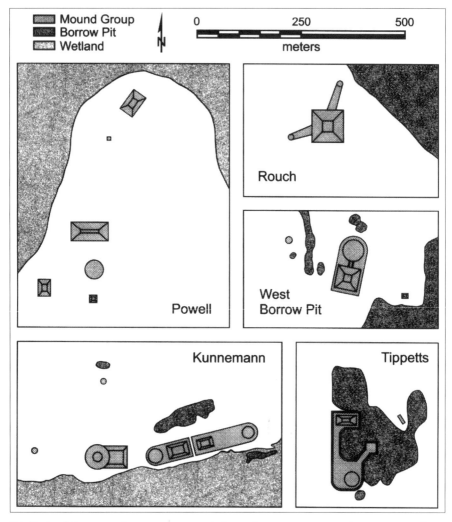

32. Each of the mound groups represented a unique arrangement that was sometimes tailored to the natural topography (Kunnemann), to the locally created topography (Tippetts), or even to adjacent mound groups (West Borrow Pit). A common feature was the use of platforms to connect mounds within a group.

kilometers) north. Other significant mound clusters are more than 10 miles from the site.

The mound groups located from 1 to 2 kilometers from Monks Mound may have been, at least for a time, interdependent with the core of the Cahokia site, unlike the politically related, but occupationally separate, centers of East St. Louis, St. Louis, and Mitchell. One of the most obvious cases of an outlying mound group that is clearly tied to the center of the site is the Powell mound group (fig. 32). It is sited on topography that is oriented diagonally along Cahokia Creek, yet the mounds, in the main, are oriented according to cardinal directions, against the grain of this topography and seemingly tied to Monks Mound (Ahler and DePuydt 1987; Reed 1973).

The location of the Powell mound group, at the sharp bend where Cahokia Creek flows south, is also notable. As travelers moved northeast up the creek to Cahokia, the Powell mound group provided a striking impression as one came around the bend—a cluster of mounds, including one large mound over 12 meters in height, standing in stark contrast to the scattered distribution of mounds that had preceded it. The General Land Office surveyors, who seldom bothered to mention the mounds in their notes, commented specifically on this attention-getting group during the initial township line surveys of the area in 1808 (Messenger 1808). They also noted that from this location a number of other mounds were discernible (twenty-four or more), including Monks Mound. Thus, from this position, the Central Precinct was clearly visible. The Powell mound group marked, or signified, one's arrival at the great Cahokia Mound Center, at least from the main corridor of the Mississippi River and Cahokia Creek.

Powell Mound (Mound 86) was largely destroyed in the early 1930s, but its form can be ascertained based on early air photos and excavation data. It was a ridgetop mound, rectangular at the base and rising to a ridge at its summit. Less than ten ridgetop mounds have been recorded at the Cahokia site. Most of them are found at distances of 1 to 2 kilometers from Monks Mound. Fowler (1997) has proposed that they functioned as marker mounds at the periphery of the site and other critical points within the community. On the south was Rattlesnake Mound, at the center of the arcuate shape formed by the southern water boundary. On the west, along Helms Ridge on the banks of Cahokia Creek, was Powell Mound. On the east, along the banks of Canteen Creek, was Mound 2, a small ridgetop mound (Fowler 1997, 59, 188–89). Construction on these ridgetop mounds appears to have been initiated early in the Mississippian sequence, right upon the heels of the central elements of Monks Mound and the Grand Plaza. Three ridgetop mounds have been excavated. All contained interior primary mounds that were expanded to form the final mounds, as well as burials and other features (Fowler 1997, 188–89) indicating their special nature.

It does not appear that the outlying mounds were tethered to subcommunities lorded over by a chief separate from Cahokia. The form of these mounds suggests that they were not substructural in nature. In other words, they did not provide a large, flat summit for the siting of buildings, such as for a chief's compound or elite residence, nor did they seem to have plaza arrangements that would be expected for a functioning center. This is also true for Rouch Mound, another large mound located at the site margins which, although not a ridgetop mound, is very tall with a relatively small summit area on top.

Powell Mound, Rattlesnake Mound, Rouch Mound, and Kunnemann Mound are tall so that they can be seen. They also exhibit an interesting relationship with the site if we broaden our focus to consider seeing as well as being seen. Earlier we discussed the 1-kilometer radius from Monks Mound within which most of the mounds at the site are located and how this corresponds to both the ring enclosed by the water-filled borrows and the distance at which one can detect a person. Monks Mound is certainly visible from at least 4 miles (6.5 kilometers). For practical purposes, however, it was not enough to see it. Part of the impact was seeing what was on it, which would only be possible within this 1-kilometer distance. The tall mounds located at the margins of the site are located at a similar distance of 1 kilometer from the next larger mounds, thus tying them all to the core of the site by this visual distance. Therefore, from these mounds one can not only see the mound groupings within the site core, but one can clearly see people on the mounds located around the fringes of this core, and vice versa.

The Kunnemann mound group (fig. 32), an outlying mound group containing one of these tall mounds, is in many respects an anomaly. It differs markedly from the other outlying mound groups in the form and function of the principal mound (Mound 11) and in the form and function of the mound group as a whole. Its separation from the site core appears to have been largely effected by Cahokia Creek, as opposed to a separation based on physical distance. It also differs from other marginal mound groups in the lateness of its construction, largely within Stirling times.

A grouping of small mounds, including a probable ridgetop mound (Mound 2), was constructed along the eastern side of Cahokia. Although many explanations for the lack of major monuments in this eastern expanse are possible, an explanation related to Mississippian land use is most plausible. The Powell mound group signaled to visitors approaching via Cahokia Creek from the Mississippi River system that they were entering Cahokia. In contrast, the eastern margins of the site would have served primarily as a path of daily movement for the Cahokians as they traveled to the fields and to the bluffs to obtain wood and other resources. Perhaps this explanation accounts for the relatively diffuse boundaries along this edge. As visitors approached Cahokia on the east, the entire site would have been spread out before them from the bluffs. The mounds located along Helms Ridge at the eastern margins of Cahokia, as well as the Kunnemann mound group, underscore the fact that our contemporary notions and applications of symmetry may not always be appropriate.

SUBCOMMUNITIES

How ordinary Cahokians were disposed lies at the heart of questions about the layout and functioning of Cahokia as a town. Was Cahokia a seamless occupational sprawl, or did it consist of a number of joined, but separate, residential areas?

We propose that residential subcommunities can be recognized by the presence of visible signatures of identity that, singly or in combination, would signify a distinct or separate community. These elements occur in a variety of forms and include features and factors such as (1) boundaries (either natural boundaries such as sloughs and creeks or culturally constructed

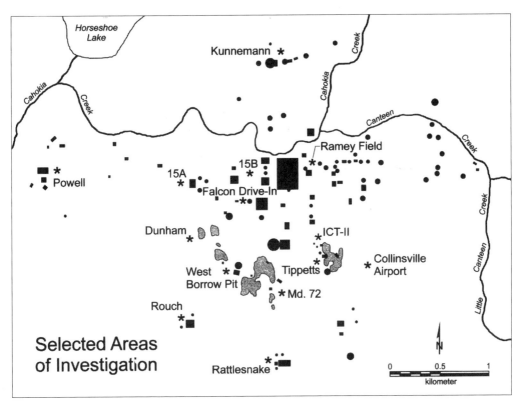

33. Only a few of the investigated areas of the site have sufficient documentation. These areas comprise a diverse assortment of areal coverage and intensity of investigation. The lack of uniform coverage inhibits our understanding of the site, although the broad coverage of investigations does provide important insights.

boundaries such as palisades); (2) central focusing elements such as posts, pits, plazas, special buildings, or even earthen monuments; (3) a change in material inventory, house form, organization, and so forth that suggests a different ethnicity, a different status group, or a specialized resident population of some sort; and (4) residential stability or continuity, derived from the seemingly simple chore of maintaining residential continuity across generations and recognized in *in situ* rebuilding.

We begin our exploration with a look at the structure and distribution of suprahousehold groupings and how these changed over time. Just as the areas where people were living changed through time (figs. 20 and 24), so did the nature of suprahousehold groupings, and with this the nature of activities, the number of people participating in these activities, and the extent to which they participated in these activities together.

Information derives mainly from four areas of the site that have been subjected to machine-blading of the topsoil, thus revealing the distribution of house plans and related subsurface features. These four areas are the Powell Tract, Tracts 15A and 15B, and the ICT-II (Interpretive Center Tract-II) (fig. 33). Hand-excavation of smaller areas has also added details important to our understanding of diverse portions of the site.

During Emergent Mississippian times there is clear evidence for segmentation in the organization of households. This is best seen in the most intensively occupied areas within the center of the site (e.g., at Tracts 15A and 15B and within Ramey Field), as opposed to the Emergent Mississippian occupation at the site margins. In a pattern also typical at other Emergent Mississippian sites (Kelly 1990b), houses were arranged around a plazuela (small plaza) or courtyard. Within this communal plaza, anchoring features such as pits, pit clusters, posts, and even buildings (Kelly 1990b) were found. These courtyard clusters consistently measure 30 to 40 meters in diameter.

Around the time of the Emergent Mississippian-Mississippian transition and continuing into Lohmann times we see a dramatic increase in the population residing at Cahokia as a result of the influx of people drawn into the site from the surrounding region. Archaeological surveys and excavations have not yielded any significant Lohmann villages within the northern American Bottom, although it is possible that deeply buried occupations have yet to be uncovered. Coinciding with the growth of Cahokia was the appearance of larger formulations (Collins 1990; Holley et al. 1989; Pauketat 1991) that perhaps correspond more closely to what we think of as neighborhoods. The first evidence for this derives from the Lohmann phase.

Tension between community-wide concerns and the desires of the different groups settling new areas of the site is evident in this process of reorganization. Continuity with Emergent Mississippian communities tends to be present only at the margins of the site (e.g., Powell Tract, Tract 15A). Within more interior sections of Cahokia, public projects and reconfiguring of the site preclude the continuation of domestic occupation during the Lohmann and into the Stirling phase (fig. 34). As a result of the upheaval of people from these areas, planned communities, such as documented at the ICT-II, were constructed in areas more distant from the center of the site. Materially, we do not observe any status differentiation during Emergent Mississippian times between houses or courtyard groups. During Lohmann times, however, we see the greatest diversity in the floor plans of structures. It could be argued that this represents differences in wealth.

Contrasting with this apparent diversity is a suburban sprawl of structures indicating the integration of people on a larger scale with an organization tied to a greater Cahokia plan. For example, the blank slate of the ICT-II was filled by an array of structures rigidly oriented along cardinal directions (fig. 35). Collins (1997) attributes this founding occupation to the guidance of an elite employing the so-called Cahokia Axis. Not only did structure size increase during Lohmann times, but the scale of organization, as evidenced by this orthogonal pattern keyed to sitewide concerns, increased as well. From excavations completed to date, it is not clear how these Lohmann communities were bounded, nor if they revolved around any internal structure. It may

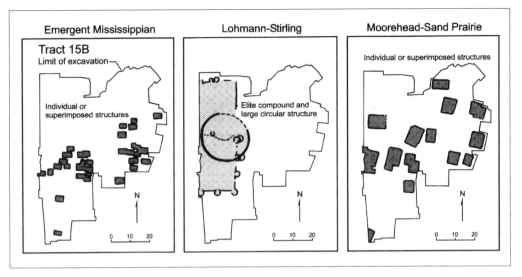

34. The transformation through time of the central area of Cahokia took a fairly consistent pattern, as shown in this Tract 15B triptych. The bracketing periods, Emergent Mississippian and Moorehead-Sand Prairie, were characterized by domestic dwellings, whereas the middle portion of the sequence, Lohmann-Stirling, was marked by specialized usage involving a large circular enclosure and a succession of palisade enclosures. This triptych depicts only structures.

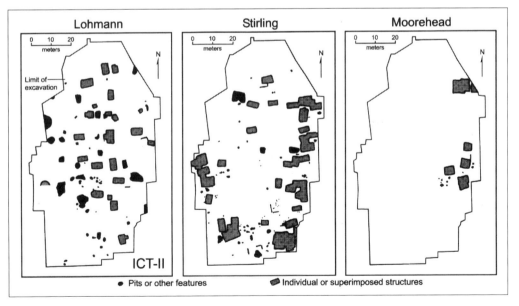

35. Residential life on the margins of downtown Cahokia, shown in this time-transgressive/resident resettlement triptych of the ICT-II, was hardly uniform. The initial domestic occupation of rigidly arranged buildings gives way to a plazalike configuration and finally ends with a reduced occupation centered on the highest ground. Dark-filled objects are subsurface pits and ancillary structures. Shaded objects represent known structures

be that we lack sufficiently large areas exposed by excavation. Though they were larger than Emergent Mississippian communities, our knowledge of the size and structure of Lohmann communities is incomplete. Our fragmentary understanding of the dating of mound construction and use, a problem that continues to haunt us for the entire Mississippian period, also adds to the difficulty of defining and understanding subcommunities at the site.

What we do know, however, is that at least at a scale of approximately 40 meters, which encompasses even the larger Emergent Mississippian communities, there are no indications of boundaries, focusing elements, or cultural differences that suggest segmentation of the Lohmann communities. It is probably safe to say that they were not physically bounded by features such as palisades; otherwise evidence of this, even in the limited areas covered, would be seen.

The Lohmann community at the Powell mound group, located at the extreme western margins of the site, accords more closely with what one would expect from a neighborhood with history, namely, a more organic orientation. Through time, this is exactly what occurred in the ICT-II, where a softening of the rigid Lohmann orientation perhaps bespeaks the emergence of a degree of local identity during the Stirling phase.

The relaxing of the geometric orientation of domestic structures, as documented at the ICT-II, is not without pattern. Large interior areas open in the form of an oval plazuela (with maximum dimensions of 30 by 50 meters) (fig. 35) and sizable posts and modest house mounds were erected. A whole Emergent Mississippian courtyard group would have fit within the plazuela at the ICT-II, indicating an increase in community size by Stirling times. As with Lohmann groupings, our understanding of the outer limits of these Stirling communities is incomplete, although we do know that they were at least as large as excavated areas covering ca. 150 by 200 meters (3 hectares). An estimated thirty-five households could have covered this area during Stirling times. Using the conservative figure of 5 people per household yields a resident population of around 175 people, a number that fits our concept of the size of smaller groupings at the site.

The founding community at the ICT-II stressed communality in terms of a relationship to sitewide concerns. Commensal groups were undoubtedly large and linked to feasting, perhaps a holdover from earlier patterns. In subsequent communities, privacy was emphasized and commensal group size contracted. We no longer find evidence of communal feasting. Storage and processing areas moved close to or into structures. Though still large, the community began to focus inward again, as evidenced by the reemergence of the plazuela at the ICT-II.

During the Stirling phase, we see a return to a focus around a cleared center or plaza as in Emergent Mississippian times, but of a completely different scale and nature. Although both communities were focused around an open center, the Stirling plazas did not contain the communal pit clusters typical of Emergent Mississippian courtyards. They were not necessarily for sharing resources. During Stirling times, the communities became more house-centered or individualized, with the pits located in the structures or right next to them.

The Stirling phase was a time of homogenization, with structures becoming more uniform in size and shape. This stands in contrast to the preceding Lohmann phase, which we can characterize as a time of experimentation. Exceptions to the cookie-cutter structures of the Stirling phase are the very large buildings that we first find at this time. Enclosing upward of 200 square meters, large buildings have been identified on the summit of Monks Mound and on ground level at the Powell Tract, Tract 15A, and possibly Tract 15B (in the form of a circular building) (fig. 34). The ground-level structures were immense and would have been obvious features in the landscape. When an ordinary house averaged 15 square meters, they were almost twelve times the size. These large structures would have required specialized building materials and labor groups. Although this was not unique at Cahokia, the brevity of such buildings is puzzling. They were not rebuilt, unlike the domestic structures or even the sweat baths, another type of specialized building. Their function is not known, although the paucity of debris and presence of unique internal features argues for a specialized function, as opposed to the house of an elite member of the society. Such a transitory construction contrasts with the permanence offered by earthen monuments.

The density and packing of domestic buildings at Cahokia, for example, at the ICT-II, Tract 15A, and the Powell mound group, far exceeds that experienced in the surrounding countryside. Although small courtyards at such important villages as the Julien site (Milner 1984a) mimic the arrangement found at Cahokia, what is absent is a nearby clustering of similar density and, most importantly, *in situ* rebuilding. For some, day-to-day life at Cahokia had a sense of permanence, because buildings and domestic locations remained unchanged for generations, at least in some portions of the site. This is especially apparent at the ICT-II and elsewhere during the Stirling phase, when there was an unparalleled flurry of rebuilding.

Subcommunities were tied intimately to the fortunes of the community at large and thus atrophied at the end of the sequence. During the Moorehead phase there was a return to the Emergent Mississippian pattern of small courtyard groupings. Houses clustered around an open area, with houses and plaza of about the same size as their Emergent Mississippian counterparts (i.e., 30 to 40 meters in diameter) (fig. 34). The Moorehead communities differed, however, in that the houses themselves were much bigger and fewer were distributed around the plaza. Households retained their privacy during Moorehead times, with domestic pits generally located inside of or immediately adjacent to house walls. Large buildings, sweat baths, and other trappings of earlier times were also gone.

During Moorehead times, occupation contracted back into the central areas around Monks Mound, returning both to Emergent Mississippian areas of occupation as well as to new areas. Moorehead occupation occurred not only within the palisaded center, but also outside the palisade along its perimeter. By the Sand Prairie phase, there is no evidence of formal neighborhoods, just a "rump" population scattered around Monks Mound.

We have traced the move from intimate Emergent Mississippian courtyard groupings to larger and organizationally disparate Lohmann and Stirling communities, and then a return to a smaller courtyard organization during Moorehead times. In outlining these transitions, we do not suggest that the Emergent Mississippian courtyard group was equivalent to the Moorehead cluster, or that the Emergent Mississippian courtyard group was transformed into the communities of the Lohmann phase. To understand the relations between these communities of different times, we need to explore more fully how coeval communities may have been articulated with each other or with other features within the community.

The traditional concept of Cahokia has been that the different mound groups represented, or were tied to, subcommunities. In this model, circum-core groups (mound groups that are located around the circumference of the core) represented residentially based subdivisions assumable under the lineage or barrio concepts (Fowler 1997; Holley et al. 1992). When we examine the limited data that we have, however, we do not find evidence that all, or even most, of the scattered mound groups represented residential centers, or small-scale versions of downtown Cahokia. First and foremost, most mound groups were not the central focus of a residential population. Two mound groups, the West Borrow Pit and Tippetts (figs. 30 and 32), illustrate this notion. The mounds in these groups formed the southern margins of residential occupation that emanated from the site core. Second, most of the mound groups lacked formal mound-plaza arrangements that were the absolute minimum for a Mississippian center. The earthen monuments were constructed and placed in a manner that made sense largely to a Cahokia plan and not to a neighborhood model. Previously we alluded to a relationship between the paired mounds of the West Borrow and Tippetts group and the principal paired-mound grouping at the site (Mounds 59 and 60). An exception is the Kunnemann mound group, which appears to have formed the nexus for a residential population and encompassed a formal mound and plaza group. Significantly, the Kunnemann mound group was physically separated from the main portion of the site by Cahokia Creek, which represented the strongest physical barrier within the limits of the site. The Rouch and Powell mound groups appear, at first glance, to be exceptions. However, in each case the principal mound was constructed with an eye toward the central area and was not a local monument.

Rather than forming rings around mound groups, domestic occupation appears to have been determined more by the natural terrain and proximity to the center of the site. Houses representing all time periods drop off in numbers as one moves south of Helms Ridge. As public projects took over land next to Monks Mound, more marginal areas were occupied, but this, by and large, did not take the form of separate communities of people situated and focused around the mounds. Again, an exception to this may be the Kunnemann mound group and perhaps also the Powell mound group (figs. 30 and 32).

We have no evidence of ethnic enclaves, such as those witnessed in Mesoamerica (Santley et al. 1987), for the Mississippian occupation at Cahokia. Work up to the present has not revealed an enclave where any archaeologically recognizable nonlocal styles concentrate. Postcontact Native American towns within the southeastern United States were often agglomerations of displaced ethnic groups, but we have no reason to assume the same for prehistory. Rather than a sea of disconformity, Cahokia appears to have been rather homogeneous in terms of the common folk. We do, however, see differences displayed at another level, with select communities displaying the appurtenances of wealth in the form of access to and manufacture of exotic goods (shell beads, stone axes, etc.) (Pauketat 1993b, 1998; Holley 1995). The Kunnemann occupation is an example of such a community.

Previously we indicated that circumcore mound groups were not lorded over by chiefs that had some degree of separation from Cahokia. This is not to say that these mound groups were not built and maintained by subdivisions of the community, but simply that, for the most part, those responsible for construction were limited in the amount of autonomy they were allowed. They did not construct local temples and high-status residences, and they were not allowed to become seats of power potentially rivaling that represented by Monks Mound.

In comprehending a town the size of Cahokia we cannot rely on the ethnohistoric record, since historic Native American towns were vestiges of the prehistoric megacenters. Valuable information from these towns is provided, however, in evidence for the presence and impact of sodalities based on consanguinity or a variety of associations such as age, gender, and task. Sodalities, cross-culturally, tend not to be residential units; yet there is no reason why such sodalities may not have physical embodiments in buildings or monuments in a center the size of Cahokia. It is not likely that the mounds forming these circumcore mound groups were built and maintained by residential groupings. By virtue of labor requirements and other evidence, several clans or even members of a sodality might have come together to build the mounds. In chapter 10 we will characterize monument building and associated ceremonies as vehicles for negotiation— a place where changing power relations were played out and where multiple nodes of society were connected through rituals associated with building, using, and maintaining the mounds—indeed, a process of socialization and empowerment manifest in spatial and temporal terms.

INTERNAL BOUNDARIES AND CONNECTIONS

In the discussion of subcommunities, we noted the paucity of evidence for boundaries that signaled community limits. Let us now consider boundaries and connecting features in general, that is, those features that would affect (preclude or encourage) the movement of people over the landscape.

Definitive archaeological evidence of streets (as we currently conceptualize them) at Cahokia or any other Mississippian site has not been found, although, at least in the case of Cahokia, coverage is limited. Whether or not formal streets existed in Mississippian mound centers is equivocal. An offhand mention of a principal street appears in a Spanish account by Garcilaso de la Vega (Varner and Varner 1951, 372) describing Native American towns in the Southeast. The formal arrangement of buildings along shared axes, however, is commonly encountered in archaeological contexts (Black 1967, 500–501; Price and Griffin 1979). This arrangement, along with those of mounds and plazas, may suggest the presence of established venues. No doubt some form of formal/informal passageways was present. It is probable, however, that they were formed after the fact rather than through deliberate construction.

Because of the lay of the land and the configuration of the mounds, however, we can speculate about the flow of traffic and its concentration at Cahokia. For instance, well-worn paths providing unimpeded access and movement probably existed along Helms Ridge and along the high ground, following the natural levees of the creeks both downstream and upstream from the site (fig. 29).

Evidence of boundaries at Cahokia are more visible to us archaeologically. The presence of water at Cahokia in the form of creeks, sloughs, and water-filled borrows delimited a center and a periphery, and separated marginal mound groups from the core of the site. It surely affected movement, but not vision. And, it was vision—seeing and being seen—that helped to hold Cahokia together.

Although the water-filled borrows generally precluded access, in some cases constructed causeways would have funneled or channeled movement across these features (fig. 17). A single causeway was noted in Patrick's 1870s map of the site, running along the edge of a borrow pit and connecting the conical and platform mounds of the Tippetts mound group (Mounds 61 and 62) (fig. 32). Excavations and topographic studies of the Tippetts causeway indicate that it was, indeed, a constructed feature. A man-made feature between (and postdating) borrow pits beside what is now Ramey Street has also been interpreted as a causeway (Collins 1990). Finally, there has been long-standing, though undocumented, speculation about a causeway extending south from the Central Precinct across low ground all the way to the Rattlesnake Mound (Mound 66) area. Perhaps these causeways are our best examples of "streets."

Palisades and screens were quite different boundaries from water at Cahokia, and a number of them have been documented. These did cut off the opposite side from view. The Central Palisade was an extensive wall that probably completely encircled the central portion of the site. The first version of this palisade was built after A.D. 1100, or in the later part of the Stirling phase. It was rebuilt at least four times, with minor changes in location, over the next hundred years.

The numerous entrances that have been documented from excavations along the eastern curtain of the palisade bring into question the idea that it functioned to limit access. The manner in which houses hugged the outer perimeter, at least in the south, also begs the question of how secure its defensive role was. Even though the form of the Central Palisade as revealed through excavations appeared imposing with its curtain wall and bastions, we are unsure exactly how high it was. If the role of the palisade was to cut off vision, was its purpose to preclude the view from outside in or from inside out—or both? The longevity of the palisade and the question whether four rebuildings over a hundred years was enough to maintain it also enters into consideration. At historic (eighteenth-century) Fort de Chartres, located in Illinois within the Mississippi bottom lands, two sequential palisaded, wooden forts built by the French lasted only about twenty-seven years (Keene 1991). Data from the fort suggest that posts emplaced in the clayey soils at Cahokia would have quickly rotted, and that at least the wall sections located between the more substantial bastions would have to have been repaired or replaced frequently, perhaps every ten to fifteen years. With just the four documented rebuildings, the palisade could not have been standing intact for the entire time span.

In addition to the Central Palisade, archaeological work has documented several other palisades and screens at the site (Gums and Holley 1991; Pauketat 1998; Wittry and Vogel 1962). These range in size from small-scale versions of the Central Palisade with fairly substantial walls and bastions to less substantial screens. We know very little about their functions.

We do have a better understanding of screens commonly found at the bases and on tops of mounds (summit and grade levels). If we think of mounds as boundaries of territory, screens at the base or around the summit of a mound might function to reinforce these boundaries. In conjunction, siting structures on the tops of mounds makes them dominant within the context of the community and visible from great distances (Lynch and Hack 1984, 168). In contrast, if a structure is situated on the shoulder of a mound, it will still provide a view of the surrounding terrain, but it will blend into the hillside and have a less visible position. The Mississippians placed their structures in a dominating position at the top of the mound and then screened them off. The screens hid these structures, but the fact that they were hidden was made prominent by virtue of their siting (location) on the summit of a mound. Through the combination of mound construction, structure siting, and screens, it was clear that certain people were not allowed to view various activities that were carried out within these mound-top structures.

Though encircling screens, particularly around mound summits, certainly functioned as described above, it appears likely that partial screens constructed at the base or along the slopes of mounds functioned to retard the downslope spread of sediments from mound erosion. These screens would have protected downslope habitation and special use areas. They would also have helped to hinder the expansion of erosional fans. Sediments collected at these fans could have been reused to patch and rebuild the mound. Screens of this sort have been documented on the First Terrace and west side of Monks Mound and on the south side of Mound 48.

If we combine our consideration of bounding and connecting features with the previous consideration of subcommunities in a time-progressive fashion, we obtain some interesting insights into the nature of the occupation at Cahokia and the competing desires being negotiated throughout it. For example, in Emergent Mississippian times, formally constructed boundaries are not evident, and there appears to have been a fairly continuous string of occupation constrained only by the natural limits inherent in Helms Ridge and Cahokia Creek. This lack of constructed boundaries contrasts with the clear organization of occupation into courtyard groupings focused around a small plaza or courtyard. Outside of the central areas of the site, these natural boundaries remained prevalent throughout the sequence.

Around the time of the Emergent Mississippian-Mississippian transition and continuing into Lohmann times, the community at Cahokia was reorganized. At this time, the Cahokians began constructing formal boundaries amidst the growing expanse of occupation, borrows, and mounds. Public construction began to co-opt most of the domestic areas around Monks Mound.

In Emergent Mississippian times, courtyard groups were organized within a fairly homogeneous and contiguous occupation area. In contrast, Cahokia, in Lohmann times was not made up of a large number of separate groupings. At least within the area that we have defined as central Cahokia, subcommunities were large and apparently seamless. Though the early Mississippian period represented the broadest expanse of people at the site, it is from this period that we know the least about community segmentation. We can, however, characterize it as a time of site differentiation where the once homogeneous domestic sprawl was segmented into areas of quite different uses.

In Stirling times, the communal versus private tension seems to have been ameliorated somewhat. Closed communities of the Stirling phase contrast with the open, formalized communities of the Lohmann phase. Palisades were constructed—the Central Palisade, one at Tract 15B, and one in an area that later became the Falcon Drive-In. In this respect, Cahokia was like other Mississippian sites in that the palisades were built during the middle or late part of the sequence (Holley 1999).

CHAPTER SIX

LANDSCAPE

CHANGE

Archeological phases tend to concentrate change at the margins between phases. In this chapter, we will explicitly consider variations in the tempo of change over the Mississippian occupation by focusing on mound building, reclamation projects, and building on a smaller scale, i.e., the construction and rebuilding of houses and subcommunities. We will also consider continuity in these landscape elements as well as change; long periods of stability can be just as informative about societal conditions as rapid periods of change. Moreover, continuity and change are not necessarily mutually exclusive; elements of change can exist within periods of stability and vice versa.

To begin, a review of the status of our knowledge regarding mound construction at Cahokia will be helpful. Upward of forty of the more than a hundred mounds at Cahokia have been investigated (for selected mounds, see appendix). Although this seems a relatively good sample (roughly one-third of the total), the information gathered from these investigations is quite variable and, with few exceptions, quite poor. For example, information for approximately half of the mounds in the sample derives from the excavations led by Warren K. Moorehead in the 1920s (Moorehead 1929). As an example of the quality of this information, we review Moorehead's excavations of Mound 56, which were reexamined as part of our 1992 research field school.

In 1921, during Moorehead's first season of exploration at the Cahokia site, Mound 56, or the Jesse Ramey Mound, was investigated. During September and October of that year, Moorehead's crews conducted excavations in eight mounds. The work at Mound 56 exemplifies the style and brevity of Moorehead's reporting. Two paragraphs on research at this mound were published in a 1922 summary report (Moorehead 1922, 22):

> This is about 20 ft. in height at the present time, the base diameter some 300 ft. It is the second mound directly south of Monks. It is not clear whether this was originally an oblong mound or of the pyramid type since it has been cultivated for many years. Some twenty-five men were employed in the work and a trench some 65 ft. in length was extended from near the base of the south side to a line some distance from the center. This trench was excavated to an average depth of 10 ft. Then test pits were sunk and post augers used. Five or 6 ft. farther down (a total of 14 to 16 ft.) we came upon rather soft, dark earth quite different from the clay and gumbo of which most mounds were composed. It resembled the earth found about burials in the several

mounds of the Hopewell group. There were a few scales of copper, and some fragments of highly finished pottery. The pottery was above the average found on the surface or in the village site. That is, the fragments recovered indicate the finer pottery such as accompanies burials.

This mound was trenched late in October and being the end of our season, we filled the excavation. While it can not be confidently confirmed, yet it is the opinion of the author that the Jesse Ramey Mound is a burial structure and should be thoroughly explored.

This same text was reproduced almost verbatim in Moorehead's 1929 summary report (Moorehead 1929, 37–38) and is the only information we have on the exploration of this mound. To date, no field notes, photos, or materials from the trenching of Mound 56 have been located. Although Moorehead's description of the Mound 56 work does provide some information on how the mound was investigated and some tantalizing, but questionable, comments on the substructure of the mound and its function, it also leaves many questions. No information on mound structure, features, or contents, and thus on mound age or function, is provided. Unfortunately, the paucity of information resulting from the investigation of this mound is not unique among those investigated by Moorehead and even later researchers.

As a result, in reviewing information produced by the investigations of approximately forty mounds, we are able to only tentatively date the initiation of construction of less than half of these (fig. 36). Though this is certainly not a large number, and though an understanding of the entire sequence of construction and use of these mounds is even more uncertain, they do suggest patterns in the tempo of mound construction and in the location and focus of these construction efforts over time.

Mound construction and other landscape-modifying activities did not start slowly and gradually accelerate at Cahokia. They began suddenly and significantly late within the Emergent Mississippian period. Evidence indicates that Monks Mound, the paramount mound at the site, was the first mound built and that work started around A.D. 900. The main body of this 30-meter-high, 7-hectare (17-acre) mound was completed by A.D. 1150, if not by the end of the Lohmann phase (Emerson and Woods 1990; Reed et al. 1968; Skele 1988).

The scale of early earthmoving achievements at Cahokia, however, cannot be gauged solely by the mass of Monks Mound. Though certainly an impressive earthwork, the mound itself represents only a portion of early efforts. We must also consider where the massive amounts of fill needed to construct Monks Mound came from, as well as subsequent landscaping necessary to reclaim these borrowed areas.

According to our calculations, Monks Mound comprised approximately 700,000 cubic meters of fill (Fowler [1997] calculates 624,000 cubic meters). Our estimates indicate that the open borrows at the site would have supplied roughly 417,500 cubic meters of fill (Fowler 1997, 171–81, estimates between 236,752 and 320,552 cubic meters), not enough for Monks Mound alone, much less for all the other mounds at the site.

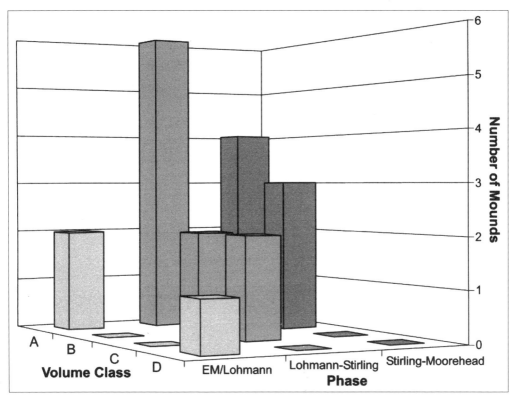

36. The size of constructed mounds declined through the history of the site. The frequency of mound construction was certainly in decline by the Moorehead phase. The graph depicts number of mounds initiated per phase and volume class. Volume classes include A—less than 10,000 cubic meters; B—10,000–30,000 cubic meters; C—30,000–100,000 cubic meters; and D—approximately 700,000 cubic meters.

Evidence indicates that fill for the construction of Monks Mound was obtained by borrowing from areas around its flanks, with the reclamation of these borrowed areas following soon after. We mapped one of these reclaimed borrows (south of Monks Mound, within the northern section of the Grand Plaza) over an area of approximately 100 square meters to a maximum depth of over 1 meter below the present ground surface. The volume of fill removed was estimated at 23,247 cubic meters, which is greater than that of seventeen of the nineteen visible borrow pits that have been mapped at the site (Fowler 1997). Moreover, this is a minimal estimate, because the lateral borrow extends both to the east and north of the area that we studied.

Not only is the scale of this feature commensurate with what would be expected for the initial construction stages of Monks Mound, but the type of sediment that would have originally covered the plaza area, a black, organic clay, forms the central, 6.5-meter-high platform at the base of Monks

Mound. Ceramics recovered from excavations of this reclaimed borrow also support the interpretation of this feature as a source of fill for Monks Mound. The presence of large ceramic rims and sherds dating to the Edelhardt phase (A.D. 950–1000) of the Emergent Mississippian period contained within the lower (primary) fill deposits suggests that the borrowed area was opened late during the Emergent Mississippian period. Subsequent filling episodes appear to have lasted into the beginnings of the Lohmann phase.

A reclaimed borrow beneath Mound 51, together with its continuation in the southern portion of Ramey Field, represents another area that likely served as a source of fill for Monks Mound. This borrow is over 2 meters in depth. Minimum north-south dimensions of this borrow, based on limited test excavations, are 53 meters, though the borrow itself is certainly much larger. It may even be part of a larger area of reclaimed ground that continues to the north. East-west dimensions are also uncertain. Based on recovered artifacts, the Submound 51 borrow appears to slightly postdate the lateral borrow identified in the Grand Plaza.

A much larger area than that documented within the Grand Plaza and beneath Mound 51 would have been borrowed from in order to supply the 700,000 cubic meters of earth needed for the construction of Monks Mound. At a depth of 2 meters, this area would have been nearly 600 meters square. Even assuming that just the early stages of the Mound (roughly 400,000 cubic meters) derived from the area immediately surrounding it, an area 2 meters deep and 450 meters square would have been borrowed from.

After the Cahokians excavated this massive amount of fill and transported it on their backs to build Monks Mound, they invested equal, or even greater, effort in reclaiming the borrowed ground and creating not only a flat, level area that served as the Grand Plaza and the substrate for Mound 51 (one of a line of mounds bordering the Grand Plaza), but also the landform of relatively low relief that extends over much of the Central Precinct. Sometime in the Lohmann phase, a ritual precinct, stretching from Monks Mound to Mound 72 and including the Grand Plaza, was for the most part complete. This was an immense undertaking in terms of size and labor requirements—earthmoving on a massive scale that had never been seen in the Eastern Woodlands and was not accomplished at any other Mississippian site.

A marked change from dispersed clusters of dwellings (A.D. 900) to a full-fledged village within three generations accompanied these early construction efforts. If one looked to the near horizon, one could see houses and smoke for a considerable distance—on the bluff edge, on the fans, on the creek margins, and on the braided sand ridges. What fueled this growth is difficult for us to imagine. Across the American Bottom, there is evidence of increasing aggregation and the integration of larger groups of people. During the Emergent Mississippian period, settlements that can be characterized as permanent agrarian communities are first documented. These are always located in the best agricultural areas. Late in the Emergent Mississippian period, sizable villages, with populations possibly numbering in the hundreds, appeared (Kelly 1990a). By the late Emergent Mississippian period, a chain-like series of single- and multimound centers had begun to form within the American Bottom (Emerson 1991; Porter 1974). What made Cahokia diverge from and eclipse these other villages is, indeed, the mystery of the site. What allowed it to amass people at a level previously unrealized and to transcend these other mound centers? Once people were drawn to the area, it is not difficult to imagine its potential, but how were they initially attracted? How did they effect the massive influx seen at Cahokia?

At other established villages of the time, for example the Range site (Kelly 1990b), the process of aggregation begins in the Late Woodland period. At Cahokia, however, it is strictly an Emergent Mississippian period issue, and this is the point from which we see a clear continuity in occupation. We must, however, add the disclaimer that if there remains at Cahokia an as yet undiscovered Late Woodland occupation, it may indeed be under the 7 hectares (17 acres) covered by Monks Mound. Nevertheless, at this point we are left with the Emergent Mississippian period as the time when this great process of aggregation begins at Cahokia, and, to us, the initiation of mound ceremonies late in the period seems a distinct possibility as the important draw.

What is striking about Cahokia is that the development of mound construction signifies an abrupt departure from earlier patterns. Smaller mound centers within the American Bottom can be viewed as having emerged gradually from progressively more integrated and aggregated communities. At a typical village of the late Emergent Mississippian period, a plaza with attendant structures and internal features formed the community core. This plaza was flanked symmetrically by a series of courtyards, possibly representative of the nucleation of a number of (ranked) kin groups within a single community (Kelly 1990b). At mound centers, mounds flanked the community plaza in a similar manner as the courtyard clusters. Yet, at Cahokia the evidence does not indicate this type of gradual development. Instead, the first mound constructed is the massive Monks Mound. Earthmoving began with the formation of a site center, but on an immense scale not realized elsewhere. Earthmoving on this large scale was not an epiphenomenon of an already "Mississippianized" society, accomplished at the peak of Cahokia's population and cultural flowering. Instead, it served as a vision of what Cahokia was to become.

Our reading of early construction at Cahokia is that this process took on an evangelistic slant. In a sense, Cahokia was a ritual "boomtown" where a vision of or plan for the future (symbolized by monumental works such as Monks Mound and the Grand Plaza and later ceremonies associated with the construction, use, and maintenance of these features) was used to convince people to join in the creation of the monumental community that it became. Mound ceremonialism, albeit on a massive scale, provided the first step in tapping the potential provided by the physical characteristics of this particular spot.

If the fervor of the times was part and parcel of the formation of Cahokia, what kept it going 250 years later? Cahokia stands in marked contrast to other early mound centers located to the south and east within the American Bottom. At these other mound centers, development was interrupted by the end of the Lohmann phase (Woods and Holley 1991). At Cahokia, however, occupation continues through the Sand Prairie phase, and mound construction activities continue through the Moorehead phase.

Let us return to the pattern and tempo of construction and change over the Mississippian occupation. Construction on Monks Mound continued into the Mississippian period in addition to a proliferation in the construction of other mounds during the period from A.D. 1000–1100 (i.e., during the Lohmann and early Stirling phases). We tentatively state, given the paucity of information we have on mound construction, that this is the period of construction of the greatest number of mounds (fig. 36). Mound construction during this period was concentrated in two areas: the core of the site, where a number of mounds were constructed along the edges of the Grand Plaza (Mounds 50, 51, 55, and 48) and at the extremes of the site (Mounds 86, 10–11, and 1).

During the period from ca. A.D. 1100 to 1200 (i.e., during late Stirling to early Moorehead times) mound building and the enlargement and internal differentiation of the site continued. Construction began on a number of new mounds, some of which were significant in size, and continued well into Moorehead times. However, in contrast to earlier construction efforts that focused on the construction of Monks Mound as well as on mounds that supported and emphasized the primacy of the center, new mound construction during the late Stirling and Moorehead phases occurred largely in intermediate areas of the site, filling in the area between the core elements and the outlying mound groups. Monks Mound acquired only minor additions and secondary mounds during the Moorehead phase. By the Sand Prairie phase, a sharp decline in construction efforts occurred. No new mounds are known to have been started.

Another indication of tempo comes from examining the pace of construction and rebuilding at the subcommunity scale and the way in which it dovetails with the sequence of mound construction. As outlined earlier, the early Lohmann phase was a time when the influx and relocation of people led to the establishment of a number of new communities. We believe that this was both a consequence of and impetus for the rise of Cahokia and the building of its great central earthworks.

After initial efforts created the ritual precinct of Monks Mound and the Grand Plaza, energies were redirected toward the construction of other mounds and the clearing of areas within the Central Precinct for the construction of woodhenges, sweat baths, large structures and enclosures, and, later, even palisades. The increase in the construction of these public or ritual areas corresponds with a trend toward a decreasing emphasis on house construction. New communities were no longer established and houses did not display the quality and variety of earlier domestic construction.

Late in the Moorehead phase, we see a snowballing of evidence indicating cultural decline in the form of atrophying of mound construction and maintenance as well as a decline in public construction. In addition, it is clear that the Mississippians were co-opting and controlling less land in conjunction with these changes. Cahokia seemed to have reached the limits of the two-hundred-year-plus time span that many Mississippian centers share (Holley 1999).

One noteworthy aspect of the Mississippian occupation is that there was a strong element of continuity in the central elements of Monks Mound and the Grand Plaza. Though this central area was almost completely reworked through massive borrowing, construction, and reclamation efforts, once completed, quite early in the Mississippian period, it remained a stable element and was not transformed like this again. There is evidence of changing land use and of the excavation of small borrow pits next to rising mounds, but there were no later modifications of terrain on the scale of the earlier efforts. The original vision and accompanying core of beliefs represented by these constructions held throughout the Mississippian period. Subsequent construction at the site can be interpreted as responding to these original elements.

In summary, it is apparent that the initial great changes accomplished over the Emergent Mississippian–Mississippian transition, including the construction of a central ritual precinct and the establishment of vast new areas of occupation, would have been observed by only a very few generations. The Mississippian period, however, for more than two hundred years, can be characterized as a period of continuity. For the Mississippians that lived during this time, mound construction was accepted and common, and mound maintenance was a continuous task. The focus of this construction changed through time, but it never again reached the heights of the early period. And though resident resettlement projects appropriated some of the energy previously devoted to the establishment of a ritual center and surrounding occupation, the upheaval of people and the landscape did not achieve the same scale as that resulting from the construction of Monks Mound and the Grand Plaza.

CONTINUED SETTLEMENT HISTORY

Landscape evolution at Cahokia does not stop with the Mississippians. A varied and complex history continues right up to the establishment of the Cahokia Mounds State Historic Site and to current efforts to create an archaeological park that is reminiscent of the Mississippian landscape. We know that this entire area was occupied by Native Americans during protohistoric times and that various groups, including Native Americans, Trappist monks, the French, and other Euro-American groups settled in and used this area during historic times.

After the effective abandonment of the Cahokia site (A.D. 1350?) there is evidence (e.g., on Mound 51, the Powell Tract [Milner at al. 1984]), and on Monks Mound) of scattered occupation on and around the mounds, symptomatic of the widespread, but diffuse, Oneota occupation of the American Bottom.

European settlement at the site began in the eighteenth century with the French, who established a mission on the lower terrace of Monks Mound and a trading post nearby (Walthall and Benchley 1987). The mission was established about 1735 on the First Terrace of the mound in association with a small Cahokia Illini village, which was also situated upon the First Terrace. Such missions were typically established at places where Native Americans gathered. At that time, Monks Mound was locally referred to as Abbey Hill or L'Abbe, and Cahokia Creek was known as the river L'Abbe (Hair 1866). The mission was abandoned around 1752, following a raid by northern tribes. Afterward the Illini fled to a Michigamea village near Fort de Chartres.

As part of the Monks Mound Stairs and Slope Stabilization Project, two pits and midden deposits dating from this period (1730–1752) were recently excavated. The pits contained remains associated with feasting activities. These excavations indicate that a substantial number of Illini were living on the First Terrace of Monks Mound in association with the chapel.

Occupation of the area resumed about 1776, with the pace of settlement increasing at the end of the eighteenth century. Land claims following the long-lot pattern were established at the village of Cahokia, presaging the "ordering of the land" brought about by the General Land Office (GLO) surveys beginning locally in 1805. In the late 1700s, Congress enacted a number of land grant initiatives pertaining to the western territories, including Illinois (Buck 1917, 72). Among these was legislation passed on March 3, 1791, that granted tracts up to 400 acres to claimants who could prove that the land they occupied had been improved, improvements consisting of "not a mere marking or deadening of trees, but the actual raising of a crop, or crops, such, in their opinion, being a necessary proof of an intention to make a permanent establishment" (Brink 1882, 69). Within the boundaries of the Cahokia site, two adjacent claims were approved, which, not coincidentally, encompassed the confluence of Cahokia and Canteen Creeks and the high ground formed by their levees. One of the claims was aligned roughly north to south, the other east to west, with a portion of their common boundary running along the western base of Monks Mound. Together they formed an inverse L that encompassed most of the northwest quadrant of the Cahokia site, extending from their nexus at Monks Mound westward nearly to the Powell mound group and northward past the Kunnemann mound group.

The east-west parcel was settled by Isaac Levy, Jean Baptiste LaCroix, and Thomas Brady around 1776, presumably for the purpose of establishing a trading post known as La Cantine. Little is known of this trading post, not even its precise location, though Walthall and Benchley (1987) surmise that it was located in the central part of the site, just west of Monks Mound. Late-eighteenth-century and early-nineteenth-century land records state that Levy, LaCroix, and Brady "made an Establishment on the River Labbe at the lower side of the Great Nobb, near where the french Church stood," residing there until 1784, whereupon "the Indians grew too troublesome and [they] were obliged to leave the same and come and live in the village" (Walthall and Benchley 1987, app. A). The village they moved to was the village of French Cahokia located approximately 8 miles (12.5 kilometers) to the southwest. The north-south parcel was settled by Jean B. Gonville, a.k.a. Rupalay, on or before 1783 (Hammes 1987, app. B).

In 1804, French residents of Prairie du Pont, led by a man named Delorm (Deloom), settled "at the edge of the timber, near the 'Big Mound' in the American Bottom, not far from Quentine (Canteen) Creek" (Hair 1866, 41; Brink 1882, 47). This settlement eventually became known as the village of

Canteen, deriving its name, as did Canteen Creek, from the trading post known as La Cantine.

By the first few months of 1811, the Levy, Brady, and LaCroix and the Gonville parcels were in the possession of Trappist monks led by the Reverend Urbain Guillet, who had first come to the area as squatters in 1809 (Hammes 1981). It is from this nearby settlement of Trappist monks that the name Monks Mound derives. General Land Office survey notes for May 31, 1810, describe a fence associated with "an improvement occupied by the monks." Within four years, in 1814, the Trappists had abandoned the site and sold the land to a local land speculator, Nicolas Jarrot. According to Charles Dickens, who viewed Monks Mound "looming in the distance" in 1842, the Trappist monks "founded a desolate convent there, many years ago, when there were no settlers within a thousand miles, and were all swept off by the pernicious climate" (Dickens 1893, 108). It was during the monks' brief tenure that Brackenridge made his historic expedition to view the mounds. Jarrot built a water mill on Cahokia Creek. According to an 1881 history of St. Clair County (Brink 1882, 46), Jarrot "had a mania for mills" and "the exposure, fatigue and sickness he experienced while at work on this mill is said to have been the cause of his death."

The nineteenth-century pioneer settlement into the areas newly partitioned by the GLO survey sought timbered areas first and only expanded onto prairie sites like Cahokia two to three decades later. In 1840 Madison County had one of the highest numbers of men employed in sawmills and the highest value of lumber products in the United States (Williams 1989, 165, 166), in large part attributable to the great period of expansion that St. Louis was undergoing at this time as well as to the provisioning of cordwood for powering the heavy steamboat traffic on the Mississippi River. Curiously, St. Clair County does not show a concurrent commercialization of its timber resources. But the answer here is the same as that in late prehistoric times and involves the relative ease of transport of wood from the uplands to the bottoms and the Mississippi through the Cahokia Creek and Wood River systems. In contrast, the major drainages in St. Clair County flow southward into the Kaskaskia and away from the market.

An 1882 account (Brink 1882, 501) describes Canteen as a "straggling village following the meanderings of Cantine and Cahokia Creeks for several miles . . . at one time a handsome village and the centre of considerable trade." Its heyday appears to have been around the mid-nineteenth century, with the main portion of the settlement just east of the Powell mound group, approximately 2 kilometers west of Monks Mound; road records from 1846 and 1847, though essentially schematics, depict a Canteen village in this general area, and twentieth-century maps indicate a number of small tracts and buildings, including Canteen School, in the same vicinity.

These 1846 and 1847 plats depict the routes of proposed roads, along with other selected features, among them "Monks Hill" and a few "little" or "small" mounds. Featured on both plats is a proposed road passing just north of Monks Mound, traversing Helms Ridge from Canteen Village at the western limits of the site to a bridge crossing Canteen Creek near "Mr. Morrison's View" and "Glover's Field" at the eastern limits. The 1847 plat also shows the route of a proposed "Plank Road to go direct to River" along the St. Clair County line, what is now Collinsville Road, or the old U.S. 40. Other roads leading to isolated properties to the southeast and southwest were not completed.

The plats and other records suggest that by the mid-1800s, and for the first time since the Mississippian occupation, the area along Helms Ridge was again becoming the focus of considerable activity. Initially it was the high land along Cahokia and Canteen Creeks that was settled, and only later did this spread out to encompass surrounding areas, including southern sections of the Cahokia site. Occupation of the area continued without interruption into the twentieth century. In the 1920s, the state of Illinois purchased the central area of the Cahokia site and made it into a park. Settlement and construction continued in surrounding areas, including the construction of modern tract housing just east of the Grand Plaza in the early 1940s (fig. 37). In 1941, salvage excavations were undertaken at Mound 55 (under the joint sponsorship of the Illinois State Museum, the Illinois State Division of Parks, and the Museum Extension Project, one of the professional programs of the Public Activities Division of the Works Project Administration [WPA] in Illinois) when it was learned that this mound, located just outside the east boundary of the Cahokia Mounds State Park, was being leveled by the building of the Mounds Acreage subdivision. The field season was terminated by the bombing of Pearl Harbor. Expansion of park boundaries continued throughout the twentieth century in efforts to curtail further modern transformations, preserve Mississippian period remains, and return the land to the look of an earlier time.

The richness of its settlement history reinforces the notion that the area encompassed by the Cahokia site is prime land. The centrality of its geographic location is attested to by state highways, interstates, and railroads. The highway that bisects the Cahokia site follows the route of the nineteenth-century plank road and is, precisely, the axis, configured by the lay of the land, which was so important to the Cahokians.

Since the abandonment of the site by the Cahokians, successive occupations by different cultures have chosen the same center to settle on and have either withered on the vine or expanded to occupy less desirable ground. It is probable that this same pattern applied to the time before the Cahokians as well.

The varied post-Mississippian settlers chose this area for much the same reasons as did the Cahokians. Natural levees along Cahokia and Canteen Creeks provided a large expanse of high, dry ground that was suitable for habitation as well as for agriculture. The creeks and the high land bordering the creeks also provided a convenient route to the uplands and to the Mississippi, allowing the settlements at Cahokia to serve as both a gathering and bulking point and as a conduit of communication and trade. For post-Mississippian settlers the mounds also provided a certain allure—if not always for their symbolism, at least for their height.

It was not until after the middle of the nineteenth century that post-Mississippian settlement spread, to any degree, to areas off the prime land

37. As if following a Cahokia master plan, a modern subdivision occupied the central area of the site. These structures have since been removed in the enlargement of the park. Courtesy of the Cahokia Mounds Historic Site.

along the creeks. It was only the latest historic occupation that covered the entire area that was the Cahokia site, and it is the only occupation that has exhibited any significant time depth. The historic pattern of settlement and growth, however, is strikingly dissimilar from the one we have observed for the Mississippian period. Examining the differences between the two provides insights into the essence of Mississippian Cahokia.

The spread of occupation during historic times occurred gradually, long after a core area had been defined. Individual farmers filed land claims and settled the more marginal areas. Expansion of the state park proceeded in much the same fashion; first a central core was defined, with subsequent efforts over the last eighty years directed toward acquiring land surrounding this center.

In contrast, the Mississippian pattern is markedly different. It does not reflect a gradual expansion from a central core, but a roughly coeval definition of both a central area and mound groups located at the site limits around the time of the Emergent Mississippian–Mississippian transition. Early Mississippian developments and growth occurred largely within this defined area.

These differences underscore why Cahokia emerged and came to dominate the Mississippian world. The Euro-American settlers did not conceptualize themselves as a community. Settlement growth was individualized and haphazard; communal features or any other trappings of planned community development were absent. An informal name developed for this rural area solely because of population density. On the other hand, it is obvious from the way that the Cahokians placed themselves on the land that they formed a planned, cohesive community. And, as we have argued, it was through the construction of Monks Mound, the Grand Plaza, and numerous marker mounds that this community was created and defined.

The evolution of the Cahokia Mounds State Historic Site differs from the Mississippian scenario in that the outlying marker mounds have been the last to come under jurisdiction. What has been similar is that the first area purchased for the park, i.e., the central area of Monks Mound and the Grand Plaza, was developed early and then left largely alone. During Mississippian times, the center was also "frozen," once defined. Fortunately for us, it is this curtailing of repeated development and evolution of the central area that has provided us with such a pristine and unsullied record of Emergent Mississippian and early Mississippian activities.

Although Euro-American settlement did eventually spread over the entire area of the Cahokia site, occupation during the historic period was always considered rural, and the big centers were located at East St. Louis and St. Louis. The overriding reasons for this relate to the difficulties of overland transportation, which rendered locations along the Mississippi River very attractive. Prehistoric settlements were established at these same locations for much the same reason, yet the Mississippian mound centers at St. Louis and East St. Louis did not rival Cahokia.

We might ask why the area of the Cahokia site remained a historic backwater when it was certainly not a prehistoric one. We know that transport was important to the Cahokians. After all, they located themselves along a creek that fed into the Mississippi River system. Exotic goods recovered at the site, together with Cahokia materials recovered across much of the eastern United States, attest to a widespread trade network. But transport was obviously not the sole factor, nor even the most important one. Obviously the Mississippians were tied quite closely to an agricultural base. Cahokia was located within a broad expanse of fertile ground, the size of which was not available near the East St. Louis and St. Louis mound groups. In addition, travel away from the Mississippi and to the uplands was important to the Mississippians. Cahokia Creek, with its large catchment, provided unparalleled access to the uplands. Finally, of course, there was an individual or a group of individuals who had the vision and power to put it all together at Cahokia.

RESIDENT RESETTLEMENT AND CHANGE

We have discussed the timing and tempo of landscape change at Cahokia and the way in which they differed from other mound centers within the American Bottom. We have also described how the Cahokia phenomenon compares to later historic developments. In this section we will examine the fluidity of the Cahokia landscape in terms of mound construction and attendant borrowing, reclamation efforts, the establishment and solidification of subcommunities, and the transformation of domestic village to sacred and public precincts and back again to domestic use. All these changes occurred within the span of several centuries, and everywhere we look at the site we see a scenario that plays differently through time. Reconstructive views depicting a model village cannot possibly capture this quality.

Smaller Mississippian mound centers characteristically maintained site partitioning for centuries, with only minor fluctuations. Mound and plaza arrangements, together with residential areas, exhibited stability, not flux (e.g., Brain 1989; Polhemus 1987; Schnell et al. 1981; Williams and Brain 1983). But at Cahokia, with the exception of Monks Mound and the Grand Plaza, change was pervasive. Both temporally and spatially, the landscape and resident population were characteristically, and even necessarily, fluid. We will call this fluidity "resident resettlement" and use the following examples to illustrate the range of transformations taking place. Though separated as to type, a broad relationship runs between them, keyed to the expansion and contraction of functional areas and to the relationship between center and periphery.

Land Reclamation in the Center

Borrowing efforts directed toward the construction of Monks Mound were the first large-scale impacts on the land by the Cahokians. As noted earlier, borrowing was sudden and massive. Concentrated around the flanks of Monks Mound, it most certainly resulted in the unprecedented upheaval of large numbers of people from previously established domestic areas. Certainly any borrowing to the east of Monks Mound displaced domestic occupation, given the intensive Emergent Mississippian occupation along Helms Ridge. It is also probable that borrowing on the southern margins of the Mound, as documented within the Grand Plaza and below Mound 51, would have resulted in the movement of habitation areas. Evidence for a spilling of occupation southward off the ridge has been documented in excavations at Mound 48 and the Falcon Drive-In, although an effective limit to this occupation was likely no more than 200 meters south of Monks Mound.

The holes created by this massive borrowing for Monks Mound were not left open but were, without exception, all reclaimed. Silty clays served as the primary source for filling sediments. They were either obtained through stripping of surface soils south of Helms Ridge, or perhaps from the open borrows that formed a ring around the Central Precinct. Garbage and midden generated from occupation areas along Helms Ridge was also used to reclaim this land.

Once reclaimed, the area surrounding Monks Mound changed little over the remainder of the Mississippian occupation. Domestic use of this area was largely precluded until late in the sequence, and at this time only minimal transformation of the landscape was effected. The fact that the rest of

Cahokia was so fluid makes this stable central complex of Monks Mound and the Grand Plaza stand in high contrast.

From Hearth to Cosmos and Back

Although we lack data regarding the impact on presumptive dwellings by massive borrowing around Monks Mound, we are nearly overwhelmed with evidence for the displacement of dwellings moving spatially out from the halo of Monks Mound and temporally forward from the initial transformations beginning in the Emergent Mississippian period. Let us consider the social implications of such uprooting.

Where you lived in a Mississippian community revealed much about who you were. Equally important, who your neighbors were was part of the fabric of social life. Appropriation of residential land was not an isolated process and did not affect families individually. Rather, it was, as were all things at Cahokia, large-scale. How was it possible then to repeatedly uproot scores of families? For this is what we know occurred at Cahokia for more than a century.

Evidence of this process comes from several areas at the site and indicates that displacement precipitated by the enlargement of a public core proceeded in a time-progressive fashion with distance out from Monks Mound. It is around the flanks of Monks Mound that we see a residential intensity of Emergent Mississippian households unequaled in the environs. To a large extent, this occupation was truncated prior to the end of the period, and the land was co-opted for other than domestic uses.

Farther west from Monks Mound (about 200 meters), domestic settings were transformed at the same time in the Merrell mound group (Tract 15B). However, this change represents a transitional zone, because pockets of occupation at this radius from Monks Mound exhibit residential stability for another century (documented by excavations at the Falcon Drive-In area and under Mound 31). But where settlements were uprooted, domestic construction was replaced by elite display and privatization—walls and more walls, with circular buildings enclosing areas of 25 meters in diameter, and bastioned walls at least 55 meters in one dimension, and large posts (fig. 34). It is no coincidence that this displacement was timed with the power display of the Mound 72 burial program.

Following a western course—because this is where the data are—and moving out another 500 meters or so to the woodhenge grouping, we find evidence that domestic tranquility lasted a century longer than that observed around the collar zone of Monks Mound. Disturbance to domestic life in this area, excluding the mounds, was effected by construction of a circle of wooden posts (i.e., a woodhenge) and associated large buildings and sweat baths. The woodhenge was rebuilt five times (with diameters ranging from 73 to 145 meters). However, a large building, enclosing some 229 square meters, apparently was not.

The redomestication of these areas, which occurred some hundred years later, was gradual and probably related both to an increasing focus on the area around the palisade and to a drop in overall population. Domestic settings of courtyard groups in Tracts 15A and 15B sprang up during the Moorehead phase. The densities of residential occupation once observed in these areas, however, were not achieved again. A comparison between late domestic structures for Tracts 15A and 15B shows that Tract 15B, which is closer to Monks Mound and the Central Palisade, had a greater number of structures in a smaller area exposed than Tract 15A, which was located farther west.

Formerly settled areas along the southern flanks of Helms Ridge, as documented by pipeline work in Fairmount City and by work in the Dunham Tract, were abandoned at the same time, making this transformation a contraction in nearly all areas of the site. To a significant extent, the palisade became the defining element for the central area and served as a magnet for domestic occupation. Although all domestic occupation was not confined to the circuit of the palisade, there was a sharp retrenchment to this position. By Sand Prairie times, the end of the Mississippian sequence, people were again living right next to Monks Mound. Along its west flanks, occupation was sufficiently dense to generate thick refuse deposits.

Subcommunity Formation and Solidification

Undoubtedly, large areas of the site were not subjected to the shuttling back-and-forth between domestic and other uses as outlined above. Indeed, there is evidence of subcommunities at Cahokia with an Emergent Mississippian foundation that did not undergo such transformations, but they are not the norm. The ones that have been documented were confined to prime land along the margins of Cahokia Creek, although these were located outside the confines of the Central Precinct. Excavations at the Powell mound group reveal a continuity from Emergent Mississippian times through the Stirling phase, occasioned only by the additions of large buildings and sweat baths over time. A similar continuity, based on controlled surface collections, can also be assumed for the collar occupations around the Kunnemann mound group.

Elsewhere on the margins, another story is revealed in the scattered dwellings south of Helms Ridge (Gums et al. 1989; Lopinot et al. 1993; Witty 1993). At these locations, housing developments blinked on and off like the lights on a Christmas tree, seldom witnessing occupational stability. This may have been one outlet for displaced people along Helms Ridge, but it surely did not account for the vast numbers affected. If entire neighborhoods were uprooted from the center, where did they go? How were the major acts of appropriation involved in the creation of the center and in the later conversion of domestic areas to other uses answered? They, as well as the continuing flood of immigrants from surrounding areas, had to be have been housed somewhere.

Excavations associated with the construction of the modern Interpretative Center (Collins 1990) offer one possibility—the construction of planned communities to accommodate, in toto, entire neighborhoods either displaced from the central area or arriving from outlying settlements. As mentioned earlier, what appears to have been a planned community in this location emerged in Lohmann times. We use the word "planned" because the structure of this community was unlike that of previous, or even many contemporary, Cahokia residential areas. It was carefully ordered, with house axes oriented to the cardinal directions (fig. 35).

It does not appear that this new community displaced earlier occupations. The environs of this tract were not featureless, although prior residential occupation was limited. Borrowing, in particular, seems to have been common—a portion of the tract was a filled borrow. The paucity of early occupation in this area, together with the fact that it was low-lying and distant both from the central area and from Cahokia Creek, reinforces the notion that people were being settled in areas that were not prime land.

No doubt exists for assigning the initial filling-up of the land at Cahokia to the Lohmann phase. We see evidence for Lohmann domestic occupation spilling out from Helms Ridge to the far south on the surface at the Rattlesnake mound group, in testing at the Rouch mound group, and in other areas in between. Points along the western margins have also been documented as having Lohmann occupation. It is only to the east that doubts exist. Some of this land was surely considered marginal—the ICT-II is a case in point. Frequently inundated during modern times, the ICT-II was once a prairie. Now, thick, silty clay soil causes water to pond in this relatively low-lying area. In other areas not affected by the broadcasting of people from areas impacted by elite or public goals, such as the Kunnemann mound group and the Powell mound group, Lohmann occupations carry over uninterrupted from the preceding terminal Emergent Mississippian occupation.

We assume that original acts of appropriation involved in the creation of central elements were answered by the creation of ICT-II-like phenomena—that is, planned communities built on the margins of the site. At the ICT-II at least, the establishment of a community appeared to have been successful, given residential continuity and the building of small mounds. Solidification occurred during Stirling times with a focus inward, around a plazuela. Residential rebuilding continued for another century or so. Upward of six rebuildings in one location through the sequence are evident, and even the construction of the Central Palisade failed to deter this community.

But even after this first massive shift, people continued to be displaced from the site core for at least fifty to seventy-five more years. The woodhenge that disrupted Lohmann houses and the palisade that disrupted late Stirling dwellings are examples of such displacement projects. But where did people go? Pauketat (Pauketat and Lopinot 1997, 119) suggests that they moved outside the site limits. Indeed, regional population does appear to jump, especially during the late part of the Stirling phase.

PART THREE

LANDSCAPE

AND

MEANING

CHAPTER SEVEN

CAHOKIANS

IN THE

LANDSCAPE

When viewing Cahokia from above, using a map or aerial perspective, it is easy to forget how big it is and the meaning and effect of the great distances involved. This is not the case when walking across the site. Not only is our experience of immensity heightened, but we are pushed to acknowledge the relationship between movement and space, and the connection between the size of our bodies, with our attendant capabilities of hearing and vision, and the scale of the landscape that we are experiencing. To simulate such an encounter and understand the meaning and social use of space on a human scale, we will discuss universals of human scale and explore an analogy with another public space of similar scale, the Capitol Mall in Washington, D.C.

The Cahokia site is roughly 2 3/4 miles (4.5 kilometers) across. A brisk (ca. 3-miles/hour) walk across the site takes roughly an hour, provided that a route with few obstacles is followed. Walking from the margins to the center takes half this time. These distances were not conducive to interaction among the entire Cahokian community on a daily basis. People living on the western edge of the site (e.g. at the Powell mound group, Mound 86 area) would probably not have been in daily contact with people living on the opposite side of Monks Mound. Thus, the frequency of interaction would not be what connected the people who lived on opposite margins with each other or with those residing in the center, for both distance and numbers of people residing at the site precluded this sort of personal interaction.

Let us use Washington, D.C., as an analog of familiar public space to provide some scale comparison. The central elements of the federal city include the U.S. Capitol building, the White House, the Washington Monument, the Jefferson Memorial, the Lincoln Memorial, and the Capitol Mall joining them. Figure 38 illustrates the distribution of these elements over an area of approximately 2 kilometers north to south and 3.5 kilometers east to west. The dimensions of Cahokia are roughly equivalent. The north-south dimension, from the Kunnemann mound group to Rattlesnake Mound, is approximately 3 kilometers. With Monks Mound at the midpoint, a 2-kilometer distance along the east-west axis includes only the area between Mounds 44 and 27, although this would enclose the main concentration of earthen monuments at the site. East-west dimensions of the entire site, from Powell Mound to Mound 1, are roughly 4.5 kilometers. For those of you who have walked the Capitol Mall, you know this is a fair distance. Imagine traveling this and even farther across swampy ground or even a creek!

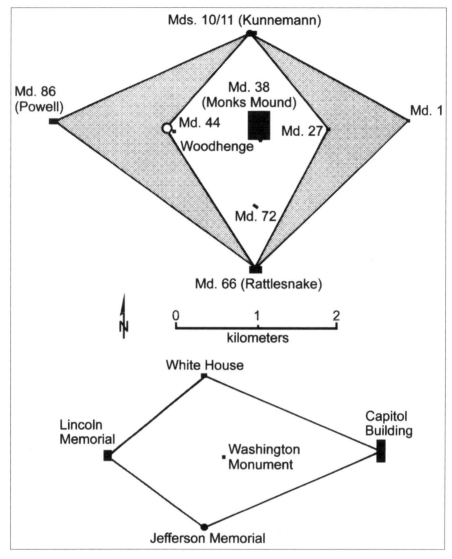

38. When compared to a known monumental place, Washington, D.C., the organization of the Cahokia site can be seen to encompass an area of similar dimensions.

If we compare the layout of the monuments in the federal city with a group of earthen monuments from the central portion of Cahokia, parallels are evident. In Washington, D.C., structures are arranged in a roughly dia-mond-shaped pattern, with the U.S. Capitol at the head. The White House and various monuments and memorials are distributed at the other corners. A similar diamond-shaped arrangement of mounds can be traced at Cahokia, with functions comparable to those at the Capitol, although this configura-

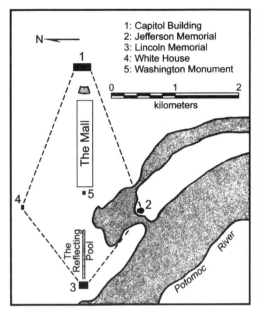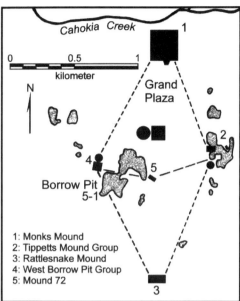

39. A comparison of central Cahokia to selected central elements of Washington, D.C., indicates a similar arrangement of monumental structures and open water.

tion covers an area only approximately half the size (fig. 39). At Cahokia, Monks Mound stands at the head of the diamond. As in Washington, D.C., this was where the governing body of the community was centered. In L'Enfant's vision of Washington, the spatial separation of the White House and the Capitol building was a symbolic representation of the separation of powers between the president and Congress. Since Cahokia was not a democracy, but was ruled by a chief, this was not the case at Cahokia. The powers of the president and Congress, as well as the church, were all centered at Monks Mound, the domain of the chief.

The relative dimensions of these two structures, the Capitol building and Monks Mound, reflect this centering of power. Although a smaller area was encompassed by the diamond-shaped configuration at Cahokia, individual monuments were not smaller than those in Washington, D.C. For example, the dimensions of the U.S. Capitol building are 751 feet by 350 feet (229 meters by 107 meters), compared to dimensions of 1037 feet by 790 feet (316 meters by 241 meters) for Monks Mound, indicating that three Capitol buildings could fit within the area covered by Monks Mound. Of course, Monks Mound was not as high as the Capitol building (100 feet as opposed to 287 feet), though this is largely due to the height of the Capitol dome.

The other points of the diamond at Cahokia are two twin-mound (platform-conical) complexes at the east and west corners and an important ridgetop mound (Rattlesnake Mound) marking the southern limits of the site. The significance of the paired mounds is inferred, based on a wealth of literature in southeastern ethnohistory and archaeology that links the platform mound to a charnel house for drying human remains, and the conical mound for entombing the remains (Knight 1981; Swanton 1946, 718–29; Waring 1968; Waring and Holder 1945). The largest example of a paired-mound grouping, in addition to an important early burial mound (Mound 72) containing the remains of a powerful individual and numerous retainers, was found at the center of this diamond. Evidence suggests that these paired-mound complexes formed a mortuary district that had special significance to the Cahokians. This ritual and memorial function was similar to the memorials found in the center of and defining the western portion of the diamond in Washington, D.C. An association of water with the memorials is present in both cases. At Cahokia, the mortuary complex was integrated with open borrow pits. In Washington, D.C., a reflecting pool is located in front of the Lincoln Memorial, a tidal basin extends between the Lincoln and Jefferson Memorials, and Arlington Cemetery is connected to extensions of the Mall by Memorial Bridge over the Potomac River.

Previously we discussed the connection between the distance at which one can detect a human being (ca. 1.1 kilometers) and physical and cultural features at Cahokia. This limit of vision appears to coincide with a site core radiating out from Monks Mound, at least during the early Mississippian period. Outlying mound groups appear to have been visually connected to this center by this 1.1-kilometer distance (fig. 31). Note that the chain of mounds leading west toward the East St. Louis group was spaced at just over this limit (ca. 1.4–1.8 kilometers).

Moving to scales smaller than this maximal limit of vision, Lynch and Hack (1984, 157) state that a person may not only be detected but also recognized at a distance of about 25 meters. As one of the Mississippian subcommunity plazuelas at the site shows (fig. 35), this distance actually corresponds to a "neighborhood" scale where daily interaction on a personal basis can be effected. The plazuela documented at the ICT-II measures approximately 25–30 meters across and 50 meters north to south. In contrast, Emergent Mississippian courtyards were typically much smaller, i.e., ca. 15 meters across in all dimensions. Interestingly enough, this corresponds to the distance given by Lynch and Hack (i.e., 14 meters) at which it is possible not only to recognize someone but to also see his or her facial expressions. Emergent Mississippian courtyard groups can be thought of, therefore, as more intimate than their Mississippian successors. Such cohesiveness was also reflected in the pits in the center of these courtyards—features that provided a well-defined focal center to the community and that were replicated at sites across the region.

Motloch (1991) considers anything greater than 3 meters as public distance. Similarly, Lynch and Hack (1984) define a distance of 1–3 meters as a personal space, in which we sense others in direct relation to us. Let us examine house spacing with this measure in mind, though we must emphasize that this issue is clouded by the fact that we do not know how many houses within an area were present and being used at any given time. Be that as it may, the spacing between adjacent houses varied from 1 to 10 meters. Given what we know about Mississippian society, together with a consideration of the personal nature of this 3-meter distance, the smaller range of house spacing, i.e., houses that are 1–3 meters apart, may have been connected (belonged to one household).

We also believe that there are important dimensions to consider between the 1.1-kilometer limits of vision and the smaller and more intimate distances outlined by Lynch and Hack. For example, perhaps we can consider the limits of vision for recognizing people in costume or for viewing pageantry, or the limits of hearing.

If we return to our Washington, D.C. analog, how are processions—military, political, civic, or religious—perceived by the pedestrian in the Capitol Mall? Similarly, what was it like to partake of such pageantry at Cahokia? We suggest that an arena or performance scale would be on the order of a hundred to several hundred meters. This dimension corresponds to the size of playing fields in contemporary sports. Formal dimensions of ballplaying fields in the Southeast obtained from ethnohistoric accounts varied considerably, i.e., up to more than 300 meters (Swanton 1946, 674–83), although a size of 100 meters would not have been unreasonable. Perhaps consideration of this dimension may help us understand better how the Grand Plaza area might have been used.

Let us first examine the structure of the Grand Plaza. The arrangement of mounds around a square, cleared area, or plaza was a typical pattern during the late prehistoric period throughout much of the eastern United States. Ethnohistoric accounts suggest that these open spaces functioned as the setting for games, such as chunkey and lacrosse, as well as for communal ceremonies (Swanton 1946). Other activities included dance, theater, monumental construction, and planting and harvesting ceremonies. Plazas were a nearly universal phenomenon, serving as a central focus for planned towns and centers, and were one of the few monumental features within Mississippian towns that displayed unlimited access, indicating that these open spaces were unequivocally public.

Various interpretations of the limits of the Grand Plaza at Cahokia have been put forward. At a minimum, it extended across a rectangular area defined by Monks Mound to the north and Mound 49 to the south. At a maximum, it included all available level land between Monks Mound on the north and Fox and Round Top Mounds (the paired mounds, Mounds 59 and 60) on the south. East-west dimensions would have extended between a linear series of mounds on the east (Mounds 50, 51, 54, and 55) and Mound 48 on the west (Fowler 1975, 96; 1989, fig. 10.1; Holley et al. 1990; Morgan 1980, 51). A maximal interpretation does not necessarily align itself with the performance dimensions postulated above. However, it does not preclude envisioning the plaza as a number of subspaces, each having a different configuration and use.

The classic description of a segmented plaza is that provided by Bartram for the historic Creek Indians (Swanton 1946, 390–93). Three functionally distinct segments are described, including town "hot house," square ground, and chunkey yard, which accommodate purification, meeting, and game playing, respectively. These functional units have not been recovered in archaeological contexts. It is likely that plazas in small, late-eighteenth-century towns would not be an ideal match for a megacenter occupied nearly seven hundred years before.

We suggest that Mound 56 may have served as an effective southern boundary to the plaza, at least in terms of ceremonies focused on Monks Mound. From Monks Mound to Mound 56 measures roughly 300 meters. If one moves much farther south, it becomes harder to see and definitely more difficult to hear what is happening on the mound. For instance, we have noted that the First and Second Terraces of Monks Mound form an amphitheater effect for broadcasting. One can clearly hear people today on Monks Mound from the area around Mound 49 (a distance of approximately 200 meters), even over the traffic traversing the road in between. Ceremonies centered on the First Terrace of Monks Mound would have been clearly visible and audible to the people in the plaza below.

Further evidence for Mound 56 as a southern boundary to the Grand Plaza is provided by the tiers of Mound 56 that form a sort of ramp which looks to the north, facing, and carefully aligned with, the southward facing ramp of Monks Mound. This inward focus and symmetry suggest that something in between was to be accessed and viewed. A ramp on the northeast corner of Mound 48 also maintains this inward focus and alignment. The fact that Mound 56 appears to have been an elite-residence mound also argues for its exclusion from, rather than inclusion within, a plaza. However, we must also allow the possibility of a temporal component to the definition of the plaza. We do not know exactly when construction on Mound 56, Mound 49, or Mounds 59 and 60 began. We only know that Mound 56 was occupied at least by Stirling times.

We might also consider how many people the Grand Plaza might have held. The size and frequency of plazas have typically been considered to be proportional to town size and presumed organizational structure. If we use Mound 56 as a southern boundary, and the space extending from Mound 48 to the linear string of mounds on the east as east-west dimensions, we are left with a space that measures approximately 300 by 500 meters, or 150,000 square meters (15 hectares). Assuming a gathering of people for an address or a ceremony centered on Monks Mound, giving each person an area of 1 meter (roughly 2 meters between people), and considering some of this space to be taken up by Mound 49, we could fit approximately thirty thousand people into this space. (This is probably a minimal estimate, because measurements employed by Harris and Dines [1998] suggest that 1 meter between people in rows and also elbow-to-elbow would be a generous space.) Of course, how close people stood (or sat) would depend on the event that they were watching or participating in. For an activity like a chunkey game, the numbers would have been significantly less. Though these numbers are conjectural, the point is that hundreds of thousands of people would not have fit into the Grand Plaza.

Estimates for the population at Cahokia have ranged from less than five thousand to over forty thousand individuals. Gregg (1975) provided the first "hard" estimate of twenty-five thousand. Since archaeological excavations have covered less than 1 percent of the site, and the methodologies employed for determining populations are subject to a great deal of uncertainty, the question of the number of individuals at Cahokia will continue to be a matter of strong debate. Recent and refined estimates by Holley (1990) and Pauketat and Lopinot (1997) generally agree that perhaps as many as ten thousand to fifteen thousand people would correspond with the maximal population reached by Cahokia. In any case, there were a lot of people there, the largest population concentration in what was to become the United States until the beginning of the nineteenth century. From a global perspective, these maximum figures are in line with those recorded for pre-industrial cities (Crone 1989, 16–18), although typically one expects the rural population to number from 80 to 90 percent of this value, and this does not appear to be in keeping with the regional population of the Cahokia polity. The Grand Plaza at Cahokia has also been interpreted as a gathering spot for the larger American Bottom region. Our estimate of thirty thousand people fitting into the Grand Plaza would then be commensurate with what would have composed this Cahokia system.

We have argued that a plaza extending from Monks Mound to the Twin Mounds (Mounds 59 and 60), a distance of about 550 meters, was too large for an effective ceremonial space, at least in terms of pageantry centered upon Monks Mound. Our experience in physically mapping this area affirms that this distance makes the discrimination of detail difficult. For example, it is common surveying practice to convey information via hand signals, e.g., "move left," "come forward," and so forth. Visual signaling between two people, one standing at the foot of Monks Mound, the other at the base of the Twin Mounds, however, involves jumping up and down while waving a brightly colored object, such as a yellow field book. Dimensions of a few hundred meters are thus more conducive to this use. We must also consider, in view of their paired association, that the space surrounding the Twin Mounds might have been ritual space of another and separate sort, though this too may have been defined according to performance dictates. It is interesting to note that if we draw a space around the Twin Mounds with these dimensions, it embraces the high ground around the mounds to the south and is bounded by Mound 56 on the north. We also know that ground around the mounds was built up, possibly to create this elevated ritual space.

If we consider the distances mandated by a performance type of space to be a few hundred meters around features, some interesting details arise. For example, other paired-mound groups, like the West Borrow Pit group and the Tippetts mound group, were surrounded by interrupted terrain, including open borrows, and did not provide space for large groups of people. They could not have served as locations for the whole community to gather. Only smaller groups could have observed or participated in ceremonies centered at these mound groups. They also did not have populations radiating out from or ringing them. These mound complexes were islands, set apart from the rest of the site, but not set apart as an arena or stage for large gatherings. Their separation appears to have been more intrinsic than this. Outlying mound groups such as Rattlesnake, Rouch, Powell, and Kunnemann, also seem to share these characteristics, though the constraints on the space around the mounds seems to be largely related to the natural terrain.

Dimensions larger than those of the site also mattered. For example, looking outward from Cahokia was as important as the inner visual layout. From the site one can see the loess bluffs as they extend along the eastern edge of the American Bottom. In the past, one would also have seen a number of bluff-top mounds along this expanse, although only a few of these mounds remain today. Few reported investigations concerning these bluff-top mounds exist, but they suggest that the mounds were primarily burial mounds that were conical in form.

From the summit of Monks Mound, one can also see the limestone bluffs where the valley constricts. This is near the present communities of Alton on the north and Columbia on the south. Posting sentinels at these points would have provided knowledge and control of the American Bottom and views of people moving into and out of this region. From these points, signals could have been sent back to Monks Mound to indicate that travelers were coming either up or down the river, and this information could have reached Cahokia while the travelers were from 15 to 30 miles (24 to 48 kilometers) distant.

Finally, let us make a few comments about the temporal dimension of a human scale. A generation for the Cahokians would have been equal to roughly thirty years. If we take the origins of village life around A.D. 900 through the winding down of mound construction around A.D. 1300, we have a site history spanning four hundred years. Dividing this span of occupation by thirty-year generational increments provides nearly fourteen generations experiencing this long sequence of change. Which of these changes would have been noticeable to a generation or to a few generations, and which would have occurred over a much longer, and hence more remote, span of time?

At the ICT-II, the construction of a planned community in an area largely devoid of occupation provided radical change that a single generation surely would have witnessed. From the first occupation of this community in the Lohmann period through its development during Stirling times (ca. A.D. 1000–1150), however, the area would have been relatively stable. Our data indicate only one major change, from the orthogonally-oriented community to a more internally focused one. Though there is certainly rebuilding, there were centuries of stasis in the form and stability of this particular area.

This was not the case in the more volatile central area of the site, where changes occurred much more rapidly. For example, during an equivalent time span (A.D. 1000–1150), the area at Tract 15A experienced the move from an Emergent Mississippian village to Lohmann wall-trench houses to the construction of four woodhenges in the Stirling phase, with a return to a domestic setting in the Moorehead phase. Thus, multiple changes of a fundamental nature occurred in this area. Each of these changes would have happened on the order of a generation or two and therefore would have been much more visible to the Cahokians.

Analysis of materials recovered from the Submound 51 borrow (Pauketat 1997a) indicate that this borrow was open for a year or so. There was little evidence of natural siltation in the old borrow, but marsh grass had grown in the pit bottom before refilling. The refilling of the Submound 51 borrow, and probably also its initial excavation, would have been events obvious to a generation of Cahokians. Indeed, what was the use of their involving themselves in all these constructions unless they could see results within their lifetime? It is our view that the plans involved in initial construction activities had to be realized in a relatively short time. Like the Submound 51 borrow, the large borrow in the Grand Plaza was not open long. These borrows were not lying open for generations upon generations of people to throw in garbage until they filled in. Though the Grand Plaza was a massive undertaking, it appears to have been completed within a time span of less than fifty to seventy-five years. This would have been comprehensible to only a generation or two.

Just as the borrows surrounding Monks Mound were filled in relatively quickly, it appears that mounds also went up relatively quickly, at least in their initial stages. Even some entire mounds appear to have been constructed within a short time. For example, four cores taken through Mound 48, which appears to date from the Lohmann phase, showed no evidence of a hiatus in construction.

The construction history of the Kunnemann Mound (Mound 11) is contained within the Stirling phase (within one hundred years). Excavations into this mound indicate that even though individual stages of a mound would have been built within a generation, an entire mound would not necessarily have been completed. The schematic of mound construction activities reconstructed by Pauketat (1993b, fig. 3.33) shows ten stages, many of which were substantial and involved shifting the mound from a group of multiple structures to a single massive monument, undertaken within about three generations. As a rough guide, a new stage would have been built on the order of every ten years, and hence each generation would have been cognizant of several different stages.

Although it appears that early borrowing efforts and the basal platform of Monks Mound may have been completed within a generation, the people involved in starting the construction of Monks Mound would have been separated by nearly nine generations from those constructing the small Moorehead phase mound on the First Terrace. This is approaching a mythical separation. Even if we consider that it only took a hundred years for the main body of Monks Mound to be completed, this time span would constitute the memory of multiple generations.

CHAPTER EIGHT

BUILDING
CAHOKIA

Earthmoving efforts at the Cahokia site involved the application of specialized knowledge. Earthen construction did not result from rows of unskilled laborers trudging up hills with basket loads of sediment and dumping this fill wherever they pleased. Rather, experts were involved. For want of better terms, it is clear that surveyors, architects, and engineers numbered among the population at Cahokia. Surveyors laid out the alignments between mounds and other features that we observe today. Architects and engineers collaborated to produce the variety of earthworks and other terrain modifications at the site, employing diverse sediments and specialized structural and drainage features. Although these specialists were intimately involved in earthmoving efforts, their visibility in Cahokian society is another matter. Our knowledge of these specialists lies solely in the results of their labors, and we have no evidence for preferential living conditions to which they might have had access. Specialization at Cahokia in general has been commented on by Holley (1995), Muller (1997), Pauketat (1994), and Yerkes (1989) as is evident in concentrations of material residues representing the manufacture of shell-bead necklaces and celts at multiple locations within the site.

TECHNICAL EXPERTISE

Engineering expertise is manifest in sediment selection and placement in mound building and land reclamation, and in structural members and drainage features placed within mounds and reclaimed borrows. It is apparent that even the mixing of diverse materials was practiced to achieve a desired medium. The permanence of the mounds despite centuries of disturbance and erosion, and the minimal slumping which has occurred in refilled and reclaimed areas, is also testimony to this expertise.

The Grand Plaza provides a sterling example of engineering expertise. On the surface, the Grand Plaza appears to be a relatively (and naturally) flat area where mounds were not built (although mounds were built around its margins). This is how we thought of the Grand Plaza for a long time. However, we discovered that this area of the site is level because it was fashioned to be so by the Cahokians. This discovery changed our ideas about earthmoving at the site: not only were the Cahokians raising mounds, they were also sculpting the terrain.

During Emergent Mississippian times, muted ridge and swale topography would have been present within the bounds of what became the Grand

Plaza. As contiguous flat areas were needed by the incoming populace, however, this rolling terrain was overcome. After borrowing from extensive sections of this area to obtain sediments for Monks Mound, reclamation efforts proceeded in a purposeful and careful manner. Into this gaping hole was first thrown garbage from occupation areas along Helms Ridge. Discontinuous and heterogeneous deposits containing occupation debris and large sections of ceramic vessels litter the bottom of the borrow. These debris-filled sediments were then sealed, or covered, by more homogeneous fills (massive, silty clays), which contain almost no cultural debris, that were used to elevate the area and create a clean and level plaza surface. More accurately, we should say not quite level, for the plaza has a slight grade (a 0.3 percent slope), encouraging drainage to the south. Ultimately this drainage may have been directed into the open borrows located at the margins of this area.

During a filling operation, the degree of compaction must be controlled to produce a soil dense enough that it will not settle during subsequent use of the site, yet loose enough that internal drainage is not destroyed (Lynch and Hack 1984, 225–26). The Cahokians had considerable expertise in the infilling and controlled settlement of these reclaimed areas. The reclamation procedure followed within the Grand Plaza is impressive. On the surface, there is no sign that an extensive portion of this area was borrowed from, that is, no obvious slump corresponding to the borrowed area is visible, nor is there a pattern of standing water to indicate its presence.

The degree to which this reclaimed area mimics, or appears to be, undisturbed ground became even more apparent when we opened test units in this area. Nearly a thousand years of soil formation is partially responsible. Soil formation within the reclaimed borrow in the Grand Plaza proceeded quite rapidly because the Cahokians used "preconditioned," or developed, soils for infilling. Fill soils were also so similar in texture and degree of compaction to naturally formed soils in this area of the site that the large borrowed area within the plaza was not located with electromagnetic surveying. Examination of reclaimed areas as part of test excavations showed that clear evidence of basket loading was uncommon and that the differences that can be used to determine that these areas were modified are much more subtle; fill sediments display slight changes in texture and in the degree of soil formation compared to surrounding natural soils. Sparse prehistoric artifacts also provide a clue to the nature of these deposits. Largely, though, it was through the magnetic analysis of soils, which allowed us to quantify and trace these subtle differences in texture and the degree of soil formation, that the reclaimed borrow within the Grand Plaza was defined.

The Grand Plaza does not stand alone. Large sections of the Central Precinct, borrowed from to obtain fill to build Monks Mound, were probably reclaimed in a comparable fashion. Below Mound 51, test excavations have documented an infilling process quite similar to that observed in the Grand Plaza. Within the Submound 51 borrow, cultural debris was concentrated in the lower fill layers, whereas relatively "clean" soils made up the

upper portion of the borrow. In the Submound 51 borrow, however, the seal-
ing of these lower, debris-filled deposits may have been more deliberate—a
layer of burned thatch effectively sealed these deposits until they were
opened by excavations in the twenty-first century (Bareis 1975a). When the
burned layer was pierced, an overwhelming stench arose, the result of the
contact of air with the underlying undecomposed debris.

Technical expertise is also indicated in the infilling of smaller borrows at
the site. As an example, we return to the Grand Plaza, to a reclaimed borrow
located next to Mound 56. A test pit centered in this borrow showed that it
extended to a depth of 2.5 meters below the present ground surface into a
naturally deposited, well-sorted, fine sandy loam. Several distinct filling
episodes were indicated. The base of the borrow appears to have been filled
through alternating periods of rapid silt inwash and more gradual clay sedimentation. Abundant worm castings, leaf imprints, and oxidation of lami-
nar surfaces within these deposits indicate that the borrow was left open and
underwent periods of wetness and desiccation. This borrow may have served
for a time as a sump to drain standing water from the northern sections of
the plaza. Given that the final landscape was not created in a short period of
time, it is possible that some form of drainage would have been necessary to
remove standing water during construction activities. Ceramics from this fill
place the drainage facility late within the Emergent Mississippian period.
Subsequent deposits within this borrow represent episodes of fill, replacing
the drainage function of the pit. Notably, a sand-filled channel documented
within upper clay fills may have served as a filter drain for overlying fills of
clay and silt (Holley et al. 1990).

Mounds at Cahokia provide further evidence of engineering expertise.
Within mounds, drainage features have also been documented, as well as
features designed to strengthen these earthworks. Monks Mound is an excellent example of the application of specialized materials and engineering
knowledge on a massive scale (fig. 40).

It appears that the construction of Monks Mound began during the late
Emergent Mississippian period about A.D. 950 with the bulk of the present
mound certainly completed by the end of the initial phase of the Mississippian period a hundred years later. This would include the vast majority of
the fill to the north of the so-called First Terrace. Subsequent additions were
completed throughout much of the Mississippian period until the mid-
thirteenth century. These additions consisted of a sequence of veneer caps
on the Third and Fourth Terraces, completion of the First Terrace, at least repairs on the Second Terrace, and the emplacement of secondary mounds on
the southeastern corner of the Third Terrace and the western end of the First
Terrace. We have evidence from our recent work and from previous excavations that the various stages and construction sequences of the Mound were
carefully planned and engineered; for the Cahokians it was not just a matter
of throwing up a huge pile of dirt and then adding to it as the spirit moved
them. Decisions were made on the selection and placement of materials and

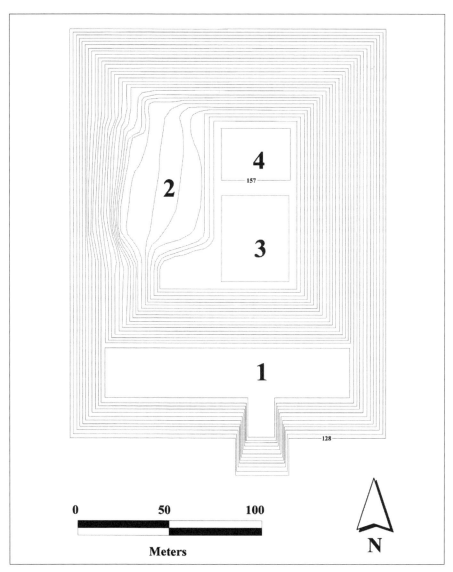

40. Our perspective of Monks Mound has changed from the four-terrace notion, coined in the early twentieth century, to only three terraces. The second terrace is illusory and resulted from slope failure of the western margins of the mound and associated prehistoric repairs.

from this, as Bareis (1975b, 13) argues, we can infer that a group, perhaps a class, of individuals with specialized knowledge of soils (soils or mound engineers) was responsible for directing the construction of the mound.

The efforts expended on engineering suggest a high degree of understanding of the problems inherent in earthen constructions of this magnitude in humid, midlatitude climatic regimes. The basic problem concerns the materials themselves. A significant portion of the mound mass was composed of clays with a high shrink-swell capacity and low hydraulic conductivity. When wet, these clays displaced significantly more volume than in the dry condition, whereas upon drying they contracted and tended to crack. The consequences of repeated episodes of drying and wetting are obvious: they produced great instability. Given a high local water table and an annual average of over 65,000 cubic meters of precipitation on the surface of the mound, continual water control was clearly essential for maintenance.

The base or core of the mound was composed of a 6- to 7-meter-high clay platform. Water pulled up into the mound by capillary action to a height of up to 10 meters kept the smectite clays in this core perennially saturated with capillary water (in an expanded state), thus forming an excellent supporting base for the enormous weight above it. A fair amount of earth would have been needed on top of this core in order to pull up the capillary water; without it, the core would have cycled through wet and dry states throughout the year and hence have been unstable. Thus, from an engineering standpoint, it made sense for the bulk of the mound to be constructed relatively rapidly.

The key to further stabilizing the mound was to keep the materials overlying the clay core dry. For this purpose, we know that the Cahokians constructed several types of drains. Above the core a series of massive clay-rich fill units were emplaced with their upper surfaces presumably sloping to the exterior of the mound. The clay members would have served to strengthen the mound. In most cases, these clayey soils were separated by coarser (sandier) materials that would have functioned as internal drains to remove atmospheric water before it infiltrated the core sediments. Puddled clay facings may also have been used to facilitate surface runoff, although there is no clear evidence for this, and the materials locally available do not lend themselves well to such a use.

Retaining buttresses incorporated into the internal structure of the mound, as well as placed externally along the southern edge, provide further evidence of prehistoric engineering. A retaining buttress composed of clay-rich sediment was defined within the slope leading to the Third Terrace, and this was capped by a zone of coarser materials. It appears that the coarser sediments were produced by mixing materials from multiple sources. This was probably done intentionally to produce a sediment with the desired texture to facilitate drainage. It is possible that various sediments were procured during seasons that were optimal for borrowing and then stockpiled together for later use in mound construction. Redigging and loading these soils would probably have been all that was required for mechanical mixing. The Cahokians also cut smaller drains into the slanting sides of the clay buttress, and these too were filled with coarser-textured material. These drains facilitated the subsurface flow of water down the face of the mound.

The degree of success of all these efforts can be measured by the long-term stability of the mound. With the exception of the prehistoric slumping evidenced by the two east lobes and a newly hypothesized prehistoric failure on the west side, no major failures occurred for a thousand years in spite of the instability of materials and the enormous mass and surface area of the structure. Only in the last two decades has the mound experienced major failure, with the several hundred years of stability testifying to the skills of the makers of this "stupendous pile."

MAINTENANCE

> We have seen the hope of complete preservation irreparably lost. The vandal and the farmer have worked wonders in obliteration. We have seen the height of all the big table mounds diminish steadily every year. We have seen the most beautiful and conical mound in the group divested of its head by men who, for all the care they took to preserve the configuration of the mound, might have been digging for worms. We have seen the kind-faced, but sharp-hoofed, cow climb over the precious face of the great Cahokia mound, until that priceless pyramid exposes trails and spots so vulnerable to the forces of erosion that every rain sees something of its immensity descend in solution, and every year sees it lose some part of its perishable configuration.

These are the comments of Clark McAdams, son of William McAdams, an early investigator of the Cahokia Mounds (McAdams 1907, 12, 35–47). Ironically, as part of these comments, McAdams presents a plea for the preservation of the mounds as well as for archaeological investigations at Cahokia, which (because they entail extensive excavations) are by nature destructive.

A visitor to Cahokia today can view the effects of centuries of disturbance and erosion. Park personnel are becoming increasingly concerned about Monks Mound and are actively working to try to preserve it. In 1984 a moderate slope failure along the eastern edge of Monks Mound called into question the future stability of this earthwork. The state of Illinois began joint archaeological and geotechnical studies to gather information on the internal structure of the mound and the causes of the slope failure. About the same time this work was in progress, a massive slope failure occurred on the western face. This slump was larger than all previously known examples (Emerson and Woods 1993). Within two years, however, movement stopped and the mound appeared to have restabilized. In response to the record rainfalls of 1993–1995, however, a renewed cycle of failure began, which has continued intermittently to the present.

It appears that the recent series of failures of Monks Mound is associated with modern changes in groundwater levels. Water use by local industries from the 1940s through the early 1960s was of such magnitude that ground-water levels in the entire northern portion of the American Bottom were lowered drastically to the point where many wells went dry. In response, capillary water within Monks Mound also dropped, and the clay core dried out for the first time. Consequently, this portion of the core contracted and probably developed cracks at numerous locations. This shrinking and crack-ing of the core and displacement of enormous volumes of material would also have disrupted the integrity of higher parts of the construction, includ-ing the drains and massive fill units. By the late 1960s, due to recycling, in-dustrial closings, and direct draw from the Mississippi River, the water table began to rise again. Within a decade, former levels were approached. The ex-pansion of the core of Monks Mound caused by rewetting exacerbated the problems caused by the earlier shrinking. With the internal drains no longer functioning efficiently and with cracks in the clay core, massive fill units, and clay caps, intrusion and retention of atmospheric water increased dra-matically. Hence, failure and slumping occurred. The careful structural engi-neering of the mound appears to have been overcome by this extreme situa-tion. The prehistoric planning that had been successful for centuries had not taken into consideration modern changes in the groundwater table.

Funded by the state of Illinois, the most recent archaeological investiga-tions of Monks Mound have been conducted by Southern Illinois University Edwardsville's Contract Archaeology Program in association with remediation procedures and concurrent replacement of the stair system ascending the south slopes of the mound. Since the slumping that occurred in the 1980s, new directional boring technology has been developed that is being em-ployed for remediation. This technology allows a narrow hole to be drilled at any angle up into the mound where it meets the zones of perched water be-fore exiting at a higher surface. Perforated pipe is then placed in the top of the hole and pulled downward to a connection with a catchment basin at the base. It is hoped that the installation of five of these drains on the western side of the mound will reduce groundwater buildup and thus eliminate, or at least slow, the slope failures that have occurred in recent times.

Investigations in areas to be affected by construction started in late July 1997. In the stairway area, narrow trenches were excavated where concrete footings had been placed to support the new step system. On the western side a deep 2-by-2-meter unit was excavated where a water collection basin will be placed; profiles were made of a historic well; and the installation of the drain system was monitored.

In addition to the recent slope failures on Monks Mound, several others have been recorded during the modern period. A slump occurred on the west face near the juncture of the First and Second Terraces in 1956 and an-other on the north face during the late 1960s (McGimsey and Wiant 1984, 1). The results of these, however, were readily patched and were not viewed as serious. Despite accounts such as that of McAdams that suggest the opposite, modern studies show that until recently there has been little change in the shape of this mound since its depiction in the early 1800s (Emerson and Woods 1993).

Just as there have been episodes of instability and stability during historic times, so there were within the Mississippian period of occupation. Evidence indicates that there were also problems with the mounds during prehistoric times. We know that slumps and failures of various kinds occurred at Monks Mound and were repaired. Therefore we have to change our conception of the mounds, as well as for the site as a whole, and think of them in more fluid terms and, furthermore, as not changing in a uniform or linear manner.

Evidence for slumping of Monks Mound during the Mississippian occupation includes the two so-called east lobes of the mound. On the west side, it has been postulated that the Second Terrace functioned as a buttress; however, evidence obtained during the recent stairway and slope stabilization project on the mound suggests that there was a large failure of the entire west side of the mound during Moorehead times and that a large patch job associated with this failure created the Second Terrace as we see it today. Increased risk of failure of the west side of Monks Mound makes sense due to the direction of prevailing winds and the force of rains, which are greatest on this side of the mound. The large Stirling phase structure documented on the summit of Monks Mound was incomplete on its west side. It is probable that this portion of the structure, or at least this portion of the remains of the structure, was lost during the failure of the west side of the mound. It seems likely that the west side of the mound was originally a mirror image of the east side and the awkward lobes and gully features evident today are the result of the subsequent erosion of the slumped area that dates to the Moorehead phase.

Over 2 meters below the current surface, within the 2-by-2-meter unit excavated at the base of the west slope (fig. 41), were portions of Late Woodland features that had been truncated by borrowing, presumably to obtain fill for Monks Mound building or repair operations. The age of ceramics (Moorehead phase) present in the infilling sediments suggests that the soils at the base of the west slope had been stripped relatively late in the sequence, perhaps two hundred years after onset of construction of Monks Mound. These activities may have been initiated by the large failure of the entire west side of the mound. What was being worked on was a massive patch job, rather than an addition to the mound. Overlying the truncated surface, a thick zone of thinly laminated layers of sands whose stratigraphy had not been disrupted by occupational trampling indicates a period of rapid deposition. This zone was formed by sediments washed down by rainstorms during the short period that the Second Terrace was being worked on. Above that were zones of loamy sands that would correlate with the period when the newly stabilized surface on the mound was subjected to a much slower rate of erosional deflation. Any sedimentary sequence within these has been obscured by subsequent pedogenesis and trampling. Artifacts dating from the Sand Prairie phase, around A.D. 1350 and well after mound construction had ceased at the site, were recovered from near the present ground surface. The proximity of these materials to the modern surface here and on the First Terrace indicates that surficial erosion has little affected the mound since prehistoric abandonment and that there has been a lengthy period of mound stability.

It appears that maintenance of the earthworks was as much a concern during prehistoric times as it is today. Mounds were, and continue to be, high-maintenance structures. Today, Bermuda short grass is used to stabilize the slopes, and visitors to the site are directed to "stay off the mounds" (with the

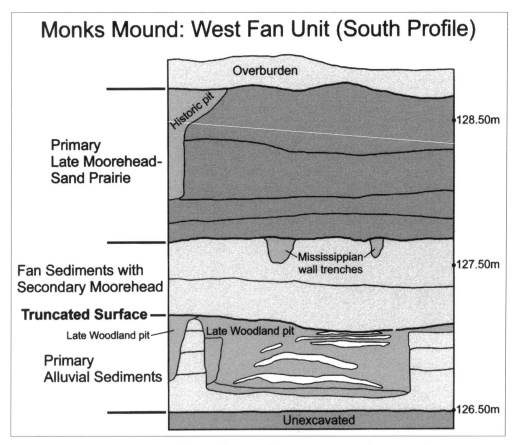

41. The episodic land use of the Monks Mound area is evident in the profile of an excavation unit from the ground level next to the mound. The earliest occupations, dating from the Late Woodland period, and portions of subsequent occupations were truncated during the Moorehead phase, presumably for patching the west slope of Monks Mound. Continued erosion of the slope followed in the form of fan sedimentation. Eventual stabilization allowed a terminal occupation with domestic structures.

exception of the constructed stairs up Monks Mound). During Mississippian times, it is probable that ramps were used to access mound summits and that for at least some mounds, only limited numbers of people were allowed to use them. Access to mounds was largely prevented through screens and palisades.

One advantage to the emplacement of the First Terrace was that it made the ascent of Monks Mound relatively easy, at least up to the top of the First Terrace. Moving from grade to this position along the ramp, the slope is about 25 degrees. From the level of the First Terrace to the Third Terrace the slope is about 45 degrees, which probably indicates that access to this portion of the mound was more restricted.

It is unlikely that the mounds were vegetated in prehistoric times. High prairie grasses were found in the environs and Bermuda short grass, an exotic, had not been introduced. For various reasons, however, we believe that prairie grasses did not grow on the mounds. First of all, high grasses would have presented an extreme fire hazard, threatening not only people but also structures on mound summits. These types of high grasses would also have made it difficult to perceive the constructed form of a mound and thus may have also been an aesthetic issue.

Some archaeologists have suggested that dark clay caps were used to surface the mounds and to prevent erosion. A clay cap, however, would have been the worst solution to the persistent problem of erosion. The type of clays found at Cahokia would, when wetted and dried, either have expanded and oozed, or cracked, and thus would not have remained on the mound. Besides, we have evidence to the contrary. The dark soil noted at the surface was not uniformly clay. This dark soil also covers surfaces of different ages, including early historic surfaces. Therefore, the dark cap noted in excavations can more correctly be ascribed to pedogenesis—a surface that was the product of mollic epipedon (a thick, dark-colored surface horizon) formation.

If neither a dark clay cap nor vegetation was employed, then how was the surface stabilized? We believe that maintenance would have been a constant issue and that the Mississippians may have used a tamped earth surface to maintain the mounds. Screens would have served as catchments for sediments eroding off the mound. Periodically these sediments would have been mined and deposited back on the mound slope and tamped. Collecting the sediments and dumping them back on the side of the mound would not have been enough. If the earth was tamped, it would stay longer, and there would be less of an erosion problem. The screens would also have controlled gully erosion and hindered the formation and spreading of erosional fans.

In addition to subsurface engineering efforts, surface maintenance would have been an essential aspect, at least until the mounds became vegetated. After the Sand Prairie phase, vegetation began to take hold, and surficial erosion slowed drastically. At Monks Mound, we see that fan development stopped when the prehistoric occupation ended. Other mounds also experienced a lengthy period of stability, however, modern cultivation renewed and even accelerated surficial erosion on many of them.

The Mississippians employed tamping for mound maintenance. It appears, however, that tamping also developed into an established practice for mound construction. At least this happened at Monks Mound. Excavations in older parts of the Mound clearly show evidence of basket loading. In the profiles of the Second Terrace observed within the historic well, however, a change in technology is apparent that correlates with this latter building phase. Sediments in this portion of the mound were tamped down into flat lenses. The Mississippians had been working on Monks Mound for two hundred years or so by the time of the west side patch. Tamping was not used in construction during this period, but we suggest that it was used in maintenance and that through its use to maintain the mound, its effectiveness as a construction method was realized.

As on Monks Mound, there has not been appreciable erosion of Mound 48 since abandonment. Here most erosion was prehistoric; it was not cultivated during historic times. Although it was necessary to maintain mounds, evidence from this mound suggests that these steps were not always taken. It appears that Mound 48 was built rather quickly during Lohmann times. In excavation units placed at the base of the slope of this mound, we would expect to see fans developing from the Lohmann phase on. But these do not

42. Artist's reconstruction of the building of Monks Mound at the end of the Emergent Mississippian period. The vantage point is from within the Grand Plaza.

Each fall the Cahokians would continue the process of building the civic structures of their growing town. We see here a number of people borrowing soil from the area in front of Monks Mound, in what is eventually to become the Grand Plaza. The Cahokians are breaking away chunks of soil directly into baskets, which are being carried to the top of Monks Mound. On top of the mound we see other men and women spreading soil and tamping it into place, layer by layer, with digging sticks. The designers of the mound have carefully considered the structure and drainage needed to support this enormous earthwork; they are on site, directing the efforts of their fellow citizens.

occur until the Moorehead phase. The implication is that the mound was maintained through the Stirling phase, at least to the point that eroded sediments were not reaching as far out as the test units that we excavated. The mound was still being used but was not being maintained by Moorehead times. At this point there was massive erosion. After abandonment, the mound stabilized, probably as it became vegetated.

THE EARTHMOVING PROCESS

In chapter 3 we described how different the Cahokia of Emergent Mississippian and early Mississippian times would have looked from traditional reconstructive renderings. As opposed to a manicured, finished product, it would have looked like a construction site with great gaping holes in the ground (fig. 42), especially during the early part of the sequence. Mud would have been everywhere during rainy seasons. We know that large reclaimed borrow pits surrounding Monks Mound remained open for a period of time before they were refilled. For example, marsh grass at the bottom of the Submound 51 borrow indicates that it sat open for a year or more before the infilling process even began. Our excavations in the small borrow located adjacent to Mound

56 revealed water-laid clays at the base of this borrow, indicating that it too sat open for some time prior to refilling. This sense of a work in progress, of construction, rebuilding, and disruption, would have been evident, albeit on a smaller scale, across the site throughout most of the sequence.

What do we know specifically about this process of borrowing and mound construction? The earth was dug out using stone hoes. Bone scapula and shell hoes may have also been used, as well as wooden digging sticks. At the base of a reclaimed borrow next to Mound 56 we could still observe the imprints of the hoes used to excavate the sediments used in building the mound. Wooden digging implements, with the haft element parallel to the shaft, were probably also used; a modern equivalent would be a spade. Sediments were transported in baskets. Filled baskets weighed approximately 50 pounds. And we know that mound construction, reclamation, and other landscaping efforts were directed by those with specialized surveying, engineering, and architectural expertise.

It appears that at Cahokia borrow pits next to mounds generally supplied the soil for mound construction. In his succinct, straightforward account describing his impressions of the site, William Oliver, who visited Cahokia in 1842, first alluded to a relationship between borrow pits and mounds: "Water sometimes occurs in the depressions of the surface, which, so far as I saw, invariably accompanied, and were always proportioned to the size of the mounds" (Oliver 1924 [1843], 171). Warren K. Moorehead, after his explorations of Cahokia in the 1920s, also mentioned a relationship between mounds and nearby borrows. He viewed this pattern as an issue of convenience, stating that "it does not seem likely that the Indians would go any distance to secure the earth for the construction. . . . It would be more convenient to obtain it from points nearby" (Moorehead 1929, 105).

We have tested the hypothesis that mounds at the site were constructed principally of earth derived from areas immediately adjacent to the mounds under construction. We have used a variety of methods, including studies of whole-soil texture and magnetic properties of soils derived from mounds and adjacent surrounding terrain. Factor analysis of fills from various mounds and from natural soils next to these mounds shows clear differences between samples derived from the different mounds. Furthermore, the samples from each mound are located closest to samples of the soils surrounding the mounds.

We have also documented that this process of local fill procurement was followed time and time again at Cahokia. In fact, it appears to have been the most common practice. The soils mined from the large lateral borrow in the Grand Plaza would have provided a local source for the initial platform of Monks Mound. Within the Grand Plaza, fill for at least the initial stages of three mounds (Mounds 49, 56, and 57) was obtained from borrows adjacent to each of these mounds (Dalan 1993b). Mounds of the Tippetts mound group (Mounds 61, 62, and 95) and within Ramey Field (Mounds 36 and 37) also reflect the pattern of locally available soils (Dalan et al. 1994). Evidence of borrowing, reclamation, and mound construction documented at the Rouch mound group likewise suggests a pattern of localized fill procurement (Holley et al. 1992).

As Oliver did in 1843, we can now point to a number of borrows located adjacent to mounds in various parts of the site. With the aid of fine-scale topographic mapping we have identified slight depressions that correspond to reclaimed borrows. We have also applied geophysical surveys within the Grand Plaza, at the Rouch mound group, and at the West Borrow Pit group to define the limits of these features. Other researchers have documented borrow pits in the vicinity of mounds as well, for example at Powell Mound, Mound 55, Rattlesnake Mound (Mound 66), and Mound 65, to name a few.

Although the evidence indicates that a process of local fill procurement was followed at Cahokia, this is not to say that other fill sources were not used besides. Fill choice at Cahokia, as previously outlined, was also dictated by engineering concerns. For example, one of the coarser-grained soils noted in our recent excavations of Monks Mound was obviously a mixture mechanically produced for its material properties and used in areas where increased porosity and drainage was desired. The same loamy material was also found within the layered soils filling the large lateral borrow in the Grand Plaza. Engineering concerns obviously worked in tandem with the pattern of local fill procurement. We must also consider other purposes that were met in choice and placement of fill. Although locally procured soils formed at least the bulk of the initial stages of a mound, nonlocal, contrasting, or symbolically charged soils may have been added as well. The small burial mound in the ICT-II had loess outlining the burials. This loess had presumably been redeposited from the bluffs in the Cahokia Creek flood plain. A selection of materials for color symbolism (black, red, white) has been documented at Mound 72. At this important early burial mound, Gartner (1999) has demonstrated male/female burial distinctions in earthen fills and caps and an alternating sequence of colors within the mound itself.

We can also speculate about the seasonality of earthmoving efforts based upon considerations of seasonal conditions that would have affected the ease with which sediments could be excavated, as well as upon what we know of the Mississippian seasonal round. These considerations apply generally to efforts involved in raising a mound or adding stages, and not to maintenance efforts, which, as we have indicated, were of pervasive concern. We assume a climate during Mississippian times similar to that of today, although summer precipitation may have been higher than at present (Chmurny 1973). The Neo-Atlantic climatic episode (ca. A.D. 800–1250), a time of relatively warm and moist conditions (Wendland and Bryson 1974), coincided with much of the Mississippian period at Cahokia.

The heavy, sticky, black clay that extends over much of the Cahokia site has appropriately been given the name "gumbo clay." During the summer, the sun bakes these clays into a brick-hard mass. During the winter, cold temperatures produce a similar effect. Neither are conducive to hand excavation.

This is something that we and others who have excavated at the site can attest to. During Moorehead's testing of Mound 61 (1929, 58), his crew found the ground to be so hard that "it required the united efforts of six strong workmen to put down six auger holes in three days time." Based on the extensive experience of his crews, Moorehead suggested that February to April were the more favorable months for excavating in this gumbo clay, because the rains had a tendency to soften the material.

Certainly the season of construction would not only have been determined by digging conditions, but also by the need to dovetail it with other activities in the Cahokian seasonal calendar. Earthmoving efforts would have been scheduled for times when the Cahokians would have had the time and energy to devote to the construction process. And surely there was a ceremonial component to mound construction and other earthmoving activities that would have been linked to seasonal celebrations and ceremonies. It is also possible that earthen stockpiles were used in mound construction at Cahokia and other Mississippian sites. Porter (1974, 336–39) interpreted two small mounds at the Mitchell site (north of Cahokia) as stockpiles of sediments destined for mound construction. Stockpiling would have allowed for the mixing of soils we often see in mound fill, and for mound construction during periods when quarrying was not feasible or efficient.

From what we know of the Cahokian and broader Mississippian seasonal round, spring was a very active time of the year for tilling garden plots and the more distant outfields. Food gathering would have been limited, with fish the primary resource, and some reliance on stored foods left from the fall. War parties would have been forming, scouting, and bringing back captives. During the summer, efforts would have concentrated on tending the outfields and refurbishing houses. Green corn ceremonialism, the first harvest from the fields, would have launched the feasting season. During fall, large groups of people would have been involved in harvesting and hunting, moving to and from the fields and throughout outlying areas. At the mound center, large gatherings of people would have come together for ceremonies, ball games, and feasting, which may have lasted for a week or more (Penicaut 1981, 88). Stored foods from harvests, hunting, and gathering nuts would have fed the Cahokians during the winter. Meat processing and hide working would have been the predominant winter activities. According to LePage du Pratz (1774, 336–42), who recorded the thirteen-month calendar of the Natchez, the new year began in March, harvest of small corn occurred in June, and harvest of great corn took place in September.

With these seasonal activities in mind, fall would have been the most likely season of construction. The ground would still have been moist enough to be soft but probably not inundated, as occurred during spring rains. Construction would have proceeded in tandem with harvesting and harvest ceremonies, when many people would have gathered at the site. Though a heady time, this would not have been as busy in terms of labor requirement as the spring, when planting would have required massive investments of time. Fall would have been a time of plenty, when energy was high, unlike the hungry times of winter and spring.

This connection between mound construction and fall harvest ceremonies makes even more sense if we consider what has been said about the association of Mississippian mounds and agricultural ceremonies. A number of researchers (Hall 1989; Howard 1968; Knight 1986; Schnell et al. 1981; Swanton 1928; Waring 1968) have argued that Mississippian mounds and their arrangements were intimately tied to agriculture through ceremonies similar in nature to those described historically for southeastern Indians (Bartram 1909 [1789]; LePage 1975; Payne 1862; Swanton 1932). Furthermore, the periodic addition of mound mantles as a significant component of these rituals served as a symbolic means of purifying and maintaining the social order (Howard 1968; Knight 1981, 1986; Schnell et al. 1981; Waring 1968). We can speculate, based on the genesis of Mississippian mounds from earlier communal burial mounds, that ancestor veneration was also a likely component of mound ceremonialism.

Symbolic ties between mound and plaza construction and maize agriculture are abundant in both the ethnohistoric and archaeological records. For example, myths of the southeastern Indians and historic accounts of agricultural practices refer to the "mounding" up of soil around the base of maize plants and to maize originating from a mound, thus portraying maize hills as small-scale versions of Mississippian mounds, replete with periodic additions or mantles (Hudson 1976, 297–98; Swanton 1929, 13; 1931, 209–10). Similarly, the clearing and preparation of maize plots (Hudson 1976, 149–56; LePage 1975, 338; Waring 1968, 51) appears to mirror the cleaning and preparation of the square ground prior to the agricultural ceremony known as "busk" (Adair 1930, 100–101).

Hudson's description of southeastern Indians connects the use of mounds and plazas with agricultural practices in a more direct manner: "Early in the morning of a working day, one of the old leaders would stand on top of a mound or in the plaza and call all the people to work" (1976, 295; see also Bartram 1909 [1789], 39–41.)

From an archaeological perspective, Mound D at the Ocmulgee site in Georgia provides a physical and symbolic association between mounds and maize fields (Kelly 1938, 10). According to Waring and Holder (1945, 23–24), "the old surface at the base of this mound was marked by two low mounds with wattle-and-daub structures on their summits surrounded by well-preserved rows of ancient cornfield. These had been carefully covered by eight feet (2.4 m) of mound fill and new structures erected on the surface."

Based on our documentation of the process of obtaining fill from the area immediately adjacent to the mound, we can also argue that a ceremonial component to mound construction existed, though the exact nature of it is not as yet known. We do not believe that this pattern is attributable to convenience, as Moorehead suggested, especially considering that many of these borrows were refilled. In fact, this process of local fill procurement increased the effort required, since following such a procedure often necessitated later land reclamation, which required the Cahokians to travel great distances to obtain fill. We maintain that the act of mound construction was just as, or even more, important than the material result (Bender 1992; Kuchler 1993) and that the process of working the landscape at Cahokia was significant. It was critical to have people together in one place to experience and to see the rising mound. This view of mound construction stands in direct opposition to that of workers trudging back from distant sources with basketloads of fill, all the while under the whip of a powerful ruler. At Cahokia, earthmoving patterns indicate communal construction, a pattern certainly consistent with the proposed ceremonial impact of this construction.

CHAPTER NINE

LANDSCAPE
ELEMENTS

We have discussed earthmoving and earth maintenance at Cahokia. Let us now examine the results of this process—specifically, the form of mounds and other earthen constructions at the site. Since the early period of study and exploration of Cahokia, the myriad forms of these mounds and features and their distributions have been of considerable interest. Today the mounds appear largely as rounded rises, bearing only slight resemblances to the different forms they originally represented.

MOUNDS

A considerable lexicon of earthworks derives from the entire span of prehistory in the eastern United States. Yet to the most prolific moundbuilders, the Mississippians, only a handful of shapes are ascribed. Nearly all of these are represented at Cahokia—platform, conical, and ridgetop. All can be classified as geometric solids with sloping sides. The primary distinction between them is summit configuration. Platforms were level across the top, conicals were rounded, and ridgetops had long, narrow summits. Platforms were generally rectangular in outline, though historic maps depict a number of variations such as ovals and truncated cones. As the name suggests, conicals were circular, their overall form being that of a rounded cone. Ridgetops were similar to platforms in planimetric outline, but the side slopes extended upward to form a narrow ridge along the summit length.

The truncated platform mound is the ubiquitous Mississippian earthwork. Many sites only have mounds of this shape. Its popularity was due to its ability to house a building on its summit. Additionally, its square shape is said to have mimicked the sacred four-corners concept of the universe (Brown 1997; Howard 1968; Knight 1981). In addition to the typical truncated platform, Cahokia contained a number of tiered platform mounds (mounds with multiple terraces) (e.g., Monks Mound and Mounds 44, 55, and 56). The conical mound, the other type considered to be an integral member of the Mississippian lexicon, was surprisingly uncommon at most Mississippian sites (Holley et al. 1998; Morgan 1980). At Cahokia, conical mounds were paired with platform mounds, reinforcing the traditional notion of conjoined function: the platform mound housed the temple/charnal house of the gods, and the conical mound housed the dead. The ridgetop mound, found only at Cahokia, seems to have been a unique means of housing the dead as well as serving as a special marker mound (Fowler 1997).

There is a great deal more variation in the mounds at Cahokia, however, than the traditional cookie-cutter nomenclature suggests. Not all platforms were created equal, and the same goes for conical and ridgetop forms. For example, platform mounds at Cahokia had summit surfaces that cover areas from 40 to 70 percent of the basal surface. An exception was the big Rouch Mound (Mound 70), whose summit comprised only about 25 percent of the basal surface and perhaps more closely resembled a truncated conical. Another variant was the elongated Mound 48, which we interpret as the setting for a temple.

Cahokia also contained mounds that consisted of a combination of two or more of the above forms. For example, Monks Mound included not only multiple terraces, but also a small conical on the Fourth Terrace. Oliver (1924 [1843], 170) describes this cone as being flat on top (i.e., a truncated cone), again, a form that was not addressed in the basic mound morphology, but one that was often depicted on the 1876 Patrick Map. Information deriving from the internal structure of mounds indicates that the form of a mound may have changed over time through additions to the mound. Certainly this was the case for Monks Mound. Another example is Mound 72, where the final ridgetop shape encompassed three smaller mounds.

Other variations in mound form included features such as ramps and connecting causeways and platforms. Though only a few of these features have presently been documented at Cahokia, it appears that they were quite common. The ramp extending south off the front of Monks Mound, now accessorized with steps, is well known to modern visitors. It faces the Grand Plaza, as did ramps off the northeast corner of Mound 48 and the northern edge of Mound 56.

In addition to causeways discussed in relation to internal boundaries and connections (chap. 5), we have documented only by a causeway connecting the main platform and conical mounds of the West Borrow Pit group. Topographic ridges may also have linked two small mounds (Mounds 69 and 71) to the principal mound (Mound 70) of the Rouch mound group. Causeways connecting mounds have been reported at other Mississippian period centers, especially by early investigators who had the good fortune to study these sites prior to extensive clearing and cultivation (e.g., Squire 1860). Some of these features have been documented only by excavation (Brain 1989, 32), which suggests that these sometimes subtle features may have been more common than we suspected, but that centuries of disturbance have rendered them invisible.

Mounds may also have been joined by a common platform. We see this in particular at the paired conical and platform mounds at Cahokia. Our excavations on the southern margins of the big twin mounds (Mounds 59 and 60) revealed massive building-up of the landscape that may represent fill associated with the construction of a Twin Mounds platform. This build-up represents careful planning, not just a dumping of soil. Exotic materials recovered from the fill, including shell, galena, hematite, quartz, a sandstone bead, and microlithic debitage, indicate the special nature of this construction. Our excavations within the West Borrow Pit group (Mounds 67 and 68; Holley et al. 1996, 1998) have also revealed a shared platform for the conical and platform mounds.

A platform not only raised mounds constructed on its surface above the surrounding grade, but also incorporated paired mounds into one solitary mass. The fact that conical and platform mound pairs at the site are generally joined together by a platform and/or causeway suggests that the Mississippians did not think of these mounds separately, but conceptualized them as a shared entity. The single mound did not have meaning; the mound complex did. Exotic materials associated with these construction surfaces, such as those found at the platform of Mounds 59 and 60, suggest that there may have been specialized use of the platform area around the mound fringe. At the West Borrow Pit mound group, the platform outline mimics the plan of the two supported mounds, that is, the truncated platform mound is housed on a square platform segment, and the conical mound rests on a circular platform segment. Harmonizing opposites, like directionality, was a pervasive New World notion and the replication of shapes emphasized the importance and power of these symbols. The merging of circle and square is common in art forms and buildings, and these two symbols are the most frequently recognized in southeastern art (Phillips and Brown 1978, 1984; Waring and Holder 1945).

Documenting the varied forms of the mounds at Cahokia is important for understanding relationships among mounds and how they were used. It is a commonly held notion that the form of a mound was linked to its function: platform mounds served as substructures for buildings, conical mounds served as burial mounds, platform-conical pairs served a mortuary function, ridgetop mounds marked special areas of the community. It is not such a leap to assume that platform mounds of different sizes and shapes perhaps housed different types of structures with different uses or that conicals with truncated tops had a different function from those that were rounded. Though our understanding of the forms of all the mounds at Cahokia is still in its infancy, it is important to develop more knowledge about them in order to understand the functional partitioning of the site and how mounds might have been linked through alignments and the associations of particular forms or other features.

Research testing the efficacy of a combination of fine-scale topographic mapping and soil magnetic studies (Dalan et al. 1996) suggests that the original form of a mound, despite centuries of erosion, can still be documented. To date we have demonstrated characteristic signatures for conical and platform mounds that can be used to identify these forms, even on mounds that are rounded beyond recognition. In addition, it is possible to identify the presence and positions of multiple terraces on platform mounds. Ridgetop mounds show intriguing differences from conical and platform mounds, although further work is still necessary to refine our understanding of this form. We can also apply these techniques to model the original form of other earthen features, e.g., the causeway joining the paired mounds in the West Borrow Pit group.

There is a tendency to pass off the numerous small mounds mentioned in historic accounts as unrecoverable and not to feel too bad about this, "because they were probably not all that important." These small mounds, however, may not be all gone. For example, although no mounds were previously identified within the ICT-II, three mounds have been identified through aerial photo interpretation and documented through excavation. Working in wooded areas of the site is profitable for mapping small mounds and other features, as the terrain in these areas was not disturbed by centuries of plowing. We are also rapidly developing methods that will allow us to identify mound remnants that are no longer visible. Significant success in this regard has been obtained by using aerial photographs, fine-scale topographic mapping, and geophysical surveys. As we learn more about the site and about planning and alignments, we are also becoming better at deciding where we might focus our attention when looking for traces of these now relatively invisible features.

The small mounds are not just polka dots on the landscape, randomly positioned. Within the ICT-II, these mounds had importance to the local community. It is important to remember that not everything at Cahokia was big and that information on the locations, function, and variability of all mounds, regardless of size, is worth recovering. Size and importance do not necessarily equate, and the meaning of the small mounds is compounded by their relationships to other mounds. Through their association with communities, with other mounds, and with sitewide planning dictates, such as alignment and location, these mounds may have assumed even greater importance.

We believe the geometric alignments of mounds and other features were planned at the Cahokia site and that these arrangements reveal much about Cahokian site planning and the culture that produced them. We examine these spatial patterns at varying scales, moving from sitewide alignments or axes to alignments between mound groups and finally to alignments or repetitive relationships within mound groups (figs. 43 and 32).

On the basis of map analysis and information gained from archaeological excavations, Fowler (1969) first proposed both a north-south and an east-west axis for the Cahokia site. The north-south axis spans roughly 1.75 miles (2.8 kilometers) along a line connecting Mound 66 (popularly known as Rattlesnake Mound) on the south, Mound 72, Mound 49, and Monks Mound, and ending at a point within the Kunnemann mound group on the north.

A problem with postulating alignments at Cahokia is that just by virtue of the sheer number of mounds at the site, it is not difficult to find any number of widely separated mounds that are situated along a north-south or east-west line. What makes Fowler's proposed north-south axis intriguing is its position near the center of the Cahokia site and the position and significance of the particular mounds that it intersects.

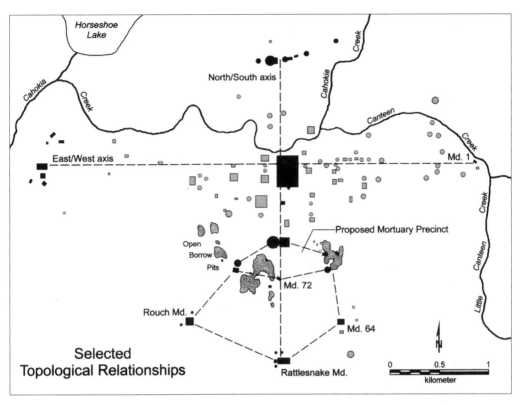

43. Orderly arrangements of the Cahokia site mounds, based on topological relationships (relative, as opposed to exact, positioning), delineate a major cardinal axis and a mortuary precinct. Another triangular pattern in the south, although asymmetrical, balanced and extended the overall site plan.

Aside from the obvious importance of Monks Mound, this north-south line also includes three ridgetop mounds (Mounds 66, 72, and 49). Fowler (1997, 188, 189) suggested that these mounds may have been positioned at strategic locations to serve as markers at the site periphery and other important areas of the site. Rattlesnake Mound marks the extreme southern limit of the site and one point of the postulated north-south axis. Mound 72 is a relatively small mound, roughly 6 feet (1.8 meters) in height, yet it has been shown by excavations to have been an important elite burial mound. Archaeological evidence indicates that there was a large post, approximately 2 feet (60 centimeters) in diameter at the base, in the southeast corner of the mound. It is through this post that the north-south axis is postulated to have run.

At the southwest corner of the First Terrace of Monks Mound there is evidence for a number of smaller superimposed posts whose positions are also on the north-south axis. It is likely that a post at this location and the Mound 72 post would have been visible from many areas of the site. The size and chronology of the Monks Mound posts in relation to the Mound 72 posts, however, are problematical. They appear much later in time, but buildings, fences, and a small platform mound on this part of the terrace may indicate that the southwest corner location had longevity as a community focal point. Also, excavation was discontinued approximately 11 meters above the base of the terrace, so whatever additional features may be below this level are unknown.

The third ridgetop mound along the north-south axis is Mound 49, located in the Grand Plaza approximately 700 meters north of Mound 72, which is also very nearly the distance between Rattlesnake Mound and Mound 72. The northern end point is located at the Kunnemann mound group, across Cahokia Creek, approximately a half mile (0.8 kilometers) north of the center of Monks Mound. This is generally considered to be the northernmost limit of the Cahokia site, although there is a small mound in an open field just over a half mile (0.8 kilometers) north of the Kunnemann mound group that lies near the extrapolated north-south line.

Two alternative, or perhaps complementary, north-south alignments, both generally paralleling the major axis of Monks Mound, have also been suggested. The first (Reed, Bennett, and Porter 1968) passes through Mound 7 of the Kunnemann mound group, a large post near the center of the Fourth Terrace of Monks Mound, and Rattlesnake Mound. The second (Rolingson 1996; Sherrod and Rolingson 1987) is similar, but includes the post in the southwest corner of Mound 72 while excluding the Kunnemann mound group. Kelly (1996) suggests that these could represent subsequent manifestations of Fowler's axis as they relate to the later construction stages of Monks Mound, i.e., the First and Fourth Terraces.

There has also been discussion of a number of potential east-west axes for Cahokia. Two possible axes suggested by Ahler and DePuydt (1987) connect the Powell mound group with Monks Mound, and end at the southwest corner of the First Terrace of Monks Mound. The first uses Mound 84, a small mound just south of Powell Mound, as the western end point; the rationale behind this configuration is that this line forms a 90-degree angle with the post in Mound 72. The second suggested axis uses Powell Mound as the western end point. During archaeological salvage work on the mound in 1931, two large rectangular burial pits and a large post were discovered. A line extended eastward through these three features ends at or near the aforementioned point on Monks Mound. Rolingson and Sherrod have proposed that the near-center post, Feature 452 of the reconstructed woodhenge at Tract 15A (Circle 2), lies along an east-west line connecting Mound 87 of the Powell mound group to Mound 27, again passing through the southwest corner of the First Terrace of Monks Mound. Additionally, Reed (1973) noted that Powell Mound, which is oriented east-west, and Mound 1 at the eastern periphery of the Cahokia site lie due west and east, respectively, of a large post discovered near the center of the Fourth Terrace of Monks Mound that also lies on a possible north-south site axis, as noted above.

These proposed alignments, oriented to the cardinal directions, may have reflected the basic Mississippian tendency of arranging mounds around a plaza, an arrangement that dictated that mounds would either be at right angles to each other or in alignment with each other (Reed 1973). The plaza, demarcated by the arrangement of mounds, took on a square shape as a manifestation of the four-quarters worldview (Knight 1981, 46). The four-corner or four-point directions were also replicated in the square plan of the platform summit. Repetition of the cardinal directions is apparent at Cahokia not only in many mound orientations, but also in the arrangement of planned communities of the Lohmann phase. Structures as well as art forms (Waring and Holder 1945) took on this form. Such redundancy in ideological concepts is not a sign of triviality, bur rather of utmost gravity in ritual expression. The cross in Christianity, for example, is used in gesture, art forms, clothing, building designs, and so forth. The four-corner concept implied a spatial reference, a topological feature, with the center point as the referent (Brown 1997, 476).

Some researchers feel that there was also a solar or celestial basis for the placement of mounds and other features (Fowler 1996). Solar alignments were based upon a concern with noting and marking the rising and setting of the sun at important times of the year, most notably equinoxes and solstices. This particularly influenced alignments within strongly east-west oriented site designs. Celestial alignments referred to positioning objects in relation to the rising and setting of significant stars or planets.

An example of a solar alignment is the woodhenge construction west of Monks Mound. In the early 1960s, salvage archaeology related to the construction of Interstate 55/70 uncovered evidence of a number of large posts clustered to the west of Mound 44. It was observed (Wittry 1996) that many of these posts could be construed as forming arcs, or portions of at least four circles, a little over 400 feet (122 meters) in diameter, with corresponding near-center posts. If one stood at a near-center post, the position of certain posts along the circle corresponded closely to the sun's position on the horizon at daybreak on the summer and winter solstices, and the vernal and autumnal equinoxes. Thus, it has been suggested that one function of the circular arrangement of posts may have been as a type of sun calendar or solar observatory.

Sherrod and Rolingson (1987) and Fowler (1996) have also hypothesized that these woodhenges served as surveying tools, i.e., alidades, and that there were other woodhenges placed in strategic locations across the site, including in the vicinity of Mound 72. An interesting aspect of Mound 72 is its diagonal orientation of 30 degrees south of east, or roughly northwest-southeast, as opposed to the predominantly north-south-east-west orientation of the majority of other rectilinear mounds at Cahokia (including other ridgetop mounds such as Rattlesnake and Powell Mounds). This angle places the mound along the winter solstice sunrise and summer solstice sunset line. If the woodhenges did serve as spatial aligners, i.e., large plane tables, one function might have been to maintain the position of important points on Monks Mound as the mound grew in height.

We also must recognize the influence of the local topography in the choice of where mounds and other cultural features were constructed. At other Mississippian sites, mound arrangements generally conformed to local conditions. As shown in figure 29, the most intensively developed portion of Cahokia lay on the highest and driest land, i.e., the natural levee (Helms Ridge) bordering the south side of the Cahokia Creek bottom lands. The northern edge of this ridge runs generally east-west. If the ridge trended on a diagonal from northwest to southeast, for example, would the site layout still have been predominantly to the cardinal directions of north-south-east-west, or would it have conformed to the orientation of the local topography, with alignments parallel and perpendicular to the diagonally trending ridge? Reed (1973) suggests the latter in that Monks Mound was aligned slightly east of north and that the other mounds and rectilinear features took their cue from its orientation.

At Cahokia we see evidence of layouts relating to the grain of local land-form and layouts oriented to the cardinal directions against the grain of lo-cal conditions; within some mound groups we see evidence of both. For ex-ample, the layout of the Powell Mound complex as a whole mirrors the local topography. The primary mound of the group, the big Powell Mound (Mound 86), however, was oriented east-west, counter to the prevailing trend of the landform it rested upon. By going against nature, the big Powell Mound stood out even more, perhaps serving as notice that one was enter-ing Cahokia. At the northern limit of the site, the Kunnemann mound group was strongly aligned with the edge of the ridge on which it was con-structed. In contrast, some groups far from the ridge edge, such as the Tip-petts mound group, displayed strong orientations to the cardinal directions.

Another aspect of spatial alignment is the topological relationships indi-cated between mound groups (fig. 43). These associations were based more on relative positioning than on precise measurements and orientations. For example, in a topological system, whether an object is located precisely along a 33-degree azimuth at a distance of 100 meters from another object is not as important as the fact that it is placed to the right (east) and above (north) of the other object. This appears to have been an important compo-nent of planning and design at Cahokia.

An example of a topological relationship is a group of mounds that in-cludes several paired-mound complexes which may have formed a mortuary district within the site. These mounds include the Fox and Round Top mound pair (Mounds 59 and 60), the Tippetts mound group (Mounds 61 and 62), and the Borrow Pit mound group (subdivided into the Mound 72 mound group and the West Borrow Pit mound group). As noted in our com-parison with the Capitol complex in Washington, D.C., these mound groups formed a diamond-shaped pattern arranged roughly symmetrically around the proposed north-south axis. This diamond was bounded by the West Borrow Pit mound group on the west, the Tippetts mound group on the east, Fox and Round Top Mounds on the north, and the Mound 72 mound group on the south. The eastern and western mound groups were approximately evenly spaced in relation to Mound 72 and Fox and Round Top Mounds. They also were approximately due east and west of each other. They appeared to mirror each other in other aspects as well. For instance, both were situated in close proximity to a large borrow pit, and both featured a conical and platform mound pair, with a possible third mound forming a right triangle with the other two. On the northwest leg, or side, of the diamond, two conicals were juxtaposed (Mound 59, or Round Top Mound, and Mound 67 of the West Borrow Pit mound group), whereas on the northeast leg it was the rectangular platforms that were nearer each other (Mound 60, or Fox Mound, and Mound 61 of the Tippetts mound group).

Moving southward from the Mortuary Precinct, we come to the Rouch mound group and the Rattlesnake mound group. The Rouch mound group is situated approximately 600 meters southwest of the West Borrow Pit mound group, and about 490 meters south-southeast of the Tippetts mound group lies the eastern portion of the Rattlesnake mound group. Mounds 66 (Rattlesnake Mound), 82, and 83 are located about 730 meters south of Mound 72. Although the pattern formed by these groups was somewhat asymmetrical and not precisely placed in terms of distance and direction from the inner core defined by the ring of open borrow pits, these outlying mound groups effectively balanced and extended the overall site plan to the south.

The importance of the regular, repetitive relationships that connect the various mound groups is apparent in their placement around Fox and Round Top Mounds, the two largest mounds (in terms of height) after Monks Mound (fig. 31). Brine (1894, 107), an early historic visitor to the site, described a parallelogram that he felt contained the group of mounds of greatest importance and noted the central position of these mounds: "In the centre, there were two conical mounds [actually a conical and a platform mound, i.e., Fox and Round Top], which must have been raised in that position for some important purpose. They were each about forty feet high, and appeared to have been so placed as to dominate the mounds forming the sides of the inclosure." Late in the Mississippian period, Fox and Round Top Mounds were segregated from the other mounds in this group by the Central Palisade, which enclosed the core of the site. But this would not have been the case during the early Mississippian period. This arrangement bespeaks a special function, perhaps a mortuary precinct, that had critical significance for the earlier Mississippian residents.

Speculation as to why the Central Palisade was erected has counterposed a defensive (for the commonwealth) versus a restrictive (for the elite) function. A third possibility may have been to divert attention away from the southern clusters of mounds, including the orchestrated arrangement of paired mounds, Mound 72, and the central open borrow. This strategy would have been consistent with the devaluation of the sacred character of

Tract 15B and other areas of the site. Regardless of the specific reason for construction, the Cahokians felt enough need for this palisade to have re-built it at least three times after its initial construction.

The Tippetts mound group exemplifies alignments within mound groups. In this group, there was a pairing of a conical mound (Mound 61) and a platform mound (Mound 62) on the banks of a large, open borrow pit. A causeway, not a common platform, connected the conical and platform mounds. Atop a narrow ridge on the other side of the borrow pit a slight rise, designated as Mound 95, formed a right triangle with the mound pair.

A peninsular feature extended from the conical mound into the borrow pit. Unlike mounds, which are constructed on top of the land, it was sculpted out of the landscape to form a square with sides oriented to the car-dinal directions. The peninsula lay at the geometric center of the mound group. By connecting the presumed center points of Mounds 61 and 62 and this peninsular feature, an equilateral triangle is formed, the distance be-tween the center of each mound to the center of the plaza being the same. This same equilateral relationship is repeated across the site. Although we describe it as a triangle, it is probably the equal spacing of the mounds that is culturally significant.

Another triangular arrangement is seen at the Rouch mound group, which is located in the extreme southwest portion of the site, well outside the ring of open borrows. This mound group was situated on high ground adjacent to the west side of a slough, which ran roughly northwest-south-east. An interesting aspect of this group is that its arrangement does not seem to mirror the local topography at this site, which is well defined by the strong visual edge of the slough and accompanying low ridge, nor does it correspond to the cardinal directions, though it appears close. The spatial geometry of this mound group closely approximates an obtuse isosceles tri-angle. The main mound, Mound 70, is one of the larger mounds at the site (fig. 31). Two small mounds, Mounds 69 and 71, though extensively worn down by years of plowing, are roughly equidistant from Mound 70.

BORROWS

The focus in Mississippian archaeology has been on mounds. However, examining the mounds is just half of the story; there would be no mounds without borrows. We need to study borrows in order to understand where the earth came from to build the mounds, the location and extent of earth-moving activities, and the construction process, which was so much a part of Mississippian life.

The rewards of doing this type of research have been amply illustrated by our work in the Grand Plaza. In general, there has been an archaeological bias toward not investigating Mississippian plazas, probably because they are perceived as being regularly shaped, open spaces that contain little in the way of domestic debris (Lewis and Kneberg 1946; Nash 1972; Neitzel 1965,

1983; Stout 1986; Wesler and Neusius 1987; Williams and Brain 1983). The Grand Plaza at Cahokia, however, is anything but flat, barren ground. As we discussed earlier, within the Grand Plaza is preserved an unparalleled record of early earthmoving activities that have informed us about the initiation of construction on Monks Mound and the complicated molding of the landscape that was required to create the level surface of the Grand Plaza.

Our work in the Grand Plaza opened our eyes to the fact that there was much more to be learned about earthmoving at Cahokia than could be gained by examining only mounds and open borrows. In all probability, there are other tracts of ground that appear undisturbed but that were significantly modified by the Cahokians. Our work in the Grand Plaza also redirected us from a focus on discrete features to investigations of more diffuse evidence of earthmoving activities.

To understand the process of borrowing and mound construction at Cahokia, it is simply not enough to identify borrows and what was removed from them. It is also necessary to look at the varied sediments used as fill in those borrows that were reclaimed as part of an ongoing and complex process that the Cahokians participated in. This perspective and this information are critical for understanding the transformation of the landscape in cultural terms. The identification of a pattern of using locally derived sediments in mound construction (from areas adjacent to the mound) helps us understand the communal nature of mound building activities. Within the Grand Plaza, the fill sequence indicates that there was a desire to create not only a level, but a clean, surface that was maintained as such throughout the sequence.

Mound 37 was recently rebuilt by park personnel using slump material from Monks Mound. This project provides a modern example of the complicated movement of soils across the site that most certainly also figured prehistorically. We can track the movement of soils that occurred prehistorically by using a variety of soil magnetic techniques (Dalan 1993a, 1993b; Dalan and Banerjee 1996, 1998). We can even unravel sources for mixed soils and forward mixing models indicating the proportions of soils from various sources that were used to create earthen features and reclaim the borrows.

Borrows are not just holes in the ground. Instead, each has a unique history relating to the history of the site, as revealed by examining changing functions over time. Initially all borrows provided fill, but their function did not necessarily stop there. Some served as garbage receptacles. Others served as drainage features. Some borrows functioned in this way first and then were later reclaimed for other uses (i.e., to function as the Grand Plaza or a location for residential development). Others were left open, which may also relate to their continuing functions.

One of the prevalent myths of Cahokia is that the large borrow pits for Monks Mound and the other mounds presented perfect containers for waste disposal and were therefore quickly filled with the enormous amounts of garbage generated by the site's prehistoric inhabitants. Let us examine the assumptions upon which this myth is based.

Investigators have discussed the accumulation rates of excreta, garbage, and other wastes at prehistoric human settlements and the resultant changes in soil chemical properties and midden (anthropogenic soil) formation (Cook and Heizer 1965; Woods 1977, 1982, 1984, 1995). From these studies it is clear that significant deposits and great chemical alterations can occur as the result of the concentration of a variety of materials associated with human habitation activities. At Cahokia, the primary additions to the site area by weight and volume would have been those related to food and wood, with the by-products of tool and ceramic production and discard largely incidental. Regardless of which of the projected population levels for the site are accepted, during the Mississippian occupation huge quantities of food-stuffs were processed, consumed, and eliminated, and wood use for construction and fuel would also have been enormous. But how much does this really amount to, and what was the ultimate disposition of the by-products from human occupation?

First of all, let us look at the trajectory of food harvesting, processing, consumption, elimination, and deposition. Whether hunted, netted, gathered, or harvested, animal and plant foods were subject to a degree of mass reduction before being brought back home. In order to decrease spoilage and lessen the weight of transport, fish and game were gutted in the field, and nonusable body parts were expediently removed. In a similar manner, only edible plant parts were retrieved; maize cobs were cut from the plant stalk, small seeds shaken from the plant body, and only the nuts were gathered from oak and hickory groves. Consequently, the volume of organic items brought into the site was greatly reduced. Processing involved removing those materials that would not be eaten and preparing the food for consumption. Much of the nonfood items would have been further processed and utilized—hides, feathers, bones, antlers, and shells being obvious examples. Of the remainder, any item that could potentially be eaten by the dogs most likely was. Food for humans was at a premium, and, without Alpo, dogs would largely have subsisted as scavengers. (During an excavation in Mexico, we witnessed an entire diseased pig carcass, with the exception of a small portion of hide and the mandible and teeth, consumed by dogs in less than a week.) After consumption and digestion by humans and dogs, materials would have been eliminated in the form of urine and feces. The deposition of both was probably in the immediate vicinity of the house, with the former immediately being incorporated into the soil matrix, whereas deposition of the latter may have taken place at specified locations, perhaps in abandoned pits. Human feces probably also would have served as part of the canine diet and, after their recycling and further reduction, were deposited haphazardly around the settled area. Again, neither form of excreta would have been available for borrow filling. Indeed, it is clear that there was not nearly the volume of remains related to food that one would expect if a model based upon our modern refuse generation patterns were used.

But what about the wood materials that were brought to the site? Lopinot and Woods (1993) have demonstrated the huge volumes of wood that would have been used by the inhabitants for fuel and construction. As with food, wood was at a premium at the settlement. The American Bottom was largely an inundated environment with a wet prairie. Water-tolerant tree species would have been predominant on elevated terrain positions that were not under water perennially. Trees within a relatively short walking distance of Cahokia would have been totally removed early in the history of Mississippian occupation, if not earlier. Wood would then have been procured from upland settings at some distance upstream to the east and northeast. As a result, materials brought to the site for construction would have been recycled where possible and ultimately used as fuel, rather than discarded. As all of us have experienced, the reduction of weight and volume of wood during combustion is exponential. Therefore, even with the huge amounts of wood brought on site, little would have remained for borrow filling and would have been largely reduced to wood ash and fine charcoal.

Given these on-site patterns of processing, consumption, and disposal, what specifically can we say about refuse materials available for borrow filling? A generous estimate for the total production of waste and refuse by each of the site's inhabitants would be on the order of 500 g/day, a little more than a pound per day. The bulk density (weight per unit volume) of these materials on a dry-weight basis, considering their organic/inorganic ratio, was perhaps $1.0 g/cm^3$ (mineral soils average $1.3 g/cm^3$ and organic soils somewhat less than $1.0 g/cm^3$). With these figures, one can project the yearly inputs for various population levels. Because the results are self-evident, we will confine this analysis to a total population number of ten thousand individuals. On a daily basis, this population would have generated 5,000 kilograms of refuse, or enough over the course of a year to fill a volume of 1,825 cubic meters. This is certainly an impressive amount by any standard, but how does it relate to the filled borrows in the Central Precinct? At this rate of deposition, it would have taken nearly four hundred years to fill the borrows responsible for the erection of Monks Mound. We know that Monks Mound borrows were filled quite rapidly after their excavation, in a matter of no more than a few years. The materials from garbage were just not there; besides, the estimate for daily individual production was purposely set high. Indeed, it is probable that disposal of wastes and garbage was primarily in the immediate zone of habitation, with those items that were not directly incorporated into the soil deposited in ready-made containers. The number of abandoned pits (ca. 0.5–1.0 m³) and house basins (ca. 15 m³) certainly would have been sufficient at any one time to have served as household dumps, and all evidence from excavation of these facilities points to the fact that they were used as such. The borrows were not incidentally filled by household debris. Rather, earthen materials were dug from other locations and transported to those borrow sites where filling was planned as part of the overall design. The peripheral borrows were allowed to remain open and water-filled, and remained so into the twentieth century before they were partially filled by agricultural sheetwash sediments.

Beyond examining borrows as sources and receptacles for fill, we can also examine the spatial patterning of borrows, noting whether they were reclaimed or not. We have talked about the borrowing of vast tracts of ground surrounding Monks Mound. Though evidence indicates that large borrows were common within the central portion of the site, all were carefully filled relatively early in the site's history. Open borrows were common and, in fact, circle the site's core. Within areas adjacent to and outside of this ring of borrows, evidence of large-scale earthmoving activities and land reclamation (beyond mound construction and discrete borrow pits) has generally not been identified despite the investigation of several large tracts of land including the ICT-I, the Dunham Tract, and Tracts 15A and 15B. What is more common outside of the central area of the site is a pattern of localized borrowing and mound construction amid unmodified natural terrain, documented by investigations at the Rouch mound group, the Powell Mound, and at Mounds 72 and 55. A few instances of reclaimed ground have been documented in outlying areas, including a borrow within the ICT-II, a refuse pit below Mound 84, a refuse deposit north of Mound 34, expansion of a tongue of land under a small promontory mound in the West Borrow Pit mound group, and evidence of ground leveling before construction began on the Powell Mound. However, these efforts were generally not on the same scale as those recorded around the margins of Monks Mound.

Why were the peripheral borrows left unfilled if it was such a common practice to fill the early borrows next to Monks Mound? We believe that there were reasons that these borrows were not reclaimed. Open borrows figured prominently in the functioning of Cahokia and were used by the people for a variety of purposes. The importance of water provides a clue to understanding their role. One possibility is that the ring of borrows functioned as a border distinguishing a central "island" from a surrounding periphery, mirroring in form an outer ring of water formed by the Spring Lake meander channel and associated cut-off chute. This ring of borrows may have been purposefully tied to certain important limits of vision. The relegation of water to site margins was common to all Mississippian sites; nowhere else in the Mississippian world do we find a site crosscut by or centered around water.

Another possibility is that at least certain of these borrows may have been used as communal water sources, in particular, those borrows penetrating buried sand ridges. Borrows extending down into these sand aquifers might have provided a reliable, pure community water supply in areas where water was not otherwise proximal. The open borrows may also have lowered the water table locally, providing "dry basements" for pit houses and other structures within the central area.

Open borrows may also have served as integral features of mound groups. The Tippetts mound group is focused around an open borrow that is not just an irregular hole in the ground. Extending out into the borrow is a sculpted extension, or peninsula, with a square platform that is located at the geometric center of the mounds. Thus the borrow was intimately connected to the layout of the mounds and probably also to the function of the mound group. Though the details of this are unclear, we do know that occupation was not centered around the Tippetts mound group, but was removed some-what to the north, with occupational intensity increasing northward. In-stead of being an anchor for a subcommunity, this mound group may have formed part of a special mortuary precinct for the site.

Borrow Pit 5-1, located just southwest of the Twin Mounds, is the largest open borrow at the Cahokia site. Though irregularly shaped, its north-south and east-west dimensions are roughly those of the Grand Plaza. Near the center it constricts to a very narrow passage that separates the West Borrow Pit mound group from the Mound 72 mound group while simultaneously connecting the two main basins of the borrow pit. In plan view, the north-eastern half bears some resemblance to the beaked head of the Cahokia Bird-man icon. If one considers the water to be positive space and the land to be negative, the eastern half of this borrow pit complex roughly mirrors itself, with the land also taking on an anthropomorphic beaked appearance.

This leads us to the issue of aesthetics, an issue that has resonated with us at the Tippetts mound group in particular. At this group, the Cahokians sub-tly wove together various key aspects of their built environment into a seam-less, balanced whole; as with the Chinese yin-yang symbol, the visual ele-ments that make up the Tippetts mound group fit together like an interlocking puzzle, discrete yet unified. The mounds are neither inordinately large nor high; the open borrow pit, although extensive, seems to both sepa-rate and unite the earthen monuments on its perimeter. The pairing of a plat-form and conical mound, linked by a causeway, contrasts with the low-lying water gently merging into the base of the mounds. On a sunny day, the sky is reflected in the smooth surface of the water-filled borrow, bringing earth, sky, and water into a single harmonious scene. Even the symmetrical, low plat-form, sculpted from the earth and oriented to the cardinal directions, which is the geometric center and perhaps cultural focus of the complex, is not domineering. It is linked to the other associated features by its location and a low causeway. The pairing of water and mounds provides an idyllic setting, and its beauty is still captivating today (fig. 44). We surmise that these aes-thetic elements were also appreciated in Mississippian times.

The association of water (in open borrows) and paired-mound complexes is a recurrent theme within our proposed mortuary district, much as it is in our modern analog of the Washington, D.C., monuments. Promontory mounds and the sculpting of rises looking out over these borrows further at-test to the importance of these water-filled features. The promontory mounds are found along the lips of the southern borrows and would have provided a spectacular setting for rituals associated with water.

Before ending our discussion of borrows, we would like to comment briefly on the discrepancy between the estimated volume of earth needed to construct the mounds at Cahokia and the volume of earth removed from the open borrows, specifically as it relates to their function. At the Tippetts

44. Photograph of the Tippetts mound group. Mounds of this group encompass a central, water-filled borrow (see fig. 32 for plan view). A sculpted central platform, visible in the middle ground, extends into the borrow.

mound group, the local open borrows could certainly have supplied the earth needed to build the earthworks in the Tippetts mound group. Indeed, these open borrows provided much more soil than necessary. As we refined our mapping of the Tippetts borrow, we calculated that roughly 17,500 cubic meters of soil had been removed from the borrow, approximately 3.5 times the mound volume. If we include the causeway, this ratio is reduced to approximately 3:1. Because of the indeterminate nature and extent of Mound 95 and the amount of mound erosion and borrow pit siltation over the years, these figures could change slightly. But even adding the volumes of mounds within the ICT-II to the northwest (one of which contained loess sediments and would not have been constructed from these borrows) would not substantially alter this disparity between borrowed earth and local mound volume. Another borrow is located just to the east of Mound 95. We must conclude that this borrow is far too big to have been used only for local concerns. Its size, as do the sizes of all the borrows within the central ring, suggests larger plans and a more communal intent than just providing fill for a single project. To what purpose was this fill used? Perhaps for the construction of other mounds or for the reclamation of the large borrows surrounding Monks Mound, in which case they represent the end of the line in the processes of earth transport.

CHAPTER TEN

LANDSCAPE
SYMBOLISM

In a consideration of symbolic aspects of the earthworks at Cahokia, we unite a number of threads that are common within archaeological, anthropological, architectural, and geographical literature. For example, landscapes have meaning to humans, and humans not only create, but also react to, landscapes and their meanings. Landscapes can function either as a narrative or symbolic legacy (Rowntree and Conkey 1980) or as one that can be manipulated or appropriated (Bender 1992). Landscape transformation may be part of symbolization in response to stress or during times when the social or political order is particularly fragile. Hence, landscape transformation may accompany the emergence of a new social or political order (Bradley 1984; Cherry 1978). And finally, communal undertakings expressed in the landscape, such as raising a monumental structure can unite communities by engaging the feelings and senses of a people in a creative act (Tuan 1972) and make them explicit (Relph 1976). Thus, we agree with Lynch and Hack (1984, 173) that landscapes, as a medium of symbolic communication, can inform about history, the future foreseen, expected behavior, politics, ownership, status, and group affiliations.

These concepts inform key aspects of the Cahokia landscape. We return to, and expand upon, the notion that the Cahokia community was first symbolically constructed, as part of a program of political manipulation. Here elements of symbolic history, symbolic transformation accompanying the Mississippian emergence, and a vision of the future intertwine. We focus on the symbolic nature of mounds throughout the period of occupation and how they reflected concepts about group affiliations, ownership and status, the nature of power relationships, and the tenor of political and social change at the site. We contend that the Cahokia landscape and its symbolic legacy were differentially experienced by various social and political during the Mississippian occupation. Finally, we examine landscape meaning inherent in planning and design concepts.

THE SYMBOLIC CONSTRUCTION OF CAHOKIA

A landscape can function as a symbolic legacy. Mississippian mounds developed out of a long tradition and probably conveyed messages based on persistent past associations. Let us take a brief look at the building of mounds and the development of mound centers in the Eastern Woodlands in order to understand this tradition.

Mounds in the eastern United States have a long history, going back to at least 1000 B.C. in mortuary contexts (Dragoo 1976; Griffin 1967; Smith 1986). Although archaeologists have documented pre-Mississippian mounds that do not serve an evident mortuary function (Atwell and Conner 1991; Charles et al. 1988; Greber 1991), cemetery contexts are definitely predominant. During the Woodland periods (600 B.C. to A.D. 800), mounds were commonly constructed in areas disengaged from the domestic sphere, often on bluff spurs overlooking a village (Atwell and Conner 1991; Bennett 1945; Bohannon 1972; Brown 1981; Griffin et al. 1970; Jenkins and Krause 1986).

The earliest known mounds in the region encompassing the American Bottom date from the Middle Woodland period (150 B.C. to A.D. 300). These conical mounds were burial mounds found in association with the major river bottoms of the region (the American Bottom, the Kaskaskia River valley, and others) in both isolated (bluff-top) settings or seemingly tethered to some form of village occupation. A viable interpretation of the latter (Farnsworth 1990; Smith 1992) is that mound construction was associated with the internment of socially important persons (either because of status or position) who derived from a wider orbit of settlements and families than those existing at the mound site. A small number of "custodial" residents made up the "village," with the bulk of the use coming from ritual gatherings as people came together for internment and feasting activities associated with honoring the ancestors. At those times, presumably harvest feasts, the commingling of harvest and ancestor veneration was a powerful draw to bring together diverse people at one location. As these ceremonies ended, most of the participants returned to scattered, dispersed communities or isolated homesteads.

The succeeding Late Woodland period (A.D. 300–800) does not appear to represent a profound increase in mound ceremonialism. Within the American Bottom, evidence for mound ceremonialism is largely lacking. In surrounding regions, there is abundant evidence for a continuation of the practice (Atwell and Conner 1991; Perino 1971) with no appreciable change, except that perhaps multiple burials were more common.

It is in the Emergent Mississippian period (A.D. 800–1000) within the American Bottom that an abrupt change in the pattern of mound construction occurs. At this time, the first mound centers appeared, i.e., habitation sites in which the mounds were fully integrated within the village area. This accompanied a noted ubiquity of settled villages with evidence for residential stability. Fly-by-night clusterings of dwellings still existed, but all major valleys had well-established villages. The Mississippians constructed bluff-top burial mounds (Harn 1971; Melbye 1963; Perino 1967) but most mounds were no longer removed from daily life. They were brought into the community where they assumed a pivotal position at the heart of the domestic sphere, providing dramatic testimony that there was no longer a clear division between the landscapes of life and death. This was a critical change in the cultural landscape between Woodland and Mississippian times.

As mounds moved into the context of the village, their function was transformed. They continued to be used for burials in Mississippian times, to "culture" death, but they also served as substructures for culture (residences, temples, and other public facilities). Emergent Mississippian mound ceremonialism is problematical. Emergent Mississippian mounds have not been extensively investigated. Ceremonialism seems to have taken the form of cardinal-direction observations in terms of marking discoidals and the arrangement of centrally located pits. It is important to note, however, that this ceremonialism was not directly associated with death and that it was centralized within house clusters.

We suggest that the Cahokians used and manipulated the symbolic association of mounds, rituals, and burials arising out of this long tradition of mound building to create their great center, partially disguising the radical shifts that were involved by retaining traditional mound features and associations. Ties with the ancestors and the gods that this symbolic legacy conveyed were appropriated to provide legitimacy and power to Cahokia's founders. The integration of multiple nodes of society through rituals associated with mounds was also retained, but in a transformed setting. Rituals were no longer conducted on neutral ground but were made an integral part of a functioning center that used them to obtain and maintain power.

Plazas also carried a symbolic legacy that was appropriated and transformed. A plaza is a landscape feature that does not necessarily owe its stature to any intrinsic physical attribute but to its effectiveness in symbolizing the sentiments of the community. Prehistoric plazas, as well as famous historic plazas such as the Boston Commons, are features of communal integration expressive of the group. Plazas, along with large, special-purpose buildings, first appeared as part of the move to larger and more permanent settlements during Late Woodland times. By Mississippian times, however, it was apparent that plazas were not just the result of organic growth around a central space but, along with mounds, served to separate the public from the domestic spheres within the village. Evidence that Mississippian plazas were constructed and manipulated to set them apart from the village area comes not only from Cahokia, but from other Mississippian sites as well (Larson 1989; Lewis and Kneberg 1946; Polhemus 1987).

Aggressive molding of the landscape, characteristic of the Grand Plaza and mound construction at Cahokia, was a salient feature of the Mississippian period. It was during this time that a marked jump in the social and ecological transformation of the landscape occurred. We believe this was not coincidental and that the transformation of mound and plaza from Woodland through Mississippian times was related to the process of integrating larger and larger communities.

It has been argued elsewhere (Dalan 1993b) that a general version of a model proposed by Sherratt (1990) linking monumental construction, settled communities, and agriculture is useful for understanding these developments.

Changes in the character and permanency of communities in the Eastern Woodlands of North America from the Woodland through the Mississippian periods (e.g., Kelly 1990a, 1990b; Morse and Morse 1990), including a proliferation of platform mound construction (Griffin 1985; Smith 1986), were linked to the transformation from horticulture to intensive maize agriculture (Asch and Asch 1985; Johannessen 1984; Keegan 1987; Smith 1985). Complex restructuring of the agricultural system, social system, and landscape occurred simultaneously in an intertwined process.

Ethnohistoric accounts suggest that maize agriculture involved communal planting and harvesting (Bartram 1909 [1789], 39–41; DePratter 1983, 139; Doren 1955, 170, 400–401; Swanton 1931, 46). By implication, this would also be the case for prehistoric maize cultivation. What we see within the American Bottom and elsewhere, in tandem with increased reliance on maize (Kelly 1990a, 1990b; Morse and Morse 1990), were settlements growing larger and often marked by features indicative of communal integration, including encircling ditches, plazas, and special-purpose structures. Significantly, it was only in areas of agriculturally productive land that these large, permanent communities developed. And it appears that aggregation of the surrounding population was part of center formation rather than an increase in population due to increased birthrates or increased survival (Emerson 1997; Holley 1991; Pauketat 1994; Woods and Holley 1991).

A communal aspect to mound construction, which joined disparate groups together, can be traced back to the Woodland period (Atwell and Conner 1991, 245; Brown 1981; Webb 1989). By virtue of labor requirements and other variables (Knight 1981; Schnell et al. 1981), mound construction is indicative of community-unifying practices. In our consideration of the earthmoving process, we discussed ethnographic and archaeological evidence that relates to a ceremonial component of mound construction, where the engagement of people through the act of construction was as important as the material result. In a retelling of a Cherokee mound building account, representatives of several clans are said to have brought basket loads of dirt and placed them in a common pile, afterward added to by the labors of the common people (Mooney 1889). Communal mound building efforts at Cahokia may have linked disparate groups of people in a similar way, most likely as part of agricultural ceremonies. Centralized rituals conducted within the site core certainly played an important role in integrating the resident and surrounding populations (Pauketat 1991). Community cohesion was not only achieved in initial construction efforts but also through the modification and use of these constructions. Reburial and purification continued as core concepts of mounds, with the periodic addition of mound mantles as symbolic means of purifying and maintaining the social order in association with community rites.

Mississippian plazas were ordered and clean; they were regularly shaped, open, and contained little in the way of domestic debris (Lewis and Kneberg 1946; Nash 1972; Neitzel 1965, 1983; Stout 1986; Wesler and Neusius 1987;

Williams and Brain 1983). They appear to have been kept clean intentionally, perhaps through periodic rites of purification and renewal such as those described for the square ground during the historic period. As part of historic busk ceremonies and other activities, the square ground was first scraped clean (with the scrapings then used for mound mantle addition) and then strewn with pure ("untrodden") soil or sand (Adair 1930, 100–101; Baillou 1961, 98–99; Doren 1955, 168–69, 399; Gatschet 1884, 127; Hawkins 1848, 75; Payne 1862, 19; Swanton 1931, 156).

Douglas (1966, 1991) links dirt and pollution with disorder and contends that the main function of purification rituals is to impose a system of order on an inherently untidy experience. Rituals regarding dirt, pollution, and purification clarify and maintain social definitions and reduce dissonance. Furthermore, pollution beliefs protect the most vulnerable domains, those whose fragile structure would be most weakened by ambiguity. As the symbol of group unity on a newly realized scale, Mississippian plazas must have been particularly in need of rules and rituals regarding dirt and pollution. The most vulnerable aspect of Mississippian society resided in its center, where harmony and order had to be maintained in order to hold the community, and the polity, together. It is no coincidence that the Central Palisade was built around this vulnerable area, though whether to protect it from internal or external threats is uncertain.

Cereal cultivation required a stable and cooperative labor pool formed by members from several household groups. Mound construction provided an effective means of societal construction via social cohesion. As marks of continuity and common descent, which crosscut family ties, mounds not only served as a basis for the symbolic construction of the community and for creating a large labor pool, but also for perpetuating social relations and maintaining this labor force. An association with the ancestors and the deities gave a mound center—and gave those controlling rituals associated with the mounds—legitimacy from above. Mounds, linked to the ancestors and tethered to a village unit, held people together and assured a commitment to place. Even though not all Mississippian mounds were burial mounds, they drew upon this ancestral connection through their common form. The durability of their construction produced an attendant message of group permanence that centuries of weathering, historic use, and disturbance have failed to erase.

The process of aggregation and integration at Cahokia, although it cannot be followed back beyond the Emergent Mississippian period, has its roots in changes that can be traced over a broader area over a longer time span. This process relates to the necessity of creating and holding together settled communities within the context of an agricultural tradition. Mound construction unfolded as part of this process throughout the American Bottom in the Emergent Mississippian period. Cahokians used mound construction to effect this nucleation process, but they did something different and managed to eclipse all other incipient centers. As discussed earlier, the scale of construction at

Cahokia differed markedly from that at other mound centers. It was truly monumental. By late in the Emergent Mississippian period, the vision of a great community, the size of which had never been seen, had arisen. This vision is what attracted people to the site.

Early mound centers nearby in the American Bottom, likely constructed during the terminal Emergent Mississippian period and ensuing Lohmann phase of the Mississippian period (i.e., Grassy Lake [Kelly 1994], Pulcher [Kelly 1993; Griffin 1977], Emerald [Koldehoff et al. 1993]), consisted of a number of (as many as thirteen) small mounds (generally under 5 meters, but up to 15 meters at Emerald) with no or poorly defined plazas. Mound groups constructed later, that is, during the Stirling and Moorehead phases (i.e., Mitchell [Bushnell 1904; Porter 1974] and East St. Louis [Kelly 1993, 1994]) had plazas, but consisted of similarly small numbers of mounds (around eleven) and also fall within this same size limit.

In chapter 1 we referred to Cherry's (1978) assertion that peaks in monument building characterize periods of drastic societal change and that monument building can be an effective means of integrating different parts of society. We see the same process at Cahokia, with the construction of the two largest features, Monks Mound and the Grand Plaza, transforming and legitimating social and political relations over the Emergent Mississippian–Mississippian transition.

Monks Mound and the Grand Plaza were integral to community definition and creation. Their construction gave structure to the community, simultaneously emphasizing the chief's power and the scale and permanence of the community and providing a centralized location for ritual activities. The chief's power, greater than any other in the region, was manifest in the size of Monks Mound. The plaza was large enough to hold much of the surrounding population in addition to the center residents. Massive earthmoving activities involved in the creation of Monks Mound and the Grand Plaza, together with other evidence of early planning at the site (Fowler 1974), illustrate the scale of the community that was envisioned and symbolize a significant commitment to this location. Notably, this scale was manifest on the land long before the achievement of population highs that followed in the Stirling phase.

RELATIONSHIPS OF POWER

> The sense of place is a political fact. What can be done to the look of a locality depends on who controls it. . . . People can be excluded, awed, confused, made acquiescent, or kept ignorant by what they see and hear. So the sense of the environment has always been a matter of moment to any ruling class. (Lynch 1976, 72–73)

The immensity of Monks Mound and other large monuments like the Egyptian pyramids and the Mayan temples have facilitated visions of vast lines of workers forced into labor to produce such constructions. Pozorski (1980) and others, however, have questioned the accuracy of this vision. Although monumental architecture may be outwardly impressive, an accurate assessment of the manpower and organizational requirements necessary for construction of these structures, as well as careful estimates of population, efficiency, and the time span of construction, often leads to a different conclusion.

For example, Abrams (1989, 1994) quantified and analyzed the energetic costs of construction of residential architecture at the Late Classic Mayan site of Copan and demonstrated that the investment of human energy was far below intuitive notions and that economic development, as expressed by the degree of economic specialization to meet construction needs and the extent of the corvée system of labor for elite construction, was relatively limited. Erasmus (1965) and Kaplan (1963) have argued, on the basis of replicative data, that monumental architecture may be built by a relatively small number of people over a long period of time and that coercive power may not always be the primary control in its construction. Calculating manpower involved in earthen mound construction, Muller (1997, 271–79) sees no great strain on the labor pool or scheduling difficulties as part of construction efforts for any Mississippian town, including Cahokia.

The 1992 Cahokia Educational Field School produced some figures on the construction of mounds using locally available soils (i.e., sand, gumbo clay, and pedogenic clay that had been collected from a soil horizon exposed in the loess bluffs) and traditional tools (stone, bone scapulae, and shell hoes; digging sticks; woven baskets; wooden bowls [which functioned well as scraping implements]; and log tampers). It took an average of sixteen individuals 7.25 hours, split between five mornings, to build a 16-foot-long by 10-foot-wide by 3-foot-high mound. What was surprising about the mound building exercise was that it took little effort to construct the mound. Clearly, this was not Monks Mound, but one can see the results of any significant expansion of man-hours.

A narrow conceptualization of power as a coercive force is perhaps also to blame for the overwhelming association of corvée labor with monument building. Geertz's (1980) study of the nineteenth-century Balinese state brought up some important points about the varied nature of power relationships. He summarized the following views of the state: (1) "great beast" views, where power lies in its threat to harm; (2) "great fraud" views, where elites extract support from the producers by concealing material conflicts; (3) "populist" views, which see the state as an extension of the spirit of the community, an instrument of the national will; and (4) "pluralistic views," where state trappings give the rules or procedures of the society a moral legitimacy (Geertz 1980, 122).

In accordance with these views, we could conceptualize monumental construction as (1) a way to strike terror, impress, or awe; (2) a means of extracting surplus, mystifying material interests, or obscuring material conflicts;

(3) a celebration or expression of the national will; and (4) a means of moralizing state rules or procedure. We can probably find elements of all of these at Cahokia for, as Geertz says, "no one remains dominant politically for very long who cannot in some way promise violence to recalcitrants, pry support from producers, portray his actions as collective sentiment, or justify his decisions as ratified practice" (Geertz 1980, 123).

At Cahokia there are certainly elements of monument building that are expressive of more than a coercive process. We have previously summarized a number of lines of evidence that lead us to conclude that, in part, mound construction at Cahokia began under the mask of a common ideology. A historic example of a cooperative construction project on a similar scale was the 1790 transformation of the Champ-de-Mars in Paris into a ceremonial ground to mark the French Revolution. Within three weeks, a labor force that included people from all walks of life was energized, not cajoled, by the Revolution to create an arena suitable for four hundred thousand people. As described in Schama (1989, 504–5):

> The vast space . . . was full of rocks that needed to be removed before the heavy soil could be worked and made even. Most of the field was excavated to a depth of four feet so that the altar area at the center would be raised by the mound, but there were no drainage ditches, and the heavy rains at the end of June had turned much of the amphitheater area . . . into a quagmire. Huge amounts of sand and gravel were required to give the surface any firmness. There were other equally arduous preliminaries that had to be completed in great haste.

We believe that Cahokia surpassed other mound centers because the populace wanted to participate in such a great undertaking.

In his consideration of the ideology of chiefdom societies, Earle (1987) suggests the following three themes or motifs of ideology: ceremonies of place associated with the creation of a sacred landscape, symbols of individual position, and symbols of warrior might. He feels that the latter two are represented best in burials, whereas ceremonies of place are tied to monumental construction. "The created sacred landscape was the property of its creators, the chiefs. Monumental construction thus probably asserts ownership. . . . in essence the monuments create a focus for space that is bounded, a product of human action, and owned by the group's earthly gods, the chiefs" (Earle 1987, 299).

If the Cahokians were the ones who built the mounds and if this was not necessarily accomplished under the whip of a coercive and powerful ruler, then it is hard to see how they could have been confused, awed, or made acquiescent by them. Raising the massive earthwork of Monks Mound may indeed have symbolized the power of the chief, but being a communal undertaking, this power was the result of empowerment by the masses. This is not to say that in succeeding generations, separated from those that created the mound, manipulation of tradition and the meaning of the mounds might not have resulted in a much different scenario. An interesting study is Frommel's (1986) examination of the papal building program, in which he demonstrates how the egocentrism of individual popes was expressed clearly in the building sequence. In Cahokia's early history, some chief had the vision and drive to attempt something different from all the other early mound centers in the American Bottom. The question then becomes: what can we learn of later visions and of the processes by which they were accomplished?

Dillehay (1990) reacts against the use of elite themes for explaining the rise of monumentalism and provides an interesting alternative to traditional conceptions of the nature of monumental construction. In his study of ceremonial fields and earthen mounds of the Mapuche, he shows that it may have been an outcome of processes that were characteristic of changing relations and strategies between different social groups. The elite were involved, because chiefs regulated the populace through public ceremony associated with these monuments, but coercive aspects of their power were not emphasized. Dillehay makes it clear that the mounds and ceremonial fields were vital to both social and political relations, playing major roles in lineage identity, the legitimization of land claims, and the recruitment of trade and marriage partners.

Linking the construction and use of monuments to a much broader base of social relations ties in with our thoughts about monuments tethered to the creation and continuity of different social groups. Beyond functioning as substructures, burial mounds, marker mounds, and so forth, the mounds probably also signified hierarchical distinctions in their size and positioning beyond the chief's mound (Holley 1999). In all likelihood, mounds served as markers of individual and collective status and as representations of group size or power. As in the chief's mound, power and legitimacy were probably gained through construction and use and exploited as currency in the social ordering of the polity. For other mounds, this might have been effected through the positioning of a mound within an area of high visibility close to the chief's mound or upon other "high status" real estate, or it might have been accomplished through access restrictions or through the scheduling of public events on the mound.

In this conception, monuments become not inherently the property of those already in power, but places where changing power relations could be played out. This ties in with ideas about landscapes as records of the process of socialization and empowerment in spatial and temporal terms, always changing and always open to contestation. If we accept this notion, we can look at the monuments at the site as clues to changing political and social relations over the course of occupation.

Transformation of an earlier mound building tradition occurred over the late Emergent Mississippian and early Mississippian periods. Mounds were not only moved into the village but were put together in new ways and embellished. The mound and plaza configuration was established (Phillips et al., 1951), and there was a definite increase in average mound size. Rough equality of mounds in dimension and form was no longer the rule, and a common pattern of aggrandizing a principal mound above all others emerged (Holley 1999; Phillips et al. 1951; Reed 1973; Williams and Brain 1983).

Through the erection of Monks Mound and the Grand Plaza the chief's power and the scale of the community were symbolized. But how was this landscape contested and reappropriated over time? How is this portrayed in changing spatial dynamics, specifically in the complex posturing of the shapes and sizes of the different mounds? It is to these questions that we now turn. As a subsidiary topic, we also consider the degree to which the Cahokia landscape was differentially experienced. We know that because of its size the entire area encompassed by the Cahokia site of today was probably not within the path of daily movement for each of the site's inhabitants. There may have been quite distinct and separate experiences of the landscape that may have corresponded to class divisions or to divisions between lineages or other social groups. Perhaps this was not so important during Emergent Mississippian times when the site consisted of a relatively homogeneous sprawl along Helms Ridge, but during the Mississippian period Cahokia was segmented into various types of spaces. Limited access to these spaces, implied by the presence of screens, fences, palisades, and the like, leads us to believe that during Mississippian times peoples' experience of the landscape became increasingly differentiated.

BORROWED SCENERY

To trace changing social and political relations at Cahokia over time, we propose a model based on the size of platform mounds and their location. By "size" we mean specifically the heights of these mounds (fig. 45) and the area of their summits. Just as the ultimate power of the chief was symbolized by the enormity and central position of Monks Mound, other mounds embodied the status of subsidiary individuals and groups. The area of the summit is an indicator of whether the mound would have been capable of serving as a substructure for an elite residence, temple, or other building. (We exclude platform mounds paired with conical mounds because of the presumed mortuary nature of these mounds and because our evidence indicates that, in the main, these mounds were not tethered to a surrounding occupational base.) The thrust of our model is that those who either lived on or held ceremonies on sizable platforms could "lord it over" all surrounding and lower-residing populations. Moreover, from these mounds, one would not only be visible but have a commanding view.

We suggest the following breakdown of platform mounds at Cahokia. Clearly, the chief's mound, Monks Mound, was separated from all else by its height, complex form, and central location. By virtue of its mass, it dwarfed all other mounds and towered over the surrounding environs. Excavations at other Mississippian towns have consistently documented the presence of large, palisaded buildings on the most prominent mound (e.g., Black 1967,

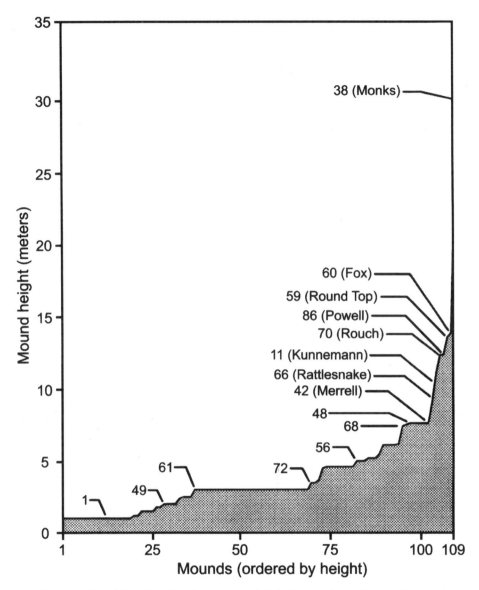

45. The overall social and political structure of Cahokia can be understood by rank-ordering the mounds by height. All mounds (of known height) are arranged in order of increasing height along the x-axis. For example, ca. 73 of the total of 109 mounds were under 5 meters in height. Monks Mound (at over 30 meters) towered over the town.

357–68; Cole et al. 1951, figs. 24 and 27; Williams and Brain 1983, fig. 3.38). Cahokia was no exception. Excavations of the Fourth Terrace of Monks Mound exposed a portion of a large structure that was palisaded.

The singularity of the chief's mound and its summit structure, in tandem with evidence from material culture, imply that the chief was superordinate—that is, overreaching the constellation of lineage and clan heads that are presumed to have occupied these towns. Today a visitor to Cahokia can climb to the top of Monks Mound and enjoy an unimpeded view of the Cahokia site and its environs. This activity is even encouraged, but it was probably not an option for the average Mississippian. This was the domain of the chief, and others likely did not enter without invitation.

Another mound, Mound 48, also appears anomalous. This mound has the largest surface area of any mound at the site (5,250 square meters, three times that of mounds of equal height), even larger than that of Monks Mound (at 3,000 square meters). The height of Mound 48, however, is middling (ca. 7.5 meters), and thus there is an imposing vertical gradient (Arnheim 1977, 17–18) established between Mound 48 and Monks Mound (at ca. 38.1 meters), which is located only 150 meters (nearest point to nearest point) from this mound. Therefore, we provisionally put this mound also under the direct control of the chief, rather than tying it to a subsidiary group. The signatures for temple mounds (Holley 1999), as identified at two major Mississippian mound centers (i.e., Kincaid and Angel), are adjacency or proximity to the chief's mound, a large surface area on the summit, and a location fronting the main plaza. At Cahokia, only Mound 48 fits these characteristics.

The issue of class in Mississippian society, outside of the chief-commoner distinction, is unresolved. Excluding the chief and his innermost circle, elites, whether priests, warrior chiefs, clan elders, or affines of the chief (Knight 1986), are cited as constituting a potential middle class, at least in terms of a social pyramid, though probably not at all equivalent to modern concepts of a bourgeois middle class. Whether achieved or ascribed, an intermediate stratum has not been well documented in the archaeological record. Elites in most societies range from around 4 to 12 percent of the population (Sanders 1984). Two lines of evidence are typically marshaled to identify elites: mortuary practices and dwelling characteristics.

Arguments for social stratification in Mississippian societies rely principally on burial data. Cahokia's Mound 72 burial program clearly documents a single individual as paramount, with little differentiation accorded to other individuals. Elsewhere examinations of a larger sample lead to a plausible suggestion of more than a two-tiered social profile of elite and commoner (Peebles and Kus 1977). Combining the limited archaeological data with the abundant ethnohistorical record, an elite stands out that would have included the chief and his family. Segregation of the chief from the commoners was all-encompassing, including dress, comportment, residence, and other markers. Warriors and priests (Knight 1981, 1986) seem the most likely candidates for occupying an intermediate position, along with lineage and clan heads. The burial program at Mound 72 could be interpreted as representing three treatments: grouped, individual, and paramount. Such a view would have been in accord with a social pyramid based on relative numbers of the three treatments.

The more mundane archaeological record of domestic life does not, at first glance, reveal profound social differences. Instead, Mississippian society looks markedly egalitarian. Though we believe that status differentiations existed, they appear to have been encoded differently than we might expect. To all intents and purposes, most people lived in the same-sized houses, used the same technology, and consumed the same foods.

The size range for residential structures of 6 to 42 square meters of floor area conforms with the range identified in the surrounding American Bottom region. But there were potentially other avenues for social differentiation involved with residential structures, including labor investment in construction, the location of a structure, and its relationship with nearby buildings.

It is possible that, as Bartram (1909 [1798], 55–56) related for the Creek, relative wealth or status was distinguished by the number of houses a family had, as opposed to the size of the house. It appears that Mississippians did not increase the size of their houses to accommodate children, in-laws, and other relatives. Instead, they may have built another house nearby to accommodate pressing demands. The presence of multiple wives or increased wealth might also have resulted in the appearance of multiple dwellings. The archaeological record does seem to support such a supposition. At the ICT-II, structure size, construction techniques, proximity, and orthogonal alignments can be used to surmise that pairs of structures were occupied in consort. Although views from this part of the site do not provide evidence for the joining of more than two houses, this can be expected, given the relative status of a community far to the south of prime occupational areas. We lack sufficient coverage for residential areas near the center. Although presumed elite deposits have been identified at the site, elite dwellings have not. Presumed elite residential mounds uncovered at other sites, for example, Mx 4 at the Kincaid site (Cole et al. 1951, 58–74), comprise a bewildering variety of structure types in close proximity. Ethnohistoric accounts and archaeological evidence also suggest that a social pecking order may have corresponded to distance from the site center. That is, those living closest to the chief's dwelling and town center were higher on the social echelon than those residing farther away.

Although our understanding is still fragmentary, we know that certain of the platform mounds at Cahokia served as elite residences. An example is Mound 56, where excavations yielded a number of likely markers indicating elite status. These included a preponderance of fancy ceramics, a disproportional representation of high-utility meat cuts, and a bead manufactured from a shark spine. A paucity of domestic debris such as hoe debitage (flaking debris from resharpening hoes) also suggests an elite use. Thus, mounds provide some of the most visible evidence about the presence of elite at Cahokia and the activities of tethered subgroups. Examining this issue of proxemics in conjunction with our model of platform mounds provides some clues to the changing relations of these groups.

A quotation from Garcilaso de la Vega (Varner and Varner 1951, 169–70) regarding the nature of southeastern Native American towns encapsulates these ideas of mounds, proxemics, and multiple dwellings:

> You may know therefore that the Indians of Florida always try to dwell on high places, and at least the houses of the lords and Caciques are so situated even if the whole village cannot be. But since all of the land is very flat, and elevated sites which have the various other useful conveniences for settlements are seldom found, they build such sites with the strength of their arms, piling up large quantities of earth and stamping on it with great force until they have formed a mound from twenty-eight to forty-two feet in height. Then on top of these places they construct flat surfaces which are capable of holding the ten, twelve, fifteen or twenty dwellings of the lord and his family and the people of his service, who vary according to the power and grandeur of his state. In those areas at the foot of this hill, which may be either natural or artificial, they construct a plaza around which first the noblest and most important personages and then the common people built their homes. They make an effort not to be far distant from the site upon which the dwelling of their lord is located.

We do not have much evidence relating to structures on top of the various platform mounds at Cahokia, but we can provide an estimate of the maximal area of a mound available for the building of multiple structures by looking at the size of the summit. Returning to our classification of platform mounds and examining mounds other than those tethered directly to the chief, we find a number of mounds whose summits ranged between 1,000 and 3,000 square meters (e.g., Mounds 5, 42, 36, 41, and 60). These are the most likely candidates for subsidiary elite residential and temple mounds. It is notable that these mounds are all located within 500 meters of Monks Mound. This is a virtual monopoly of large surfaces that could have been used for elite residential segments and public buildings. Farther away from this orbit, summit areas dwindled in size, while height was emphasized. Mounds with summits under 1,000 square meters (e.g., Mounds 70, 44, 28, 56, 55, 51, and 61) probably served a hodge-podge of functions, but this certainly included subelite residences, as evidenced by our investigations of Mound 56.

Monks Mound, the primary temple mound (Mound 48), and the presumed subsidiary elite residential and temple mounds were all confined to what we have defined as "downtown" Cahokia. Even though taller mounds existed on the margins outside of the central area, they did not have a large surface area on the summit where one could have lived in affluence, along with many wives or relatives, or have displayed one's wealth. These marginal mounds were made to be seen (visible to the downtown area and to Monks

Mound, and visible to those coming toward the site from beyond), but they were not made to be seen from. It is important here to discriminate between a privileged view and being visible to others. At the margins of the site, members of the subsidiary elite were not allowed a privileged view. Even though construction of sizable monuments was allowed, the subsidiary elite were not permitted to live on these monuments in opulent display as did the chief who resided on Monks Mound.

It appears that high living on the mounds was granted or allowed only within the strictly defined downtown area. Mounds within the central area had large summit areas, but they were not tall. They were far smaller than those on the margins, and, in addition, their proximity to, and the marked gradient between them and Monks Mound, further deemphasized their importance in relation to that of the chief.

Unfortunately, the paucity of dated mounds at Cahokia hinders attempts to look at patterns in the construction of these platform mounds over time and, in particular, the construction of platform mounds with relatively large summits (1,000 to 3,000 square meters). We do know that construction first commenced on Monks Mound and the Grand Plaza, elements that represented empowerment of the chief and the establishment of a great community. Mounds at the margins of the site were constructed soon after, but again, though tall, were not permitted to serve as substructures for rival leaders and their kith and kin. Our best evidence for the construction of other platform mounds is at the Lohmann-Stirling interface. By the end of the Lohmann phase, the borrow beneath Mound 51 was reclaimed, and construction soon began on this mound. Other early mounds (Mounds 50 and 55) completed a linear alignment along the east side of the Grand Plaza. Mounds 48 and 56 also faced the plaza, and, together with the linear string of mounds, both supported the primacy of the center through their focus on the Grand Plaza and location directly under the view and control of Monks Mound. This pattern of construction most closely approximates that considered typical of the Mississippian mound-plaza arrangement. With the exception of Mound 48, which we suggest served as a community temple, these mounds were all members of the lower class of platform summits, with most being 500 square meters or less in platform size.

The early Mississippian period at Cahokia was a time of enlargement and internal differentiation, with this mound grouping on a trajectory to becoming the dominant regional center. Homogenization and dissolution of subcommunity solidarity, perhaps best reflected in the establishment of new, orthogonally oriented communities, were part and parcel of this goal. Though Lohmann phase remains provide the most visible evidence of wealth differences (through a relatively greater diversity of house floor plans than that seen throughout the entire sequence), this diversity, as well as mound construction, is seated within a well-controlled environment focused on the broader community, as evidenced by community layouts and communal feasting activities.

Not only were subcommunities reconfigured at Cahokia, villages and incipient mound centers throughout the entire American Bottom region appeared to suffer at the expense of Cahokia's growth (Emerson 1997; Pauketat 1998; Woods and Holley 1991). What was once a sea of undifferentiated courtyard groups surrounding Cahokia during Emergent Mississippian times became notably contracted in size. Lohmann villages are hard to find in the flood plain, although they are present in the nearby uplands (Bareis 1976; Pauketat 1998). In bottomland areas, large-village aggregates were replaced by scattered and smaller units (Emerson and Milner 1982; Kelly 1990b; Mehrer 1995; Mehrer and Collins 1989; Milner et al. 1984). Life at isolated mound centers, such as Pulcher to the south and Emerald to the east, was truncated sometime during the Lohmann phase. The dispersed settlement pattern of the rural areas is presumed to indicate that households had replaced traditional subgroups as the base unit of articulation with the larger Cahokia community (Johannessen 1993; Pauketat 1991, 309–20). It was not until late in the Stirling phase that villages composed of courtyard groups appeared, and these may have been integrated with the Cahokia site through a series of ritual and political nodes (Emerson 1997). By Moorehead times, the rural countryside was restructured again. What resulted appears to have been autonomous households, courtyard groups, and villages.

Restructuring of the socio-political system allowed political centralization at Cahokia on a previously unrealized scale (Pauketat 1991, 327–28), yet the inherent weakness of a system that emphasized the greater community at the expense of lower-level controls is obvious. The path was open for the formation of new socio-political factions.

We see signs of decay in the break from a formalized community pattern during the Stirling phase to more inwardly focused subcommunities where structures were oriented to local features. Attendant changes include signals of increased privatization and hoarding of surpluses (Collins 1990; Holley et al. 1989). These changes are apparent not only at Cahokia, but at other Mississippian sites within the American Bottom (Mehrer 1995) together with a centrifugal trend, quite the opposite of the centripetal pattern that was characteristic of the Lohmann phase (Harn 1980; Milner et al. 1984; Woods and Holley 1991). Elite subgroups moved out of Cahokia into the surrounding bottom (Emerson 1991), settlements continued in the uplands, and new mound centers arose in close proximity to Cahokia. At Cahokia, conflict and social unrest are indicated by the construction of the Central Palisade late in the Stirling phase. Rebuilding of this structure into the succeeding Moorehead phase implies a growing concern with protecting the vulnerable, community-unifying center of the site. The construction of palisades, fences, and screens restricting access indicates the closure of groups into themselves, rather than the earlier focus on communitywide concerns.

Social unrest and fractionalization are also indicated by a marked change in the positioning of platforms mounds built at Cahokia during late Stirling into Moorehead times. Not only were elite moving out of Cahokia, they were also building in new areas of the Cahokia site. In marked contrast to early mound building efforts, new mound construction during the late Stirling and Moorehead phases focused on intermediate areas of the site. These mounds were concentrated along Helms Ridge, within the shadow of Monks Mound and in more distant arenas, and continued to segment areas where elite and public functions displaced residences throughout the sequence.

In a sense, this new pattern of construction introduced a sense of discord to the landscape created during early Mississippian times, in which construction of platform mounds was controlled by centering this activity around the Grand Plaza. We suggest that this new pattern of construction represented the efforts of various groups jockeying for power and position. The break with earlier locational patterns challenged the power base represented by Monks Mound and corresponded to a decline in centralized power. It is significant that the larger of these late-dating mounds were confined to the area around Monks Mound and all had relatively small summits (400 square meters or less), indicating that the chief still reigned supreme. Other mounds that appear to date exclusively to the Moorehead phase, such as the Boy Scout Mound at the West Borrow Pit mound group, the burial and platform mounds at the ICT-II, and the mound on the First Terrace of Monks Mound, were quite small. There is almost no evidence of new mound construction during late Moorehead and into Sand Prairie times. Ultimately, the decline of centralized power at Cahokia led again to an increase in household autonomy, and neither the chief nor subsidiary groups were able to muster the labor for construction. Social unrest and fractionalization, obvious as early as late Stirling, would have left the society increasingly vulnerable to environmental problems and other factors (Griffin 1960a, 1960b, 1961; Lopinot and Woods 1993; Rindos and Johannessen 1991).

PLANNING AND DESIGN

Applying a landscape approach at Cahokia has raised a series of questions about the planning and design of this great community. Was Cahokia planned? If so, what were its organizing principles? What was its meaning and purpose? How did the physical structure of the community change over time? That is, is there evidence of both harmonious organization and disjointed development? How was a site of such monumental size and scale constructed? Are there similarities between the design principles used to build Cahokia and those used to build other past and present urban places? Here we summarize our thoughts about the deliberate design and construction of ancient Cahokia.

Evidence suggests that Cahokia was deliberately planned and designed, whether on a plan drawn in the sand or as a grand vision in someone's mind. Four characteristics of the site support this hypothesis. First, the Cahokians clearly chose this site for development because it possessed the physical features and resources necessary to support long-term occupation by large numbers of people. The sheer scale of Monks Mound and the Grand Plaza, far greater than that of any other mound center developed in the American Bottom, suggests the conscious planning of a community that could sustain a larger number of people than Cahokia's own population. Second, the major organizational elements of the site—Monks Mound and the Grand Plaza—were built very quickly, perhaps within one generation, and most of the subsequent mounds and site developments were organized in relationship to them. Third, the geometric shape of Cahokia's mounds, their varying heights and sizes, their physical arrangement, and the technical expertise used in their construction indicate deliberate, careful design. Finally, the Cahokians clearly used paired combinations of platform and conical mounds to create the physical structure of their settlement and to establish the legitimacy and power of their leaders. These paired combinations were, we believe, physical representations of the relationship between life and death and nature and culture.

Possible generative sources for the development of Monks Mound and the Grand Plaza are worth reiterating here. First, communal construction by the Cahokians—what Relph (1976) would call the creation of authentic place—gave important spatial structure to the site, social order to the community, and physical character and form to the chief's power. Second, in creating Monks Mound, the Cahokians used, manipulated and transformed the symbolic association of mounds with life and death, nature and culture to create a cultural icon that symbolized the legitimacy and power of leadership. Third, competition with other Emergent Mississippian communities in the American Bottom may have influenced the Cahokians' decision to create these monumental structures.

What were the organizational principles used to create the structure of Cahokia? What was the meaning or purpose of this design or, at least, what were the effects of the final design form? These two interrelated questions are perhaps the most difficult to answer of any that we have posed. The extant structure of Cahokia suggests the deliberate use of space-defining principles such as directionality, focus-center-goal, symmetry, boundary, and domain (see chapter 2) to construct the primary core area and the major relationships between features at Cahokia. If we use these spatial design principles as a guide for analysis, there are three primary elements that gave shape to Cahokia, namely, lay of the land, including natural topography and related site features; the location, structure, and scale of Monks Mound and the Grand Plaza as focal features; and the ordered pair combination of the platform mound and conical mound with their associated adjacencies. In addition, alignments of the mounds with each other, visual connections between mounds, and the need for visual recognition by the Cahokian elite on Monks Mound from the Grand Plaza and adjacent mounds reinforced the social structure and political hierarchy.

The surrounding natural topography formed by the course of the Mississippi River, Cahokia Creek and its adjacent lowlands, flood plains and other water bodies influenced the structure of Cahokia. Mound concentrations, housing patterns, and other data indicate that Helms Ridge was an important east-west development spine and possible movement corridor. The highest ground near the ridge was settled first, and lowlands were avoided or used for agriculture, wood resources, and borrow pits. The latter were settled only when population increased and development pressure intensified. Later, as the population decreased and "public land" near Helms Ridge became available, residents resettled the more desirable high ground.

Monks Mound and the Grand Plaza formed the focus of the settlement. All other development of the site appears to have occurred in relation to them through the use of alignment, visual orientation, or location and proportion (e.g., the lesser height and size of flanking mounds that border the plaza). More importantly, the superhuman scale and implied symbolism of Monks Mound and the Grand Plaza created a spirit of place for Cahokia that is still evident today. Spirit of place is an intangible quality that certain physical and social settings possess that is easily, often intuitively, recognized by the majority of people who experience those settings (Relph 1976). As mound-plaza, the pair functioned spatially much in the same way as other monumental spaces (e.g., Saint Peter's Basilica and Piazza, in Rome). Monks Mound represented the spiritual, cultural, and political power structure, whereas the Grand Plaza was the ritual setting for the community to recognize and celebrate that power. Both locations (either from above, standing on Monk's Mound and looking out as a member of the elite family, or from below, standing in the Plaza as a commoner and looking up) reinforced the concept of power and leadership and its relationship to life and death. Finally, Monks Mound was the largest mound at Cahokia and in the American Bottom, clearly dominating the settlement and surrounding landscape as a visual and regional landmark.

Ordered pairs of platform and conical mounds and their associated adjacencies—conical to conical, platform to platform—played an important role in organizing the space of Cahokia (fig. 43). The repetitive presence of these pairs throughout Cahokia established their dominance as a landscape form and gave the overall site visual continuity. The combined results of form, shape, and function (i.e., platform charnel house mounds and conical burial mounds symbolizing square as culture and circle as nature) originated in the use of mounds to "culture" death. Burial mounds, once separated from the settlement, were moved into the "living" areas of Cahokia and transformed into substructures for culture (i.e., elite residences, temples, and other public facilities), thus linking life and death. The platform and conical mound pair was also used to organize civic space. Representing a spiritual belief system, similar to the cross in Christianity, they repeatedly marked social order and worldview. Several pairs defined the space of the Grand Plaza and determined the edges of the Central Precinct by their location and scale. The largest pair combination, Mounds 59 and 60, served as the southern boundary of the Grand Plaza and acted as a counterpoint, both physically and symbolically, to Monks Mound on the north. There appears to have been a connection between the base shape of the conical and platform mounds and the circle and square arrangement used in Emergent Mississippian times, as evident in the marking of cardinal directions, discoidals, the arrangement of central pits, and the form of symbolic artifacts.

The alignment of mounds with each other and the visual connections between mounds also contributed to the spatial structure of Cahokia. Axial alignments of mounds are seen in both east-west and north-south directions. The east-west alignment followed Helms Ridge. The Powell group formed the far western edge, Monks Mound was in the center, and the east group along Canteen Creek formed the eastern edge. A north-south alignment included the Kunnemann group on the far northern edge of the site, the western edge of Monks Mound, Mounds 59 and 60 to the ridgetop elite burial mound (Mound 72), and the Rattlesnake group on the southern edge (fig. 43). A diamond alignment, described in chapter 7, is also visible (fig. 39). Monks Mound appeared at the head of the diamond; two platform-conical complexes formed the east and west points. An important ridgetop mound, Rattlesnake Mound, marked the southern point. Another diamond-shaped alignment occurred in the mortuary district. Mounds 59 and 60 formed the northern point, the Tippetts group formed the eastern point, the Borrow Pit group formed the western point, and Mound 72 formed the southern point. Finally, there were frequent alignments between ordered pairs where conical mound matched conical mound, and platform mound matched platform mound, but the significance and meaning of this relationship is not yet clear.

Human senses such as sight and hearing also appear to have played a role in the layout of Cahokia. The eye recognizes another human being at 4,000 feet, or approximately 1.1 kilometers. This distance seems to coincide with the distance from Monks Mound to the edge of the site core. Outlying mound groups were connected back to the core by the same distance (1.1 kilometers), as was the chain of mounds leading west toward the East St. Louis group. In addition, data suggest that housing settlements from Emergent Mississippian times forward were organized in visual relation to Monks Mound, not to other individual mounds or mound groups, with the possible exception of settlements in late Stirling times, when the Central Palisade blocked views back to the center. The ability to orally communicate ideas and inspire one's constituency was also critical for the leader of a society that had no known written language. Our field observations indicate that Monks Mound was constructed so that the sound of an unamplified human voice could be heard clearly across the area of the Grand Plaza when projected from the front of the First Terrace. It appears that the elevation of the terrace helped carry the sound over the Plaza and, in addition, sound bounced off the front of the Second Terrace; thus an unaided human voice could have been heard at the far edge of the plaza. Such evidence suggests that this distance was deliberately measured and the space laid out to facilitate auditory and visual control over the community, a goal that also affected the final form and scale of the central core.

Several types of boundaries, both physical and implied, were constructed at Cahokia. At elite dwelling sites and on temple mounds, screens or fences were probably used to mark boundaries and limit access to private or sacred space. Mounds surrounding Monks Mound and the Grand Plaza suggest an implied boundary by their scale and proportion and by the absence of housing in this area during Lohmann and early Stirling times. Borrow pits on the southern side of Mounds 59 and 60 defined and emphasized a boundary surrounding the central core. Ridgetop mounds on the east, south, and west of the site may have served as outer boundaries of Cahokia. Finally, the Central Palisade, erected for the first time in the late Stirling phase, enclosed a central core. Interestingly, it may have signaled the breakdown of stronger organizing forces. In other words, the palisade divided the central core, creating an inside and outside within the heart of the settlement that prevented direct visual access to Monks Mound and the Grand Plaza. It also broke up the ordered pairing of platform and conical mounds established over much of the site.

If Cahokia was consciously designed, what was its meaning or purpose, and what was the impact of its form? We believe that Cahokia was deliberately designed as the seat of power of the Mississippian culture in the American Bottom. Monks Mound and the Grand Plaza were built to inspire, inform, and dominate. By means of sheer scale and the appropriation of life/death symbolism, Monks Mound established the legitimacy and strength of Cahokia's ruling elite. The Grand Plaza held the entire community and surrounding populations. The layout of the community was manifest on the land long before the population reached its maximum height in the Stirling phase.

Evidence suggests that, although well planned, Cahokia suffered from population overgrowth, political decline, and resource depletion over time. In its earliest stages, civic structure was determined by Monks Mound and the Grand Plaza. Emergent Mississippian courtyard clusters were located adjacent to Monks Mound and the northern edge of the Plaza along Helms Ridge (figs. 20 and 21). As the settlement grew, new mounds and public works were constructed around the central core and along the ridge, and people moved out into lowlands south of Monks Mound (figs. 20 and 22). In Lohmann and early Stirling times (fig. 35), the orthogonal distribution of houses, continued mound building, and digging and reclaiming of borrow pits indicate deliberate planning and urban resettlement. In late Stirling times, a palisade was erected. Although clearly planned, its insertion contradicted the organization of the original layout and, as noted earlier, blocked visual access to Monks Mound. What was its purpose? Did its construction as an internal boundary indicate a change in the social structure and perhaps a decline in centralized power? Mound construction patterns, including the construction of platform mounds in intermediate areas of the site, suggest that this is so. Cessation of construction of paired platform and conical mounds located in relation to Monks Mound and the Grand Plaza may also indicate a breakdown in social order. In Moorehead and Sand Prairie times, the population moved back into the central core and returned to the earlier domestic pattern of the courtyard cluster. These later stages of occupation may indicate a disjointed settlement pattern by disparate groups of people, rather than a deliberate or more cohesive activity.

CHAPTER ELEVEN

ABANDONMENT

To create Cahokia, a site of monumental scale, the Cahokians used soil and wood. The availability and characteristics of both materials affected the form and structure of the settlement and the time and effort required for its construction and maintenance. Perhaps the materials themselves facilitated the success and decline of Cahokia. The archaeological record indicates that the Cahokians understood quite well the technical aspects of earthen construction, such as layering and compaction, and the need for internal drainage and constant maintenance. In addition to the maintenance of earthworks, the longevity and maintenance of wood structures was also problematic, especially because of contact with soil and wind. But what about the greater environmental affects of resource acquisition? Does this also figure into the abandonment of the Cahokian site as a functioning center in Mississippian times?

We find it more difficult to explain the decline of Cahokia than to explain its ascendence. Perhaps this relates in part to the length of the decline (beginning at least as early as the latter part of the Stirling phase, ca. A.D. 1100) in contrast to the rapidity of the rise of this great mound center. By A.D. 1350, the complex, aggregated community present during the previous centuries at Cahokia had been largely abandoned, and evidence indicates a regional settlement pattern of sporadic, relatively short-term, low-density habitations.

It is relatively easy to identify the by-products of this decline. These include a break in the formalized community pattern and population loss, with the remaining residents tending to move back toward the center. By the terminal Sand Prairie phase a "rump" Mississippian community occupied the site (Holley et al. 1989). Just as population growth was a regional phenomenon, so was population loss, resulting in what might be called a Cahokian diaspora. Centripetal forces were in operation by the end of the Stirling phase, with many residents choosing to repopulate surrounding environs. Exotic goods may have become more equalized (Pauketat 1992), if in smaller volume, during this decline. Even the spectrum of wood taxa used at the site gives every indication of shrinking access to highly desired and exotic species (Lopinot 1991). And then, of course, there was the continued revamping of fortifications. Emerson and Woods (1990, 102) point out that on Monks Mound a Sand Prairie phase domestic structure was present on the First Terrace secondary mound with refuse distributed around its periphery, possibly indicating a greatly diminished ceremonial status of this facility (Benchley 1975, 19).

Over the years, many causes have been advanced for the decline and abandonment of Cahokia. Currently the idea that individual great towns in

the Southeast dissipated in response to the political instability of the chiefdom is the vogue (e.g., Anderson 1990; Earle 1991, 13). This is probably a
reasonable scenario and one that is consistent with our discussion in chapter
10 about patterns of mound construction and competing political groups.

It is important, however, to look at contributory factors to this instability
within the local setting. When we are concerned with landscape, it does not
make sense to restrict interpretation to a purely social world. Our view that
political instability exacerbated by environmental degradation ultimately led
to the decline of Cahokia is one that integrates human factors with the
physical environment. It recognizes that the physical environment continued to be modified by human action. Thus, in understanding the contin-
uum of habitation at Cahokia, it is important to consider how the physical
environment affected humans and how they in turn reacted.

Environmental degradation resulting from human actions occurred
widely and exerted a great impact on the food production capabilities of the
Cahokian society (Lopinot and Woods 1993). Intensive cultivation of maize,
coupled with population nucleation, had disastrous consequences. Demands
on wood resources were great and timber clearance was extensive. Huge
amounts of timber were used for fuel, the construction of buildings and
other structures, and the Central Palisade and its subsequent rebuildings.
Major changes in the local hydrology would have resulted from overexploitation of wood resources in bottomland, slope, and bluff settings. Rapid
runoff, coupled with decreased channel capacity from sedimentation, would
have produced major flooding after each heavy midsummer rain. The results
of such flooding would have been catastrophic for bottomland maize fields,
and Cahokia, with its heavy reliance on such settings for crop production,
would have been particularly vulnerable.

Significantly, these projected events coincided with a documented movement of structures to higher elevations within the main bottom and a general
migration back into interior upland settings. Evidence for elevational resiting
within the bottom derives from investigations at a Mississippian village
known as the Julien site. Investigations at this site as part of the FAI-270
mitigation project resulted in the identification of structures that dis
played a movement upslope through time (Milner 1984a) because of rising
water levels. A similar—though less dramatic because of the absence of
relief—pattern was noted at the ICT-II at the Cahokia site (Collins 1990). Both
examples document a shift to higher ground during the Moorehead phase.

It is reasonable to speculate on flooding in flood-plain contexts. One caveat
is important. Both locations, the Julien site and the ICT-II, were characterized
by a decline in resident population, as measured by the number of structures.
Thus the "avoidance of wet feet" hypothesis may simply represent a selection
of more desirable ground within the context of a reduced population. In
short, the greater the number of people, the greater the diversity of structure
sitings; the lesser the number of people, the more restricted the house siting.
There is no extant physical evidence of flooding at these locations.

Knowledge of record rainfalls, which have resulted in Mississippi River flood events, leads people to assume that flooding was a major factor during prehistoric times. The historic and prehistoric situations, however, cannot be compared. The notoriety of the Mississippi River for flooding, for example, in 1993, is a function of river channelization and the destruction of watersheds and wetlands. Even the catastrophic floods of early historic times, during which steamboats are said to have traveled from bluff to bluff, derived from extensive clear-cutting along the river for steamboat fuel. Interestingly enough, during the massive floods of 1993, when nearly all areas around the Cahokia site were inundated, Cahokia was not, with the exception of minor sections of low-lying land. We presume the Mississippi River was sluggish during the Mississippian period; at least, we have no evidence that tells us otherwise. We have no data to support the idea that the Cahokians were being regularly flooded, if ever, above the 127-meter-contour level.

Griffin (1960a, 1960b, 1961) has hypothesized that within the Midwest warmer climatic conditions fueled the growth and expansion of Mississippian culture, whereas the onset of cooler conditions, which adversely affected agricultural practices, led to the contraction of Mississippian culture. Support for Griffin's model includes documentation of climatic effects in the upper Mississippi River valley (e.g., Baerreis and Bryson 1965; Baerreis et al. 1976; Bryson and Wendland 1967; Penman 1988), yet none of these climatic variables would have significantly affected the American Bottom region because of its lengthy growing season.

Ultimately the question of flooding revolves around whether the source of the flood was external (the Mississippi River) or internal (creeks emanating from nearby bluffs). The greatest challenge to an agricultural community would not have been flooding by the great Mississippi, but internal flooding by Cahokia Creek and its tributaries. Mississippi River flooding occurred annually during the spring, prior to planting. Internal flooding, in contrast, could have occurred from torrential rains during the spring, summer, and fall. Standing water resulting from these floods would have drowned water-sensitive maize crops and would have critically affected the Mississippian occupation at Cahokia and elsewhere in the bottom.

The Julien site and the ICT-II, with their structure resiting, provide circumstantial evidence for such flooding. There are also two specific, well-documented contexts showing internal flooding and environmental degradation associated with the Mississippian occupation of the region. The first example derives from work at the Goshen site (11-Ms-1273) (Holley and Brown 1989), where the sequence of sediments and soils demonstrates the impact of late prehistoric pressure on wood resources. This site is situated on an alluvial fan between the bluffs and the former channel of Cahokia Creek. Here, a buried Emergent Mississippian village was identified resting on a surface that had long been stable. Pit features relating to this occupation emanated downward from the top of this surface, but their orifices were obscured by continued pedogenesis after site abandonment, presumably resulting from movement of the population to Cahokia. Only a few artifacts relating to Mississippian period occupation were recovered from this site. The Mississippian presence, however, was indicated by a sequence of laminated sediments overlying the stable surface. These sediments were the result of forest clearance and, perhaps, cultivation of the bluff top but not the fan, as they show no evidence of tillage disturbance. A renewed period of pedogenesis and melanization is indicative of slope stabilization occurring after the depopulation of the area in late Mississippian times. Renewed instability during the historic period, probably beginning with forest clearance activities in the late eighteenth and early nineteenth centuries, produced another zone of laminated sediments. We are struck by the parallels between historic and prehistoric patterns. The historically produced laminated sediments were surmounted by a series of nineteenth- and twentieth-century plow zones aggrading with deposition from upslope disturbances that continue to the present.

The second example was revealed in excavations conducted on an alluvial fan where Indian Creek enters the northern American Bottom. This location is immediately downslope from the Willaredt site (11-Ms-110). Here, on a slightly lower fan position than at the Goshen site, an identical stratigraphy was revealed. In addition, a series of undulating features, clearly the result of tillage, was revealed at one of the test excavation units within the laminated prehistoric sediments. These features, interpreted as planting beds, were separated stratigraphically by undisturbed sediments originating upslope and from the adjacent Indian Creek. Although aerial photography has suggested the presence of ridged fields at Cahokia and other American Bottom mound sites, this is the first unquestioned excavated evidence of such features in the American Bottom region. Moreover, the association of sequential fields with aggrading sediments is unprecedented in this portion of the Mississippi River valley. Thus, this site provides evidence that agricultural practices were being affected by erosive events.

So, here we have a smoking gun. The agricultural basis for life at Cahokia was literally being smothered. On the sloping fields at the margins of the valley, each rain eroded planting surfaces and deposited a blanket of less fertile sediments. In fields at lower elevations, the increased rates of sedimentation accompanied by flooding and standing water would have suffocated crops through drowning during the growing season. The economic and social consequences of such localized crop failure and resultant declining production would have been disastrous, particularly at Cahokia with its downstream location and large resident population reliant on the production of maize outfields near the site.

We can speculate that the Cahokians had the ability to deal with these problems, given their engineering expertise, knowledge of materials, and ability to construct drainage features within mounds, borrows, and the Grand Plaza. It is probable that future investigations will reveal evidence of their attempts to resolve these flooding problems as well as their expertise with irrigation and drainage within Mississippian fields, but the data we have to date suggest that alterations of the regional hydrology caused by the Cahokians were not treated with adequate countermeasures. This pattern is not uncommon worldwide. The environmental effects seen in the American Bottom are similar to those documented for Neolithic societies associated with the initial adoption of food production in western Europe, the Mediterranean, the Near East, China, India, the highlands of Mexico, and the lowland Mayan area of Central America. Perhaps the relatively slow rates at which human practices altered the regional hydrology caused these changes not to be recognized until too late. This is also a familiar scenario. Presumably these changes occurred over a number of generations, and flooding was not an issue every year. Or perhaps, by the time the danger was recognized, the Cahokians no longer had the manpower or desire to reverse the situation.

CONCLUSION

While writing the conclusion for this book, we read Norman Hammond's review (1997) of *Cahokia: Domination and Ideology in the Mississippian World*, edited by Timothy Pauketat and Thomas Emerson. Hammond commenced his review with a mention of Monks Mound, as he notes, "the most prominent and most discussed remnant of the pre-Columbian community of Cahokia." What struck us about this review was not that Monks Mound provided the lead—we have commented that it is common for accounts of Cahokia to begin in this manner—but that Hammond also felt compelled to cite the same material from Brackenridge to describe the mound that we used in the introduction to this volume, i.e., "What a stupendous pile of earth!" and "I was struck with a degree of astonishment, not unlike that which is experienced in contemplating the Egyptian pyramids."

We debated among ourselves about using the Brackenridge quotes as an opening for this volume. Inasmuch as the Brackenridge material is a much-used source in writings on Cahokia, we questioned the advisability of quoting him. For example, Fowler's (1997) comprehensive atlas of the Cahokia site also begins with a discussion of Brackenridge and his observations. In the end, we decided that it was worth repeating this material for the sense of wonder—"astonishment"—and excitement that it so aptly conveys.

When we saw the Hammond review, however, our discussions began anew. This time, though, we did not question whether to cite Brackenridge, instead, we asked why it was that so many, both Cahokia archaeologists and non-Cahokia archaeologists, felt compelled to quote Brackenridge instead of using their own words to describe Monks Mound and the Cahokia site. We concluded that Brackenridge seems to have captured an impression that we secretly share but cannot seem to express within the confines of our profession. Hammond's characterization of Monks Mound as "a strange, large hump rising from the flood-plain of the American Bottom" pales in comparison. It is somehow unseemly to express one's personal excitement about archaeological remains, yet without such an expression we fail to provide statements that resonate with our readers in the manner that Brackenridge seems to have done.

Dunlop (1995, x, 5) comments on the collective enthusiasm expressed in nineteenth-century travel literature and on the thunder of nineteenth-century interpretive efforts. Though often misguided, comparisons to the great Egyptian pyramids or the temples of Mexico provide an evocative means of describing the mounds of the Eastern Woodlands. Probably for this reason such quotes also commonly find their way into modern writings on Cahokia.

The nineteenth-century accounts offer a freshness, because everyone who wrote, as well as those who read, was new to the landscape (Dunlop 1995, 5). For the modern reader, they not only provide an unjaded view of the landscape but also one that is unsullied by twentieth-century development. It is this ageless vista that we have come to desire for our archaeological properties. Hammond says that a visit to Cahokia is "depressing" due to modern developments, which include roads, housing, and industry (fig. 46). "No wonder," he says, "publishers prefer either old photographs or artists' impressions. . . . Cahokia is best seen in the mind's eye."

However, Cahokia is not a myth for us, and, we argue, it should not be a myth for others. Brackenridge was writing from experience, and so are we. Experience of place is what makes landscape. Seeing Cahokia as it is today, together with knowledge arising from our work at the site, has provided for us an entree into a more robust inquiry into what was Mississippian Cahokia. Nineteenth-century accounts furnish a view of Cahokia that is unmarked by twentieth-century developments. Although we have resorted to Brackenridge's words to communicate the marvel that is Cahokia, it is our experiences at the site, modern warts and all, that have allowed us to delve further into how the Cahokians may have related to the land.

We have endeavored to provide a much broader visual array than aesthetically pleasing old photographs and artists' impressions. Throughout this book we have interwoven with the text a sequence of representations that mirror and emphasize the underlying structure of the volume. Through the course of the text, we replaced historic photographs and sketches by more clinical representations, a graphic device that is meant to symbolize the gradual illumination of Cahokia. The shroud that cloaks the site in the mysteries of time is slowly lifted, revealing a progressively clearer, more focused image. Artistic concepts of landscape representation parallel changing trends in archaeological research, becoming more precise over time, yet more removed from the scene. Subsurface interpretations, made possible through excavation and remote sensing technology, of the land beneath the site eventually come into play, adding to our understanding of the site.

Over the years, the Cahokia landscape has been depicted in diverse ways, including the standard overhead topographic and schematic portrayals. Although these views are extremely useful in archaeological site interpretation, we have chosen to supplement them with a series of on-the-ground perspectives of the site, placing Cahokia in the context of a lived-in space. These interpretive drawings incorporate not only day-to-day cultural activity but other elements of time as well, both short-term, as in seasonal cycles, and over longer periods, as exemplified in the evolution of subcommunities at Cahokia.

It is true that the interior's landscape as it looks today is not a direct guide to the past. Dunlop (1995, 18) writes that nineteenth-century settlement meant erasure: "settlers took the ground cover, took the mounds, took the trees, took every acre for use." In a sense, this is what the Cahokians did too with their massive program of earthmoving. So how do we respond to a landscape that is no longer visible?

46. Aerial view of the central portion of the Cahokia Mounds site as viewed from the east. The since demolished Falcon Drive-In is in the foreground, with housing developments visible in the background.

Removal of modern landscape elements does not return Cahokia to its Mississippian-period state. It does serve to remove or distance us, the modern inhabitants, from the scene. We argue that one way to approach the prehistoric situation is to learn from the ways that not only we but also historic groups have related to this land. Our landscape approach has allowed a broader perspective that incorporates change across time as well as across space. Using this approach, we have tapped elements of historic and modern land use that have allowed us to appreciate both the commonalities and the uniqueness of human experience at this place. The Cahokians dealt with problems, such as the maintenance of the mounds, that are still being grappled with today. On the other hand, a settlement on the scale of Mississippian Cahokia was not attained here before or since. Cahokia was unparalleled in the Eastern Woodlands throughout the entire prehistoric sequence.

Nearly all medium- to large-sized Mississippian towns had a principal mound that was grand in scale and multiterraced and that, together with a temple mound and other mounds, was arranged around a plaza—the basic components that made up a Mississippian mound center. The central area of Cahokia that is defined by these elements is approximately 200 hectares. This is about the same size as the entire site of Moundville (ca. 150 hectares), the next largest Mississippian site. The central area of Cahokia is three to ten times the size of what are considered large Mississippian towns, such as Kincaid, Angel, Lake George, and Winterville.

We have taken great pains to document how much bigger Monks Mound, the Grand Plaza, and the central core of Cahokia are in reference to other Mississippian sites. Yet, it is not simply the size of things that makes Cahokia different. It is the organization behind the multiplicity of the mounds and their integration that required another tier to maintain—demands and skills that would not have been required at other towns.

Though Cahokia was unparalleled in the Mississippian world, Cahokia was commensurate with other New World megacenters to the south. For example, site cores in the Mayan lowlands, as defined by the central plaza and major monuments at such Classic-period sites as Tikal, are on the order of 1 to 1.5 kilometers on a side. This is the distance that we noted as defining Cahokia's core. As we noted earlier, this distance, which defines a core area of massed monuments at Cahokia, appears related to the common human dimension of sight. We should point out that we are not comparing energetics involved in erecting and finishing the monuments, nor the density of structures within the core area.

Paleontologists are often confronted with size or scale transformations. The lesson learned is that profound size changes require structural changes, and we feel that this applies to the Cahokia/Mississippian situation too. Cahokia was not just a large Mississippian site; it was both structurally and organizationally different from other Mississippian centers. Regardless of what population estimate is ultimately accepted, Cahokia was certainly larger than any other Mississippian-period town. In addition, its population crossed a threshold that generates a multiplier effect. Lekson (1989) has argued, based on a cross-cultural study, that a resident population of around 2,500 is sufficient to initiate this multiplier, or accelerator, effect. We can infer that provisioning for feasts and lean times, mediating local and extralocal disputes, and orchestrating feasts and war parties were not carried out by a chief with a small retinue—and large retinues demand logistical support. In short, an infrastructure was needed to operate such a town.

Understanding changes in the organization of the Cahokia community in the context of the process of growth and decline is at the heart of understanding the site. A number of changes were effected at the beginning of the sequence that allowed Cahokia to diverge not only from its Emergent Mississippian roots but also from other settlements in the American Bottom and throughout the entire Southeast. Organizational changes at the interface of the Emergent Mississippian and Mississippian periods that are broadly defined across the Southeast include the formation of large, sedentary communities with relatively well developed community centers and the presence of mounds within village settings. Another change was the construction of subcommunities with orthogonal layouts tied to community-wide planning. Orthogonally aligned residential groupings are not limited to Cahokia. Examples abound in the Mississippian world of orthogonal structure alignments, from small villages without mounds, such as the Snodgrass site (Price and Griffin 1979) to larger mound towns such as Angel (Black 1967). We can even glean such arrangements from the descriptions of the Spanish entrada and from eighteenth-century accounts, like Bartram's.

Several other changes are seen at Cahokia that appear to be unique to this community. One of these is the change in scale signified by the construction of the immense Monks Mound and Grand Plaza. Another is that Cahokia also seems to have either hidden or obliterated organizational structures responsible for mid-range controls as part of a program that emphasized the importance of the community above all. In early Mississippian times there is evidence of a chief/commoner distinction but few other differentiations in the social structure. We have argued that this was a necessary component of the build-up of this great mound center.

Splintering the courtyard structure of Emergent Mississippian times and forcing people to reorganize in a way that emphasized communality created a vacuum that left the door open for subsequent power jockeying: when community-wide controls failed, mid-range controls arose again, although in a form different from those of earlier times. Hence, structural changes that allowed the creation of Cahokia provided the roots for its ultimate demise.

By the end of the Stirling phase (after A.D. 1100) at the latest, Cahokia began to lose both the orthogonality and the expansiveness of its subcommunities. Through a diversification in mounds, building sizes, and household arrangements, further distinctions in the social structure beyond that of chief/commoner became visible. The proliferation of mounds, even in places such as the ICT-II, harbored the roots for the emergence of mid-level organization and expression. Concomitantly, the move away from orthogonal planning in this community to that of a plazuela is a sign of growing independence. Emerson (1997) sees the emergence of civic-ritual nodal centers in the surrounding bottomlands as part of a Cahokia-driven process of sacralization (Pauketat 1994). In this view, the process is conceived of as a building-up from the top down, whereas the same process could be seen as a bottom-up disintegration.

We argue that these changes signal not only an increased visibility but also a strengthening of mid-level controls. These groups were arising at the expense of the community and challenging the chief's power, as mirrored in the deterioration of community-wide signatures and overall site organization. For example, the construction of the Central Palisade cleaved the early and important connections revolving around the southern mortuary precinct. It was this process of reorganization, with various groups and individuals jockeying to gain power, exacerbated by problems of environmental stress, that led to Cahokia's decline. The courtyard groups formed at this time were not the same as their Emergent Mississippian counterparts, which indicates that the social structure in Moorehead and later times was different as well. Though the size of the open area around which the houses cluster was approximately the same, Moorehead houses were much bigger and fewer of them were distributed around the courtyard. The countryside returns to a simpler lifestyle harking back to earlier times (Emerson 1997).

Understanding the history of the site, which involved first the symbolic construction of a community center that was then challenged over a lengthy period of instability, has been the result of the synthesis of our data, using an approach based on the landscape concept. Reanalysis of diverse data using this approach has also allowed us to make inroads into seeing Cahokia as a lived-in place. We have considered aspects such as spatial and temporal relationships on a human scale, immediate problems of living, including issues of land renewal and reclamation, planning and design, maintenance of earthworks, and technical ability. For these accomplishments we do not claim to have provided all the answers. We have presented an approach, not a theory. We can only hope that what we have done will encourage others to bring their theories and ideas to the table to explore these issues in more depth. It is also up to others, not to us, to decide if the direction we have taken is appropriate for use in their research and, if so, to choose those aspects that will be important in their conceptions of landscape, for landscape is always some chosen part of a whole.

Utilizing a landscape approach to understand the design and planning of Cahokia has enabled us to develop the most comprehensive theory to date concerning the spatial organizing principles behind this great mound center. Whether we are ultimately correct about all aspects of the design and planning of Cahokia remains to be seen; nevertheless, our analysis has demonstrated that Cahokia was consciously designed, built to inspire, support, and, some would say, celebrate a culture for over four hundred years. The designers of Cahokia used many design principles that are still used today with great effect to create urban spaces, namely, (1) the use of monumental scale to create a spirit of place, (2) the creation of a central focus and verticality to establish domain, (3) the use of cultural symbols in built forms to communicate social and political structure, (4) the placement of key features in the landscape to create visual recognition, (5) the repetition of similar forms and elements to reinforce cultural messages, (6) the use of proportion and alignments based on directionality to establish order and hierarchy, and, finally, (7) the creation of site symmetry based on directionality.

Nineteenth-century travel literature is characterized by an emotional connection with the landscape. It is also distinguished by what we now know were often misguided attempts at explanation and interpretation. Dunlop (1995, 15–16) describes the modern moundscape as having become a very quiet place. In contrast to accounts of a century ago, contemporary travel literature supplied to visitors does not offer conclusive explanations of the mounds and earthworks. This literature uses phrases such as "seems to indicate" and "offers clues to." At the interpretive center, visitors are not given an answer to what happened to Cahokia. Instead, they are given the opportunity to vote on this question. See-through boxes, labeled with different theories, are provided in a display. Visitors are invited to deposit coins in the box of their choice, providing a visual tally of the running debate on the question of the decline of this great mound center.

Cahokia, like many other mound centers, is controlled by park systems and managers that limit access. Exhibits and interpretive programs are offered, but rarely cabins, picnic areas, and the like. The shelters, pavilions, and camping spots found across Cahokia as recently as ten years ago are now gone. Unlike nineteenth-century visitors, tourists are not permitted to take souvenirs or otherwise disturb the site—these properties are no longer to be touched by travelers. Though it is a necessary aspect of preservation, this policy reinforces the distancing of the visitor from the landscape.

We do not argue with policies that act to preserve the Cahokia site for the future; rather, we suggest that we need to find alternative means to make the experience of Cahokia, for both visitors and readers, more immediate. We must find an acceptable means for them to connect with Cahokia and to provide an explanation of the past. We think that one avenue is a landscape approach that incorporates personal experience. A call to relate to this place on a personal, or human, level, as we have done, rather than as detached scholars, may supply an answer.

Envisioning the evolving landscape that is Cahokia on a more personal, or human, level has raised some interesting questions in our minds. Did the Cahokians of A.D. 1200 and later think that things were getting worse or better? Houses were bigger than before, exotic goods were more widely distributed among individuals within the society, there were reduced demands in terms of construction, the site was less crowded, there was evidence of increased household autonomy, and habitation was again concentrated in areas of prime real estate surrounding Monks Mound. All of these changes could be seen as convincing signs that individuals were faring better than before. Yet, certainly by A.D. 1150 at the latest, the Mississippians were aware of the disintegration of Cahokia as they knew it.

Another question returns us again to a consideration of Monks Mound. Do we consider this seminal mound a work in progress or was it finished? Perhaps work halted on the mound because the focus of power changed. For example, the major structure on Monks Mound, rebuilt after the Stirling phase, was considerably smaller and lacked the complexity of the earlier building. The work that goes into such a mound is a direct corollary of the power that the chief can muster, or at least a mark of his power to convince people to participate in such projects. If the tenor of chief-directed architecture of Lohmann and early Stirling times had continued, instead of being challenged by more private concerns, we wonder how much bigger

Monks Mound might have become. In view of the instability of the slopes, however, further additions could only have been made to interior portions of the summit.

In the nineteenth century, descriptions of Monks Mound and other mounds were couched in comparisons to the pyramids and other great human achievements. We have compared Cahokia to Washington, D.C., in hopes that this modern analog will resonate with our readers not as something ancient and foreign, but as something that many of them may have experienced, that will encapsulate for them the magnificence and monumentality of moving through this space. Analogs such as these are important, but in concentrating on the behemoth nature of these earthworks, on the greatest, the biggest, the most populated, and so forth, it seems that the smaller details are lost.

We have argued that new ways to evoke a response to the past are needed and that one means is to cull it from the store of common human experience. Charles Dickens (1893, 211–12) talks about the "pernicious climate" of the American Bottom: "There was the swamp, the bush, the perpetual chorus of frogs, the rank unseemly growth, the unwholesome steaming earth." Dickens offers a view that is not myth, at least in the sense of a cleaned-up version of the past, and we think that people can relate to this vision as well. Landscape—humans relating to the land—is the essence of our approach: a means of engaging ourselves and our readers with Cahokia. And this is why we have used Brackenridge's words and ideas so extensively—because we feel that his call for a widespread appreciation of the mounds still needs to be answered.

The physical landform of Cahokia today is not a direct guide to the past—indeed, there have been many distinctive changes. But the present-day Cahokia landscape, as a place experienced by us, has provided a new way to respond to a past that also occurred at this place. With the professionalization of archaeology, the mounds became separated from the public milieu. No longer were the mounds as open to public investigation and explanation; they were increasingly restricted to a growing group of professionals. This separation also led to restricting public experience, public involvement, and, ultimately, public interest. The efforts of the first professional archaeologists demonstrated that the mounds were not built by a race far removed from us, but somehow it has taken us until now to appreciate that Cahokia was lived in by ordinary people engaged in ordinary activities.

We have employed a landscape approach to provide a view of Cahokia and the relationship the Cahokians had with the land that is informed both by archaeological knowledge and our experiences at the site. Lessons learned from countless ethnographies of the Americas and the cross-cultural study of chiefdom level societies are often employed to set the parameters for a generalized understanding of Native American conceptualizations of the human-environment relationship. We have touched upon these briefly, but will leave it to others to delve into this subject more deeply.

At the cornerstone of this understanding is the distinction between

47. The Birger figurine, recovered from a Stirling-phase mortuary precinct near the boundary of the Cahokia site along with the Keller figurine (fig. 48), depicts a women cultivating the ground. She rests on a circular base that is in the form of a snake, which could be conceptualized as the circular base of a conical mound. A. Front view. B. Rear view. Courtesy of the Illinois Transportation Archaeological Research Program, University of Illinois.

humans and nature. As bearers of culture, humans separate themselves from the natural world while at the same time embracing it. This separation derives from a bundle of psychological necessities concerning fear of the natural world, a need for group cohesion, and as part and parcel of fitting humans metaphysically into a conceptualization of the world. Objects and relationships are selected from the natural world as moralizing tales (myths), survival mechanisms (taboos), and symbols (totems and icons).

The Cahokians would have pondered on and created dynamic relationships with the natural world in this fashion. We will never fathom most of the specifics of this. The Cahokians did not leave us with written records; hence our interpretations of their landscape have been based on archaeological remains of their designs on the land. Another potential source for understanding the relationship that the Mississippians had with the land is

48. The Keller figurine complements the circular base of the Birger figurine with a square base that has analogies with the square base of the truncated platform mound. This figurine, possibly of a woman, is either transforming corn into flour or causing rain. Either interpretation would contrast with the Birger figurine, which represents the underworld and vegetative growth. A. Side view. B. Front view. Courtesy of the Illinois Transportation Archaeological Research Program, University of Illinois.

Mississippian art, yet depictions of phenomena other than people and animals are rare. This is not because they lacked the technical ability to depict them in exacting detail (Emerson 1989). The decorative arts executed in wood, stone, shell, bone, and ceramics from the eleventh through fifteenth centuries in the Mississippian world rival those of others around the globe (e.g., Philips and Brown 1978, 1984). Appropriately for us, a glimpse into the Mississippian way of thinking is evident in the Birger figurine (fig. 47), recovered from the American Bottom region. This figurine was found 3.5 kilometers east of Monks Mound (Emerson and Jackson 1984).

Emerson (1989, 1997) and others (Prentice 1986) have argued that the figurine depicts a scene that could be taken out of a myth or story involving important themes such as fertility, serpents, horticulture, and female deities. In simple terms the scene depicted is a woman who is both rooted to and cultivating the earth, which takes the form of a snake. The prominent position of a woman is rare in other Mississippian media. To our knowledge, the only time land is depicted in Mississippian art it is connected with a woman. Cosmological elements signified are the underworld as the snake and regeneration/fertility as the woman. The woman is the necessary ingredient to growth; gourd tendrils entwine her body. It is significant that the sculpture, as is the snake, is in the round, encapsulating the cyclical view of time. Signs of the upper world, the sun or birds, are lacking; these are often associated with males, specifically chiefs and warriors. Women are rooted to the earth, commune with it, and mediate with the underworld. The Birger figurine shows land connected with women, revealing a glimpse into Mississippian thought that we have not incorporated into our understanding of the landscape. Perhaps future landscape scholarship should consider, along with Mississippian symbolism, the role of gender in the creation of landscape and in the actions performed within this landscape.

Recovered from the same occupation together with the Birger figurine was another that introduces a different perspective. In this case, the figure (fig. 48), presumably a woman, is depicted grinding grain with a mano and metate. The figure rests on a rectangular or squared base. This shape reintroduces the question of platform and conical, or square and circle, that appear throughout the Cahokia site. In the case of the figurines, the circular base is entwined with nature, growth, and the underworld or death, whereas the squared base is associated with the transformation of a natural product (grain) into a cultural product (flour). Rain symbolism around the squared base also links it with the sky or upper world.

Squares or other shapes that imply orthogonality are easy to decipher for westerners raised in the Cartesian system. Thus, we have readily noted elements of them in the layout of the site. Circles, on the other hand, we have only hazily identified. We have noted a circular element in the configuration of the borrow pits, which in turn circumscribed, we argue, the Central Precinct. We recognize that we need to continue to reorient ourselves to recognize circular relationships that may have been important in the Mississippian landscape.

In terms of mounds, we have contrasted squares and circles, conicals and platforms, and have suggested that together they served as a basic design or ordering principle at Cahokia. We have pointed out how, within a topological system, these ordered pairs defined the Grand Plaza, the Central Precinct, and a southern mortuary precinct. It has been suggested that the squared, or platform, mound, as a substructure for culture, was symbolically tied to chiefs, warriors, and the upper world, whereas the circular, or conical, mound tied the earth to the underworld and to a cycle of regeneration. In tandem, the pairing of conical and platform mounds thus made sense of the world, connecting the basic elements of underworld-earth-upper world and encompassing the transformation of nature into culture and the cycle of birth, death, and regeneration.

Continuing to unravel the varied threads involved in change at Cahokia remains our goal. Removing modern features from the landscape serves to mask the visible signs of change. The essence of the nineteenth century was that it was a period of intense change. This was also the nature of Cahokia during the Emergent Mississippian and Mississippian periods. The rates of discernible change certainly surpassed that of anything we see at the site today. Without an understanding of this, we cannot hope to capture what was prehistoric Cahokia.

Throughout the period of intense change, Monks Mound provided a centralizing and stabilizing element. It is this stupendous earthwork that has become synonymous with Cahokia. Is the behemoth nature of this mound and site, however, Cahokia's only claim to fame?

For us, the Grand Plaza has also become a metaphor for the site. In tandem with Monks Mound it seems to embody much that we find fascinating and illuminating. Like Monks Mound it is immense. Unlike Monks Mound, however, its message is not so obvious. Like an iceberg, much of the story of the Grand Plaza is hidden below the surface.

Continuing work on Monks Mound has produced data that resonate with our research in the Grand Plaza, encapsulating critical elements of the site's history. The 2-by-2-meter excavation unit at the base of the west slope of Monks Mound captures this sequence of transitions, gaps, and erasures (fig. 41). Testing in this area revealed remains dating to the beginning and end of the sequence, enveloping the occupation that was Mississippian Cahokia. At the base of the unit were truncated Late Woodland features overlain by Moorehead and Sand Prairie materials. Missing is the stuff in between relating to the florescence of Mississippian culture (or the essence of what has become known as Cahokia) that was realized during the late Emergent Mississippian period and into the Lohmann and Stirling phases of the Mississippian period. This gap, though, provides an important story. It aptly illustrates that landscape is not necessarily cumulative. It also indicates a break with earlier patterns and that change and residence resettlement were commonplace at Cahokia. Most buildings and residential areas present during the initial buildup of the site were disturbed or removed. Earthmoving, including borrowing, building, and reclamation, was continuous. Reoccupation of this portion of the site late in the sequence was mirrored elsewhere in the Central Precinct.

As the Mississippians struggled to patch the west side of Monks Mound, sediments washed down from the Second Terrace, covering the exposed Late Woodland and Emergent Mississippian features. In their efforts to repair the mound, the Mississippians employed new technologies, i.e., tamping, developed over centuries of mound maintenance. Even though we have postulated that Monks Mound provided a stabilizing influence during the Mississippian occupation, recent work shows that we cannot conceptualize this earthwork as a big pile of dirt that sat there unchanged since it was raised. This mound, like the others, was not something built at a single point in time. Yes, it went through a building process, but it was also rebuilt, modified, maintained, and perhaps even restructured. Failure of the mound and the cost of maintenance were issues during prehistoric times, as they still are today. Another way of seeing landscape is to view it not as a final product, such as promoted by a contour map or a reconstruction, but as an ongoing human product.

Currently managers have to deal with issues of preservation and maintenance that are in some ways different from those faced by the Mississippians, yet in some ways the same. The slope failures of Monks Mound during the 1980s precipitated a flurry of activity directed ultimately toward the preservation of this earthwork. Instead of making emergency repairs, site managers decided to step back and first gather information on the internal structure of the mound and the causes of the slope failure. Not only would geotechnical and archaeological studies be employed to arrive at an approach for maintaining the mound, but this information would also funnel into an evaluation of the impacts that these actions would have on the architectural and archaeological integrity of the mound. In addition, information derived from a parallel process undertaken to assess the philosophical and ethical implications of any proposed stabilization and restoration efforts figured prominently in this evaluation.

A variety of engineering solutions were put forward in response to the slumping problem. Among other things they included reinforcement by building a massive 10-meter-high berm around the entire mound; capping it with a thick veneer of concrete; pinning the mound in place like a captured beetle by pounding 35-meter-long pins through it at close intervals; and the perennial crowd favorite, vitrification. This latter solution cries for an explanation: it was suggested that the mound could be stabilized by running enormous amounts of electrical energy through it and producing what would be in essence the world's largest brick.

A working meeting was convened to discuss issues of restoration, stabilization, investigative excavations, and public interpretation. A number of opinions regarding potential solutions to the problem resulted from differing perceptions of the mound as primarily an "architectural monument," a "data base," or a "public interpretive resource." Those perceiving the mound as architecture strongly urged the construction of a large, surrounding berm to preserve its form. Researchers focusing on the informational aspect suggested excavations to retrieve information that might be lost through the slumping process. Those responsible for interpreting the site to the public were concerned about any approach, such as massive berming, that would drastically modify the visual fabric of the mound and surrounding area.

Managers faced a basic dilemma in reconciling the various camps, for it seemed that all engineering actions to "save" or "preserve" the mound carried negative impacts on the integrity of either the archaeology, architecture, or visual fabric of the mound. Ultimately, none of the proposed solutions were attempted; a course of passive management was chosen instead. For a time, managers breathed a sigh of relief—monitoring of the slump zones showed little movement for almost a decade. Then came the renewed cycle of failure that followed the record rainfalls of 1993–1995. It is hoped that installation of five drains on the western side of the mound will preserve Monks Mound's visual and architectural integrity by eliminating or at least slowing the rate of slope failures while minimizing the loss of archaeological information.

Cahokia fascinates people. A visual interpretation of what Cahokia was like during Mississippian times, whether it is on the land in an archaeological park or in a drawing, such as the landscape drawings we have presented (figs. 21, 22, 23, and 42), can serve as an immediate and effective way to impart a sense of the past. Visual fabric is critical to an archaeological landscape approach; we cannot imagine how a landscape could be captured solely with heights, widths, volumes, counts, and other measures. The awe one feels when viewing the imposing Monks Mound cannot be imparted by a description of its height or areal extent. And without archaeological data, how are we to comprehend the problems and methods involved in and even the reasons for construction, modification, and maintenance? Our visual representations need to be informed with archaeological data in order to provide a more accurate and robust idea of how the site appeared, was utilized, and was reacted to over the entire time of use. We have combined both visual images and archaeological data in our landscape analysis of Cahokia.

The recognition of the monuments at Cahokia as architectural features has also been an important component of our landscape approach. Consideration of design and planning lend a new and profitable perspective. In many people's minds, however, viewing the mounds as architectural monuments presupposes that they are unchanging. We hope, if nothing else, that our approach has demonstrated the fallacy of this view.

SELECTED REFERENCES

SITE AREA	REFERENCE
General site data	Fowler 1997; Moorehead 1929
Dunham Tract	Bareis 1967; Dalan and Ollendorf 1991; Pauketat 1991, 1993a
Falcon Drive-In	Gums and Holley 1991
Fairmont City, west margins	Gums et al. 1989; Lopinot et al. 1993; Witty 1993
Grand Plaza	Dalan 1993b; Holley et al. 1993
ICT-I	Benchley and DePuydt 1982; Fowler et al. 1980
ICT-II	Collins 1990; Holley 1989; Woods 1993a
Kunnemann mound group	Holley 1995; Pauketat 1993b
Palisade, east	Anderson 1973; Dalan 1989a, 1989b; Iseminger et al. 1990
Palisade, south	Holley et al. 1990
Powell mound group	Ahler and DePuydt 1987; Bareis 1975b; Griffin 1960b; O'Brien 1972; Titterington 1938
Ramey Field	Benchley 1981; Vander Leest 1980
Rouch mound group	Holley et al. 1992
Tippetts mound group	Benchley and DePuydt 1982; Dalan et al. 1994; Fowler et al. 1980; Holley et al.1995
Tract 15A (woodhenge)	Pauketat 1993a, 1994; Wittry 1996
Tract 15B, Merrell Tract	Kelly 1980, 1996; Salzer 1975
West Borrow Pit group	Holley et al. 1996, 1998; Watters et al. 1997

MOUNDS	
31	Caldwell 1959
34	Perino 1957
38 (Monks Mound)	Bareis 1975a, 1975b; Benchley 1975; Collins et al. 1986; Emerson and Woods 1990; Mc Gimsey and Wiant 1984; Reed et al. 1968; Skele 1988; Walthall and Benchley 1987; Williams 1975
48	Ringberg 1996
49	Pauketat and Rees 1996
51	Bareis 1975a; Chmurny 1973; Pauketat 1997b
55	Smith 1973
56	Dalan et al. 1993
57	Dalan and Watters 1994
59, 60	Watters et al. 1997
72	Fowler 1991

BIBLIOGRAPHY

Abrams, E. M.
    1989   Architecture and Energy, an Evolutionary Perspective. In *Archaeological Method and Theory,* edited by M. B. Schiffer, 1:47–87. University of Arizona Press, Tucson.
    1994   *How the Maya Built Their World.* University of Texas Press, Austin.

Adair, J.
    1930 [1775] *The History of the American Indians.* Wautauga Press, Johnson City, Tenn.

Adler, M. A., and R. H. Wilshusen
    1990   Large-Scale Interactive Facilities in Tribal Societies: Cross-Cultural and Southwestern Examples. *World Archaeology* 22:133–46.

Ahler, Steven R., and P. J. DePuydt
    1987   *A Report on the 1931 Powell Mound Excavations, Madison County, Illinois.* Reports of Investigations, no. 43. Illinois State Museum, Springfield.

Anderson, D.
    1990   *Political Change in Chiefdom Societies: Cycling in the Late Prehistoric Southeastern United States.* Ph.D. diss., Department of Anthropology, University of Michigan. University Microfilms, Ann Arbor, Mich.

Anderson, J.
    1973   A Cahokia Palisade Sequence. In *Explorations into Cahokia Archaeology,* edited by M. L. Fowler, 89–99. Rev. ed. Bulletin 7. Illinois Archaeological Survey, Urbana.

Appleyard, D., G. T. Moore, and R. G. Golledge
    1976   *Environmental Knowing: Theories, Research, and Methods.* Dowen, Hutchinson, and Ross, Stroudsburg, Pa.

Arnheim, R.
    1977   *The Dynamics of Architectural Form.* University of California Press, Berkeley and Los Angeles.

Asch, D. L., and N. B. Asch
    1985   Prehistoric Plant Cultivation in West-Central Illinois. In *Prehistoric Food Production in North America,* edited by R. I. Ford, 149–204. Anthropological Papers of the Museum of Anthropology, no. 75. University of Michigan, Ann Arbor.

Atwell, K. A., and M. D. Conner
    1991   *The Kuhlman Mound Group and Late Woodland Mortuary Behavior in the Mississippi River Valley of West-Central Illinois.* Kampsville Archaeological Center, Center for American Archaeology, Kampsville, Ill.

Baerreis, D. A., and R. Bryson
    1965   Climatic Episodes and the Dating of Mississippian Cultures. *The Wisconsin Archeologist* 46:203–20.
Baerreis, D. A., A. B. Reid, and J. E. Kutzbach
    1976   Climate and Culture in the Western Great Lakes Region. *Midcontinential Journal of Archaeology* 1:39–57.
Baillou, C. de
    1961   A Contribution to the Mythology and Conceptual World of the Cherokee Indians. *Ethnohistory* 8:93–102.
Bareis, C. J.
    1967   *Interim Report on Preliminary Site Examination Undertaken in Archaeological Section A of FAI 255 South of Business 40 in the Interstate Portion of Area S-34–4 of the Cahokia Site, St. Clair County, Illinois.* Research Reports, no. 1. Department of Anthropology, University of Illinois, Urbana.
    1975a Report of 1971 University of Illinois-Urbana Excavations at the Cahokia Site. In *Cahokia Archaeology: Field Reports,* edited by M. L. Fowler, 9–11. Research Series, Papers in Anthropology, no. 3. Illinois State Museum, Springfield.
    1975b Report of 1972 University of Illinois-Urbana Excavations at the Cahokia Site. In *Cahokia Archaeology: Field Reports,* edited by M. L. Fowler, 12–15. Research Series, Papers in Anthropology, no. 3. Illinois State Museum, Springfield.
    1976   *The Knoebel Site, St. Clair County, Illinois.* Circular no. 1. Illinois Archaeological Survey, Urbana.
Bareis, C. J., and J. W. Porter, eds.
    1984   *American Bottom Archaeology: A Summary of the FAI-270 Project Contribution to the Culture History of the Mississippi River Valley.* University of Illinois Press, Urbana.
Barker, A.W., and T. R. Pauketat, eds.
    1992   *Lords of the Southeast: Social Inequality and the Native Elites of Southeastern North America.* Archaeological Papers, no. 3. American Anthropological Association, Washington, D.C.
Barrell, J.
    1972   *The Idea of Landscape and Sense of Place 1730–1840.* Cambridge University Press, Cambridge.
Bartram, W.
    1909 [1789] Observations on the Creek and Cherokee Indians. Reprint, *Transactions of the American Ethnological Society* 3:1–81.
    1955 [1792] *Travels of William Batram.* Reprint, Dover Publications, Mineola, N.Y.
Baum, Rev. Henry Mason
    1903   Antiquities of the United States: The Cahokia Mounds. *Records of the Past* (Washington, D.C.) 2:215–22.
Benchley, E. D.
    1975   Summary Report of Excavations on the Southwest Corner of the First Terrace of Monks Mound: 1968, 1969, 1971. In *Cahokia Archaeology: Field Reports,* edited by M. L. Fowler, 16–20. Research Series, Papers in Anthropology, no. 3. Illinois State Museum, Springfield.
    1981   *Summary Report on Controlled Surface Collections of the Ramey Field, Cahokia Mounds Historic Site, Madison County, Illinois.* Reports of Investiga-

tions, no. 51. Archaeological Research Laboratory, University of Wisconsin-Milwaukee.

Benchley, E. D., and P. DePuydt
    1982 *Final Report of 1980 Test Excavations at the Interpretive Center Tract, Cahokia Mounds Historic Site.* Reports of Investigations, no. 61. Archaeological Research Laboratory, University of Wisconsin-Milwaukee.

Bender, B.
    1992 Theorising Landscapes, and the Prehistoric Landscapes of Stonehenge. *Man* 27:735–55.
    1993 *Landscape Politics and Perspectives.* Berg, Providence, R.I., and Oxford.

Bennett, J. W.
    1945 *Archaeological Explorations in Jo Davies County, Illinois.* University of Chicago Press, Chicago.

Berger, J.
    1980 *About Looking.* Pantheon Books, New York.

Black, G. A.
    1967 *Angel Site.* 2 vols. Indiana Historic Society, Indianapolis.

Bohannon, C. F.
    1972 *Excavations at the Pharr Mounds and Bear Creek Site.* USDI-NPS, Office of Archaeology and Historic Preservation, Washington, D.C.

Bourdieu, P.
    1973 The Berber House. In *Rules and Meanings: The Anthropology of Everyday Knowledge,* edited by M. Douglas, 98–110. Penguin Books, Harmondsworth, England.
    1977 *Outline of a Theory of Practice.* Translated by R. Nice. Cambridge University Press, Cambridge.

Brackenridge, H. M.
    1811 Unsigned article. *Missouri Gazette,* January 9.
    1818 On the Population and Tumuli of the Aborigines of North America. Letter from H. M. Brackenridge to Thomas Jefferson. Read October 1, 1813. *Transactions of the American Philosophical Society* 1:151–59, Philadelphia.
    1868 *Recollections of Persons and Places in the West.* 2d ed. Lippincott, Philadelphia.
    1962 [1814] *Views of Louisiana Together with a Journal of a Voyage up the Missouri River, in 1811.* Quadrangle Books, Chicago.

Bradley, R.
    1984 Studying Monuments. In *Neolithic Studies,* edited by R. Bradley and J. Gardiner. BAR British Series, no. 133.

Braidwood, R. J.
    1937 *Mounds in the Plain of Antioch: An Archaeological Survey.* Oriental Institute Publications, no. 47. University of Chicago, Chicago.

Braidwood, R. J., and L. S. Braidwood
    1960 *Excavations in the Plain of Antioch.* Oriental Institute Publications, no. 61. University of Chicago, Chicago.

Brain, J. B.
    1989 *Winterville: Late Prehistoric Culture Contact in the Lower Mississippi Valley.* Archaeological Report no. 23. Mississippi Department of Archives and History, Jackson.

Brand, S.
    1994 *How Buildings Learn.* Penguin Books, New York.

Brine, L.
    1894   *Travels Amongst the American Indians, Their Ancient Earthworks and Temples.*
           Sampson Low, Marston, London.
Brink, McDonough, and Company
    1882   *History of St. Clair County, Illinois.* Brink, McDonough, Philadelphia.
Brown, J. A.
    1981   The Search for Rank in Prehistoric Burials. In *The Archaeology of Death,*
           edited by E. Chapman, I. Kinnes, and K. Randsborg, 25–37. Cambridge
           University Press, Cambridge.
    1997   The Archaeology of Ancient Religion in the Eastern Woodlands. *Annual
           Review of Anthropology* 26:465–85.
Bryson, R. A., and W. M. Wendland
    1967   Tentative Climatic Patterns for Some Late Glacial and Post-Glacial
           Episodes in Central North America. In *Life, Land, and Water,* edited by W.
           G. Mayer-Oaks, 271–98. University of Manitoba Press, Winnipeg, Canada.
Buck, S.
    1917   *Illinois in 1818.* University of Illinois Press, Chicago.
Bushnell, D. I., Jr.
    1904   *The Cahokia and Surrounding Mound Groups.* Papers of the Peabody Mu-
           seum of American Archaeology and Ethnology. Harvard University, Cam-
           bridge, Mass.
    1967 [1904]*The Cahokia and Surrounding Mound Groups.* Reprint, Kraus, New York.
Butlin, R. A.
    1993   *Historical Geography: Through the Gates of Space and Time.* Edward Arnold,
           London.
Butzer, K. W.
    1978   Cultural Perspectives on Geographical Space. In *Dimensions of Human Ge-
           ography: Essays in Some Familiar and Neglected Themes,* edited by K. W.
           Butzer, 1–14. Research Paper no. 186. Department of Geography, Univer-
           sity of Chicago, Chicago.
    1982   *Archaeology as Human Ecology: Method and Theory for a Contextual Ap-
           proach.* Cambridge University Press, Cambridge.
Caldwell, J. R.
    1959   Illinois Archaeology and the Museum. *Living Museum* 21:414–15.
Charles, D. K., S. R. Leigh, and J. E. Buikstra, eds.
    1988   *The Archaic and Woodland Cemeteries at the Elizabeth Site in the Lower Illi-
           nois Valley.* Kampsville Archaeological Center Research Series, vol. 7. Cen-
           ter for American Archaeology, Kampsville, Ill.
Cherry, J. F.
    1978   Generalization and the Archaeology of the State. In *Social Organisation
           and Settlement: Contributions from Anthropology, Archaeology, and Geography.*
           Part 2, edited by D. Green, C. Haselgrove, and M. Spriggs, 411–37. BAR
           International Series, no. 47 (ii), Supplementary.
Chmurny, W.
    1973   *The Ecology of the Middle Mississippian Occupation of the American Bottom.*
           Ph.D. diss., Department of Anthropology, University of Illinois. Univer-
           sity Microfilms, Ann Arbor, Mich.
Cole, F. C., R. Bell, J. Bennett, J. Caldwell, N. Emerson, R. MacNeish, K. Orr, and R. Willis
    1951   *Kincaid: A Prehistoric Illinois Metropolis.* University of Chicago Press, Chicago.

Collins, J. M.
1990   *The Archaeology of the Cahokia Mounds ICT-II: Site Structure.* Illinois Cultural Resources Study no. 10. Illinois Historic Preservation Agency, Springfield.
1997   Cahokia Settlement and Social Structures as Viewed from the ICT-II. In *Cahokia: Domination and Ideology in the Mississippian World,* edited by T. R. Pauketat and T. E. Emerson, 124–40. University of Nebraska Press, Lincoln.

Collins, J. M., and M. L. Chalfant
1993   A Second-Terrace Perspective on Monks Mound. *American Antiquity* 58:319–32.

Collins, J. M., M. L. Chalfant, and G. R. Holley
1986   *Archaeological Testing of the Slump Area on the West Face of Monks Mound, Madison County, Illinois.* Report submitted to Illinois Historic Preservation Agency, Springfield.

Collins, J. M., M. Skele, and C. A. Sweitzer
1993   Some Modern C-Transforms at Cahokia: A Conversation with Clyde Sweitzer. In *Highways to the Past: Essays in Illinois Archaeology in Honor of Charles J. Bareis,* edited by T. E. Emerson, D. L. McElrath, and A. J. Fortier. *Illinois Archaeology* 5:4–13. Illinois Archaeological Survey, Urbana.

Conzen, Michael P., ed.
1990   *The Making of the American Landscape.* Unwin Hyman, Boston.

Cook, S. F., and R. F. Heizer
1965   *Studies on the Chemical Analysis of Archaeological Sites.* University of California Press, Berkeley and Los Angeles.

Cosgrove, D.
1985   Prospect, Perspective, and the Evolution of the Landscape Idea. *Transactions of the Institute of British Geographers* 10:45–62.

Cosgrove, Denis E.
1978   *Women Take Issue.* Centre for Contemporary Cultural Studies, Hutchinson, London.
1983   Towards a Radical Cultural Geography. *Antipode* 15:1–11.
1984   *Social Formation and Symbolic Landscape.* Croom Helm, London.

Crone, P.
1989   *Pre-Industrial Societies.* Basil Blackwell, Oxford.

Crook, A. R.
1916   The Composition and Origin of Monks Mound. *Transactions of the Illinois Academy of Science* 9:82–84, Springfield.
1922   The Origin of the Cahokia Mounds. Bulletin of the Illinois State Museum, Springfield, May 1922.

Crumley, C. L., and W. H. Marquardt
1990   Landscape: A Unifying Concept in Regional Analysis. In *Interpreting Space: GIS and Archaeology,* edited by K. M. S. Allen, S. W. Green, and E. B. W. Zubrow, 73–79. Taylor and Francis, London.

Cutts, S., D. Reason, J. Williams, L. Burckhardt, G. Murray, J. Bevis, and T. A. Clark
1987   *The Unpainted Landscape.* Corale Press, London.

Dalan, R. A.
1989a Electromagnetic Reconnaissance of the Central Palisade at the Cahokia Mounds State Historic Site. *The Wisconsin Archeologist* 70:309–32.

1989b *Geophysical Investigations of the Prehistoric Cahokia Palisade Sequence.* Illinois Cultural Resources Study no. 8. Illinois Historic Preservation Agency, Springfield.

1991 Defining Archaeological Features with Electromagnetic Surveys at the Cahokia Mounds State Historic Site. *Geophysics* 56:1280–87.

1993a Issues of Scale in Archaeogeophysical Research. In *Effects of Scale on Archaeological and Geoscientific Perspectives,* edited by J. K. Stein and A. R. Linse, 67–78. Special Paper no. 283. Geologic Society of America, Boulder, Colo.

1993b *Landscape Modification at the Cahokia Mounds Site: Geophysical Evidence of Cultural Change.* Ph.D. diss., University of Minnesota. University Microfilms, Ann Arbor, Mich.

1997 The Construction of Mississippian Cahokia. In *Cahokia: Domination and Ideology in the Mississippian World,* edited by T. R. Pauketat and T. E. Emerson, 89–102. University of Nebraska Press, Lincoln.

Dalan, R. A., and S. K. Banerjee

1996 Soil Magnetism: An Approach for Examining Archaeological Landscapes. *Geophysical Research Letters* 23:185–88.

1998 Solving Archaeological Problems Using Techniques of Soil Magnetism. *Geoarchaeology* 13:3–36.

Dalan, R. A., G. R. Holley, and H. W. Watters Jr.

1993 *An Assessment of Moorehead's Investigations at Mound 56, Cahokia Mounds State Historic Site.* Submitted to Illinois Historic Preservation Agency, Springfield.

Dalan, R. A., and A. L. Ollendorf

1991 *Report on the 1990 SIUE-Cahokia Mounds Field School in Geoarchaeology.* Submitted to Illinois Historic Preservation Agency, Springfield.

Dalan, R. A., and H. W. Watters Jr.

1994 *Determining the Original Form of Mississippian Mounds.* Report on file. Illinois Historic Preservation Agency, Springfield.

Dalan, R. A., H. W. Watters Jr., and S. K. Banerjee

1996 The Application of Soil Magnetic Techniques for Determining the Original Form of Prehistoric Earthworks. In *Proceedings of the Sixty-sixth Annual Meeting of the Society of Exploration Geophysicists,* 1:790–93.

Dalan, R. A., H. W. Watters Jr., G. R. Holley, and W. I. Woods

1994 *Sixth Annual Cahokia Mounds Field School: Understanding Mound Construction.* Submitted to Illinois Historic Preservation Agency, Springfield.

Deetz, J.

1990 Prologue, Landscapes as Cultural Statements. In *Earth Patterns: Essays in Landscape Archaeology,* edited by W. M. Kelso and R. Most, 1–4. University Press of Virginia, Charlottesville and London.

DePratter, C. B.

1983 *Late Prehistoric and Early Historic Chiefdoms in the Southeastern United States.* Ph.D. diss., University of Georgia. University Microfilms, Ann Arbor, Mich.

Dickens, C.

1893 *American Notes and Reprinted Pieces.* Chapman and Hall, London.

Dillehay, T. D.

1990 Mapuche Ceremonial Landscapes, Social Recruitment and Resource Rights. *World Archaeology* 22:223–41.

Donley-Reid, L.
    1990   A Structuring Structure: The Swahili House. In *Domestic Architecture and the Use of Space,* edited by S. Kent, 114–26. Cambridge University Press, Cambridge.

Douglas, M.
    1966   *Purity and Danger: An Analysis of Concepts of Pollution and Taboo.* Praeger, New York
    1991   [1975] *Implicit Meanings: Essays in Anthropology.* Reprint, Routledge and Kegan Paul, London and Boston.

Dragoo, D. W.
    1976   Some Aspects of Eastern North American Prehistory: A Review. *American Antiquity* 41:3–27.

Duncan, J. S.
    1980   The Superorganic in American Cultural Geography. *Annals of the Association of American Geographers* 70:181–98.
    1990   *The City as Text: The Politics of Landscape Interpretation in the Kandyan Kingdom.* Cambridge University Press, Cambridge.

Duncan, J. S., and N. G. Duncan
    1988   (Re)Reading the Landscape. *Environment and Planning D: Society and Space* 6:117–26.

Dunlop, M. H.
    1995   *Sixty Miles from Contentment: Traveling the Nineteenth-Century American Interior.* Basic Books, New York.

Dunnell, R. C.
    1992   The Notion Site. In *Space, Time, and Archaeological Landscapes,* edited by J. Rossignol and L. Wandsnider, 21–42. Plenum Press, New York.

Earle, T. K.
    1987   Chiefdoms in Archaeological and Ethnohistorical Perspective. *Annual Review of Anthropology* 16:279–308.
    1991   *Chiefdoms: Power, Economy, and Ideology.* Cambridge University Press, Cambridge.

Emerson, T. E.
    1989   Water, Serpents, and the Underworld: An Exploration into Cahokia Symbolism. In *The Southeastern Ceremonial Complex Artifacts and Analysis,* edited by P. Galloway, 45–92. University of Nebraska Press, Lincoln.
    1991   Some Perspectives on Cahokia and the Northern Mississippian Expansion. In *Cahokia and the Hinterlands: Middle Mississippian Cultures of the Midwest,* edited by T. E. Emerson and R. Barry Lewis, 221–36. University of Illinois Press, Urbana.
    1997   *Cahokia and the Archaeology of Power.* University of Alabama Press, Tuscaloosa.

Emerson, T. E., and D. K. Jackson
    1984   *The BBB Motor Site.* University of Illinois Press, Urbana.

Emerson, T. E., and R. B. Lewis, eds.
    1991   *Cahokia and the Hinterlands: Middle Mississippian Cultures of the Midwest.* University of Illinois Press, Urbana.

Emerson, T. E., and G. R. Milner
    1982   Community Organization and Settlement Patterns of Peripheral Mississippian Sites in the American Bottom, Illinois. Paper presented at the

Forty-seventh Annual Meeting of the Society for American Archaeology, Minneapolis, Minn.

Emerson, T. E., and W. I. Woods

1990   The Slumping of the Great Knob: An Archaeological and Geotechnic Case Study of the Stability of a Great Earthen Mound. In *Sixth International Conference on the Conservation of Earthen Architecture: Adobe 90 Preprints*, edited by N. Agnew, M. Taylor, and A. A. Balderramma, 219–24. Getty Conservation Institute, Los Angeles.

1993   Saving the Great Nobb: Preservation through Passive Management. In *Highways to the Past: Essays in Illinois Archaeology in Honor of Charles J. Bareis*, edited by T. E. Emerson, D. L. McElrath, and A. J. Fortier. *Illinois Archaeology* 5:100–107. Illinois Archaeological Survey, Urbana.

Erasmus, C. J.

1965   Monument Building: Some Field Experiments. *Southwestern Journal of Anthropology* 21:277–304.

Fairbrother, N.

1972   *New Lives, New Landscapes*. Penguin Books, Middlesex, England.

Farnsworth, K. B.

1990   The Evidence for Specialized Middle Woodland Camps in Western Illinois. *Illinois Archaeology* 2:109–32.

Fenneman, N. M.

1911   *Geology and Mineral Resources of the St. Louis Quadrangle Missouri-Illinois*. Bulletin 438. U.S. Geological Survey, Department of the Interior, Washington, D.C.

Flagg, E.

1838   *The Far West; or, A Tour Beyond the Mountains*. Harper and Brothers, New York.

Fowler, M. L.

1969   The Cahokia Site. In *Explorations into Cahokia Archaeology*, edited by M. L. Fowler, 1–30. Bulletin 7. Illinois Archaeological Survey, Urbana.

1974   *Cahokia: Ancient Capital of the Midwest*. Addison-Wesley Module in Anthropology no. 48. Addison-Wesley Publishing, Reading, Mass.

1975   A Precolumbian Urban Center on the Mississippi. *Scientific American* 233:92–101.

1977   Aerial Archaeology at the Cahokia Site. In *Aerial Remote Sensing Techniques in Archaeology*, edited by T. R. Lyons and R. K. Hitchcock, 65–80. Reports of the Chaco Center, no. 2. Chaco Center, Albuquerque, N.M.

1991   Mound 72 and Early Mississippian at Cahokia. In *New Perspectives on Cahokia: Views from the Periphery*, edited by J. B. Stoltman, 1–28. Prehistory Press, Madison, Wis.

1997   *The Cahokia Atlas: A Historical Atlas of Cahokia Archaeology*. Rev. ed. Studies in Archaeology, no. 2. Illinois Transportation Archaeological Research Program, University of Illinois, Urbana.

Fowler, M. L., E. D. Benchley, and P. DePuydt

1980   *Final Report of the 1979 Archaeological Investigations at the Interpretive Center Tract, Cahokia Mounds Historic Site*. Reports of Investigations, no. 40. Archaeological Research Laboratory, University of Wisconsin-Milwaukee.

Fowler, M. L., ed.

1996   The Ancient Skies and Sky Watchers of Cahokia: Woodhenges, Eclipses, and Cahokian Cosmology. *The Wisconsin Archeologist* 77.

Frommel, C. L.
   1986   Papal Policy: The Planning of Rome during the Renaissance. In *Art and History: Images and Their Meaning,* edited by R. I. Rotberg and T. K. Rabb, 39–65. Cambridge University Press, Cambridge.

Gallagher, J. P.
   1992   Prehistoric Field Systems in the Upper Midwest. In *Late Prehistoric Agriculture: Observations from the Midwest,* edited by W. I. Woods, 95–135. Studies in Illinois Archaeology, no. 8. Illinois Historic Preservation Agency, Springfield.

Gartner, W. G.
   1996   Archaeoastronomy as Sacred Geography. In *The Ancient Skies and Sky Watchers of Cahokia: Woodhenges, Eclipses, and Cahokian Cosmology,* edited by M. L. Fowler. *The Wisconsin Archeologist* 77:128–50.
   1999   Architecture as Allegory, Sediment as Text: Native Myths and Earthen Monuments in the New World. Paper presented at the Ninety-fifth Annual Meeting of the Association of American Geographers, Honolulu, Hawaii.

Gatschet, A. S.
   1884   *A Migration Legend of the Creek Indians.* Library of Aboriginal American Literature, no. 4. D. G. Brinton, Philadelphia.

Geertz, C.
   1980   *Negara: The Theatre State in Nineteenth-Century Bali.* Princeton University Press, Princeton, N.J.

Giddens, A.
   1979   *Central Problems in Social Theory: Action, Structure, and Contraction in Social Analysis.* University of California Press, Berkeley and Los Angeles.

Glacken, C. J.
   1967   *Traces on the Rhodian Shore.* University of California Press, Berkeley and Los Angeles.

Gleason, K.
   1994   To Bound and to Cultivate: An Introduction to the Archaeology of Gardens and Fields. In *The Archaeology of Garden and Field,* edited by N. F. Miller and K. L. Gleason, 1–25. University of Pennsylvania Press, Philadelphia.

Grant, F. S., and G. F. West
   1965   *Interpretation Theory in Applied Geophysics.* McGraw-Hill, New York.

Greber, N.
   1991   Review of *The Archaic and Woodland Cemeteries at the Elizabeth Site in the Lower Illinois Valley,* edited by D. K. Charles, S. R. Leigh, and J. E. Buikstra. *Illinois Archaeology* 3:105–6.

Gregg, M. L.
   1975   A Population Estimate for Cahokia. In *Perspectives in Cahokia Archaeology,* edited by J. A. Brown, 126–36. Bulletin 10. Illinois Archaeological Survey, Urbana.

Griffin, J. B.
   1949   The Cahokia Ceramic Complexes. In *Proceedings of the Fifth Plains Conference for Archaeology, the Laboratory of Anthropology, University of Nebraska Notebook* 1:44–58, Lincoln.
   1960a Climatic Change: A Contributory Cause of the Growth and Decline of Northern Hopewellian Culture. *The Wisconsin Archeologist* 41:21–33.

1960b A Hypothesis for the Prehistory of the Winnebago. In *Culture in History: Essays in Honor of Paul Radin,* edited by S. Diamond, 809–65. Columbia University Press, New York.

1961 Some Correlations of Climatic and Cultural Change in Eastern North American Prehistory. *Annals of the New York Academy of Sciences* 95:710–17.

1967 Eastern North American Archaeology: A Summary. *Science* 156:175–91.

1977 The University of Michigan Excavations at the Pulcher Site in 1970. *American Antiquity* 42:462–90.

1985 Changing Concepts of the Prehistoric Mississippian Cultures in the Eastern United States. In *Alabama and the Borderlands: From Prehistory to Statehood,* edited by R. R. Badger and L. A. Clayton, 40–63. University of Alabama Press, Tuscaloosa.

Griffin, J. B., R. E. Flanders, and P. F. Titterington

1970 *The Burial Complexes of the Knight and Norton Mounds in Illinois and Michigan.* Memoirs of the Museum of Anthropology, no 2. University of Michigan, Ann Arbor.

Groth, P., ed.

1990 *Vision, Culture, and Landscape.* Department of Landscape Architecture, University of California, Berkeley.

Gums, B. L., B. C. De Mott, N. H. Lopinot, G. R. Holley, and L. S. Kelly

1989 *Archaeological Investigations for the Mississippi River Transmission Corporation Alton Line in Madison and St. Clair Counties, Illinois.* Submitted to Illinois Historic Preservation Agency, Springfield.

Gums, B. L., and G. R. Holley

1991 *Archaeology at the Cahokia Mounds State Historic Site: Limited Excavations at the Falcon Drive-In, St. Clair County, Illinois.* Submitted to Illinois Historic Preservation Agency, Springfield.

Hair, J. T.

1866 *Gazetteer of Madison County.* Compiled and published by J. T. Hair, Alton, Illinois.

Hall, R. L.

1989 The Cultural Background of Mississippian Symbolism. In *The Southeastern Ceremonial Complex: Artifacts and Analysis,* edited by P. K. Galloway, 239–78. University of Nebraska Press, Lincoln.

1991 Cahokia Identity and Interaction Models of Cahokia Mississippian. In *Cahokia and the Hinterlands: Middle Mississippian Cultures of the Midwest,* edited by T. E. Emerson and R. B. Lewis, 3–34. University of Illinois Press, Urbana.

Hammes, R. H.

1981 The Cantine Mounds of Southern Illinois. *Journal of the Illinois State Historical Society* 74:146–56.

1987 Appendix B. A Chronology of Early Land Transactions in the Monks Mound Area. In *The River L'Abbe Mission: A French Colonial Church for the Cahokia Illini on Monks Mound,* by J. A. Walthall and E. D. Benchley. Studies in Illinois Archaeology, no. 2. Illinois Historic Preservation Agency, Springfield.

Hammond, N.

1997 Secrets of Tract 15A. *Times Literary Supplement,* no. 4927:6–8.

Harn, A. D.
  1971 An Archaeological Survey of the American Bottoms in Madison and St.
        Clair Counties, Illinois. In *Archaeological Surveys of the American Bottoms
        and Adjacent Bluffs, Illinois,* by P. J. Munson and A. D. Harn, 19–42. Re-
        ports of Investigations, no. 21. Illinois State Museum, Springfield.
  1980 Comments on the Spatial Distribution of Late Woodland and Mississip-
        pian Ceramics in the General Cahokia Sphere. *Rediscovery* 1:17–26.
Harris, C. W., and N. T. Dines
  1998 *Time Saver Standards for Landscape Architecture.* 2d ed. McGraw-Hill, New York.
Hart, J. F.
  1995 Reading the Landscape. In *Landscape in America,* edited by G. F. Thomp-
        son, 23–42. University of Texas Press, Austin.
Hartshorne, R.
  1939 *The Nature of Geography: A Critical Survey of Current Thought in the Light of
        the Past.* Association of American Geographers, Lancaster, Pa.
Harvey, P. D. A.
  1980 *The History of Topographical Maps: Symbols, Pictures, and Surveys.* Thames
        and Hudson, London.
Hawkins, B.
  1848 *A Sketch of the Creek Confederacy in the Years 1798 and 1799.* Vol. 3 of *Geor-
        gia Historical Society Collections,* Savannah.
Higuchi, T.
  1983 *The Visual and Spatial Structure of Landscapes.* MIT Press, Cambridge, Mass.
Hodder, I.
  1990 *The Domestication of Europe: Structure and Contingency in Neolithic Societies.*
        Basil Blackwell, Oxford and Cambridge.
Holden, C., ed.
  1996 The Last of the Cahokians. *Science* 272:351.
Holley, G. R.
  1989 *The Archaeology of the Cahokia Mounds ICT-II: Ceramics.* Cultural Resource
        Study Series, no. 11. Illinois Historic Preservation Agency, Springfield.
  1990 *Investigations at the Kunnemann Tract, Cahokia Mounds Historic Site, Madi-
        son County, Illinois.* Submitted to Illinois Historic Preservation Agency,
        Springfield.
  1991 Cahokia as a State? Paper presented at the Fifty-sixth Annual Meeting of
        the Society for American Archaeology, New Orleans, La.
  1995 Microliths and the Kunnemann Tract: An Assessment of Craft Production
        at the Cahokia Site. *Illinois Archaeology* 7:1–68.
  1999 Southeastern Great Towns. In *Great Towns and Great Polities: Comparing
        the Southeast and Southwest,* edited by J. Neitzel, 23–46. Amerind Founda-
        tion, University of New Mexico Press, Albuquerque.
Holley, G. R., and A. J. Brown
  1989 *Archaeological Investigations Relating to the Glen Carbon Interceptor Sewer
        Line, Divisions 3 through 7, Madison County, Illinois.* Archaeological Pro-
        gram Research Report no. 1. Office of Contract Archaeology, Southern
        Illinois University Edwardsville.
Holley, G. R., R. A. Dalan, and P. A. Smith
  1993 Investigations in the Cahokia Site Grand Plaza. *American Antiquity*
        58:306–19.

Holley, G. R., R. A. Dalan, and H. W. Watters Jr.
  1992 *Archaeological Investigations at the Rouch Mound Group, Cahokia Mounds State Historic Site.* Submitted to Illinois Historic Preservation Agency, Springfield.
  1996 *Investigations at the West Borrow Pit Mound Group, Cahokia Mounds State Historic Site.* Submitted to Illinois Historic Preservation Agency, Springfield.
  1998 *Promontory Mounds at the Cahokia Mounds State Historic Site: Results of the 1997 Field School Investigations.* Submitted to Illinois Historic Preservation Agency, Springfield.
Holley, G. R., R. A. Dalan, H. W. Watters Jr., and J. N. Harper
  1995 *Investigations at the Tippetts Mound Group, Cahokia Mounds State Historic Site.* Submitted to Illinois Historic Preservation Agency, Springfield.
Holley, G. R., R. A. Dalan, and W. I. Woods
  1994 Dynamics of Landscape Modification at the Cahokia Mounds Site. Paper presented at the Ninetieth Annual Meeting of the Association of American Geographers, San Francisco.
Holley, G. R., N. H. Lopinot, R. A. Dalan, and W. I. Woods
  1990 South Palisade Investigations. In *The Archaeology of the Cahokia Palisade.* Illinois Cultural Resources Study no. 14. Illinois Historic Preservation Agency, Springfield.
Holley, G. R., N. H. Lopinot, W. I. Woods, and J. E. Kelly
  1989 Dynamics of Community Organization at Prehistoric Cahokia. In *Households and Communities: Proceedings of the Twenty-first Annual Chacmool Conference,* edited by S. MacEachern, D. J. W. Archer, and R. D. Gavin, 339–49. Archaeological Association of the University of Calgary, Canada.
Howard, J. H.
  1968 *The Southeastern Ceremonial Complex and Its Interpretation.* Memoir no. 6. Missouri Archaeological Society, Columbia.
Howett, C.
  1990 Where the One-Eyed Man is King: The Epistemological Premises of Visual Analysis. In *Vision, Culture, and Landscape,* edited by P. Groth, 205–20. Department of Landscape Architecture, University of California, Berkeley.
Hudson, C.
  1976 *The Southeastern Indians.* University of Tennessee Press, Knoxville.Illinois General Land Office
  1810 *Illinois Land Records, Original Field Notes.* Illinois State Archives, Springfield.
Iseminger, W. R., T. R. Pauketat, B. Koldehoff, L. S. Kelly, and L. Blake
  1990 East Palisade Investigations. In *The Archaeology of the Cahokia Palisade.* Illinois Cultural Resources Study no. 14. Illinois Historic Preservation Agency, Springfield.
Jackson, J. B.
  1984 *Discovering the Vernacular Landscape.* Yale University Press, New Haven, Conn., and London.
  1995 In Search of the Proto-Landscape. In *Landscape in America,* edited by G. F. Thompson, 43–50. University of Texas Press, Austin.
Jenkins, N. J., and R. A. Krause
  1986 *The Tombigbee Watershed in Southeastern Prehistory.* University of Alabama Press, Tuscaloosa.
Johannessen, S.
  1984 Paleoethnobotany. In *American Bottom Archaeology: A Summary of the FAI-*

270 Contribution to the Culture History of the Mississippi River Valley, edited by C. J. Bareis and J. W. Porter, 197–214. University of Illinois Press, Urbana.

1993   Food, Dishes, and Society in the Mississippi Valley. In *Foraging and Farming in the Eastern Woodlands,* edited by C. M. Scarry, 182–205. University Press of Florida, Gainesville.

Johnston, R. J., ed.

1986   *The Dictionary of Human Geography.* 2d ed. Basil Blackwell, Oxford.

Joiner, D.

1971   Social Ritual and Architectural Space. *Architectural Research and Teaching* 1:11–22.

Judd, N. M.

1948   "Pyramids" of the New World. *National Geographic Magazine* 93:105–28.

Kaplan, D.

1963   Men, Monuments, and Political Systems. *Southwestern Journal of Anthropology* 19:397–410.

Kaplan, R., and S. Kaplan

1989   *The Experience of Nature: A Psychological Perspective.* Cambridge University Press, Cambridge.

Keegan, W. F., ed.

1987   *Emergent Horticultural Economies of the Eastern Woodlands.* Occasional Papers, no. 7. Center for Archaeological Investigations, Southern Illinois University at Carbondale.

Keene, D.

1991   Fort De Chartres: Archaeology in the Illinois Country. In *French Colonial Archaeology: The Illinois Country and the Western Great Lakes,* edited by J. A. Walthall, 29–41. University of Illinois Press, Urbana.

Keller, G. V., and F. C. Frischknecht

1966   *Electrical Methods in Geophysical Prospecting.* Pergamon Press, Oxford.

Kelly, A. R.

1938   *A Preliminary Report on Archaeological Explorations at Macon, Ga.* Bulletin 119. Smithsonian Institution, Bureau of American Ethnology. U.S. Government Printing Office, Washington, D.C.

Kelly, J. E.

1980   *Formative Developments at Cahokia and the Adjacent American Bottom: A Merrell Tract Perspective.* Ph.D. diss., University of Wisconsin. University Microfilms, Ann Arbor, Mich.

1990a   The Emergence of Mississippian Culture in the American Bottom Region. In *The Mississippian Emergence,* edited by B. D. Smith, 113–52. Smithsonian Institution Press, Washington, D.C.

1990b   The Range Site Community Patterns and the Mississippian Emergence. In *The Mississippian Emergence,* edited by B. D. Smith, 67–112. Smithsonian Institution Press, Washington, D.C.

1993   The Pulcher Site: An Archaeological and Historical Overview. *Illinois Archaeology* 5:434–51.

1994   The Archaeology of the East St. Louis Mound Center—Past and Present. *Illinois Archaeology* 6:1–55.

1996   Redefining Cahokia: Principles and Elements of Community Organization. In *The Ancient Skies and Sky Watchers of Cahokia: Woodhenges, Eclipses, and Cahokian Cosmology,* edited by M. L. Fowler. *The Wisconsin Archeologist* 77:97–119.

Kennedy, R. G.
    1994 *Hidden Cities: The Discovery and Loss of Ancient North American Civilization.*
          Free Press, New York.
King, A.
    1990 The Politics of Vision. In *Vision, Culture, and Landscape,* edited by P.
          Groth, 171–86. Department of Landscape Architecture, University of Cali-
          fornia, Berkeley.
Knight, V. J., Jr.
    1981 *Mississippian Ritual.* Ph.D. diss., Department of Anthropology, University
          of Florida. University Microfilms, Ann Arbor, Mich.
    1986 The Institutional Organization of Mississippian Religion. *American Antiq-
          uity* 51:675–87.
Koldehoff, B., T. R. Pauketat, and J. E. Kelly
    1993 The Emerald Site and the Mississippian Occupation of the Central Silver
          Creek Valley. *Illinois Archaeology* 5:331–43.
Krogstad, A.
    1989 The Treasure House of Smell: From an "Unsensing" to a "Sensual" An-
          thropology. *Folk, Dansk Etnografisk Forening* 31:87–104.
Kuchler, S.
    1993 Landscape as Memory: The Mapping Process and Its Representation in a
          Melanesian Society. In *Landscape Politics and Perspectives,* edited by B. Ben-
          der, 85–106. Berg, Providence, R.I., and Oxford.
Kus, S., and V. Raharijaona
    1990 Domestic Space and the Tenacity of Tradition among Some Betsileo of
          Madagascar. In *Domestic Architecture and the Use of Space,* edited by S.
          Kent, 21–33. Cambridge University Press, Cambridge.
Larson, L. H., Jr.
    1989 The Etowah Site. In *The Southeastern Cermonial Complex: Artifacts and
          Analysis,* edited by P. Galloway, 133–41. University of Nebraska Press,
          Lincoln.
Lash, K.
    1995 Notes on Living with Landscape. In *Landscape in America,* edited by G. F.
          Thompson, 15–22. University of Texas Press, Austin.
Lawrence, D. L.
    1986 Design, Behavior, and Evolving Urban Morphology. In *Purposes in Built
          Form and Culture Research,* edited by J. W. Carswell and D. G. Saile, 59–62.
          University of Kansas, Lawrence.
Lawrence, D. L., and S. M. Low
    1990 The Built Environment and Spatial Form. *Annual Review of Anthropology*
          19:453–505.
Lekson, S. H.
    1989 The Community in Anasazi Archaeology. In *Households and Communities,*
          edited by S. MacEachern, D. J. W. Archer, and R. D. Garvin, 181–85. Ar-
          chaeological Society of the University of Calgary, Canada.
Leone, M.
    1984 Interpreting Ideology in Historical Archaeology: Using the Rules of Per-
          spective in the William Paca Garden in Annapolis, Maryland. In *Ideology,
          Power, and Prehistory,* edited by D. Miller and C. Tilley, 25–35. Cambridge
          University Press, Cambridge.

LePage du Pratz, M.
  1975 [1774] *The History of Louisiana.* Translated by J. G. Tregle. Louisiana State University Press, Baton Rouge.
Lewis, P.
  1983 Learning from Looking: Geographic and Other Writing about the American Cultural Landscape. *American Quarterly* 35:242–61.
Lewis, T. M. N., and M. Kneberg
  1946 *Hiwassee Island: An Archaeological Account of Four Tennessee Indian Peoples.* University of Tennessee Press, Knoxville.
Ley, D.
  1985 Cultural/Humanistic Geography. *Progress in Human Geography* 9:415–23.
Lopinot, N. H.
  1991 Archaeological Remains. Pt. 1. In *The Archaeology of the Cahokia Mounds ICT-II: Biological Remains,* by N. H. Lopinot, L. S. Kelly, G. R. Milner, and R. Paine. Illinois Cultural Resources Study no. 13. Illinois Historic Preservation Agency, Springfield.
  1992 Spatial and Temporal Variability in Mississippian Subsistence: The Archaeobotanical Record. In *Late Prehistoric Agriculture: Observations from the Midwest,* edited by W. I. Woods, 44–94. Studies in Illinois Archaeology, no. 8. Illinois Historic Preservation Agency, Springfield.
  1997 Cahokian Food Production Reconsidered. In *Cahokia: Domination and Ideology in the Mississippian World,* edited by T. R. Pauketat and T. E. Emerson, 52–68. University of Nebraska Press, Lincoln.
Lopinot, N. H., A. J. Brown, and G. R. Holley
  1993 Archaeological Investigations on the Western Periphery of the Cahokia Site. In *Highways to the Past: Essays in Illinois Archaeology in Honor of Charles J. Bareis,* edited by T. E. Emerson, D. L. McElrath, and A. J. Fortier. *Illinois Archaeology* 5:407–20. Illinois Archaeological Survey, Urbana.
Lopinot, N. H., and W. I. Woods
  1993 Wood Overexploitation and the Collapse of Cahokia. In *Foraging and Farming in the Eastern Woodlands,* edited by C. M. Scarry, 206–31. University Press of Florida, Gainesville.
Lynch, K.
  1960 *The Image of the City.* Technology Press, Cambridge, Mass.
  1976 *Managing the Sense of Region.* MIT Press, Cambridge, Mass.
Lynch, K., and G. Hack
  1984 *Site Planning.* 3d ed. MIT Press, Cambridge, Mass.
Madison County Historical Society
  1913 *The Mound Builders, the Greatest Monument of Prehistoric Man.* Pamphlet on file. Madison County Historical Society, Edwardsville, Ill.
Martin, G.
  1996 Keepers of the Oaks. *Discover* (August 1996): 44–50.
McAdams, C.
  1907 The Archaeology of Illinois. *Transactions of the Illinois State Historical Society for 1907* 12:35–47.
McAdams, W. H.
  1882 Antiquities. In *History of Madison County, Illinois,* edited by W. R. Brink, 58–64. W. R. Brink, Edwardsville, Ill.

McGimsey, C. R., and M. D. Wiant
    1984 *Limited Archaeological Investigations at Monks Mound (11–MS-38): Some Per-
          spectives on Its Stability, Structure, and Age.* Studies in Illinois Archaeology,
          no. 1. Illinois Historical Preservation Agency, Springfield.
McGuire, J. M.
    1996 A Tale of Two Mounds. *St. Louis Post-Dispatch Magazine,* June 9, 1996, 5–11.
Mehrer, M.
    1995 *Cahokia's Countryside: Household Archaeology, Settlement Patterns, and Social
          Power.* Northern Illinois University Press, DeKalb.
Mehrer, M. W., and J. M. Collins
    1989 Household Archaeology at Cahokia and Its Hinterlands. Paper presented
          at the Fifty-fourth Annual Meeting of the Society for American Archaeol-
          ogy, Atlanta, Ga.
Meinig, D. W.
    1979a *The Interpretation of Ordinary Landscapes.* Oxford University Press, New
          York.
    1979b Reading the Landscape: An Appreciation of W. G. Hoskins and J. B. Jack-
          son. In *The Interpretation of Ordinary Landscapes,* edited by D. W. Meinig,
          195–244. Oxford University Press, Oxford and New York.
Melbye, J. C.
    1963 *The Kane Burial Mounds.* Report no. 15. Archaeological Salvage, Southern
          Illinois University Museum, Carbondale.
Melnick, R. Z.
    1981 Capturing the Cultural Landscape. *Landscape Architecture* 71:56–60.
    1983 Protecting Rural Cultural Landscapes: Finding Value in the Countryside.
          Landscape Journal 2:85–96.
Messenger, J.
    1808 Field Notes for the South Edge of Township 9 North, Range 3 West of the
          Third Principle Meridian. Saturday, January 9, 1808. In *Illinois Land
          Records, Original Field Notes.* Vol. 12. Illinois State Archives, Springfield.
Milner, G. R.
    1984a *The Julien Site.* University of Illinois Press, Urbana.
    1984b Social and Temporal Implications of Variation among American Bottom
          Cemeteries. *American Antiquity* 49:468–88.
    1991 American Bottom Mississippian Cultures: Internal Developments and Ex-
          ternal Relations. In *New Perspectives on Cahokia: Views from the Periphery,*
          edited by J. B. Stoltman, 29–47. Prehistory Press, Madison, Wis.
Milner, G. R., T. E. Emerson, M. W. Mehrer, J. A. Williams, and D. Esarey
    1984 Mississippian and Oneota Periods. In *American Bottom Archaeology: A Sum-
          mary of the FAI-270 Project Contribution to the Culture History of the Missis-
          sippi River Valley,* edited by C. J. Bareis and J. W. Porter, 158–86. University
          of Illinois Press, Urbana.
Monmonier, M.
    1991 *How To Lie with Maps.* University of Chicago Press, Chicago.
Mooney, J.
    1889 Cherokee Mound-Building. *American Anthropologist* 11:167–71.
Moore, H. L.
    1986 *Space, Text, and Gender: An Anthropological Study of the Marakwet of Kenya.*
          Cambridge University Press, Cambridge.

Moorehead, W. K.
  1922 The Cahokia Mounds: A Preliminary Report. Bulletin 19. University of Illinois, Urbana.
  1929 The Cahokia Mounds. Pt. 1. Explorations of 1922, 1923, 1924, and 1927 in the Cahokia Mounds. Bulletin 26. University of Illinois, Urbana.
Morgan, W. N.
  1980 *Prehistoric Architecture in the Eastern United States.* MIT Press, Cambridge, Mass.
Morse, D. F., and P. A. Morse
  1990 Emergent Mississippian in the Central Mississippi Valley. In *The Mississippian Emergence,* edited by B. D. Smith, 153–73. Smithsonian Institution Press, Washington, D.C.
Motloch, J. L.
  1991 *Introduction to Landscape Design.* Van Nostrand Reinhold, New York.
Mrozowski, S. A., and M. C. Beaudry
  1990 Archaeology and the Landscape of Corporate Ideology. In *Earth Patterns: Essays in Landscape Archaeology,* edited by W. M. Kelso and R. Most, 189–208. University Press of Virginia, Charlottesville.
Muller, J. D.
  1997 *Mississippian Political Economy.* Plenum Publishing, New York.
Naipaul, V. S.
  1995 *A Way in the World.* Vintage International, New York.
Nash, C. H.
  1972 *Chucalissa: Excavations and Burials Through 1963.* Occasional Papers, no. 6. Anthropological Research Center, Memphis State University, Memphis, Tenn.
Neitzel, R. S.
  1965 *The Archaeology of the Fatherland Site: The Grand Village of the Natchez.* Anthropological Papers, pt. 1, no. 51. American Museum of Natural History, New York.
  1983 *The Grand Village of the Natchez Revisited: Excavations at the Fatherland Site, Adams County, Mississippi, 1972.* Archaeological Report no. 12. Mississippi Department of Archives and History, Jackson.
Norton, W.
  1989 *Explorations in the Understanding of Landscape.* Contributions in Sociology, no. 77. Greenwood Press, New York.
O'Brien, P. J.
  1972 *A Formal Analysis of Cahokia Ceramics from the Powell Tract.* Monograph no. 3. Illinois Archaeological Survey, Urbana.
Oliver, W.
  1924 *Eight Months in Illinois; with Information to Emigrants,* by William Andrew Mitchell. Torch Press, Cedar Rapids, Iowa.
Olwig, K. R.
  1996 Recovering the Substantive Nature of Landscape. *Annals of the Association of American Geographers* 86:630–53.
Parasnis, D. S.
  1986 *Principles of Applied Geophysics.* 4th ed. Chapman and Hall, London and New York.
Pauketat, T. R.
  1991 *The Dynamics of Pre-State Political Centralization in the North American*

Midcontinent. Ph.D. diss., Department of Anthropology, University of Michigan. University Microfilms, Ann Arbor, Mich.

1992   The Reign and Ruin of the Lords of Cahokia: A Dialectic of Dominance. In *Lords of the Southeast: Social Inequality and the Native Elites of Southeastern North America,* edited by A. W. Barker and T. R. Pauketat, 31–52. Archaeological Papers, no. 3. American Anthropological Association, Washington, D.C.

1993a Preliminary Observations of Building Density at Cahokia's Tract 15A and Dunham Tract. In *Highways to the Past: Essays in Illinois Archaeology in Honor of Charles J. Bareis,* edited by T. E. Emerson, D. L. McElrath, and A. J. Fortier. *Illinois Archaeology* 5:402–6.

1993b *Temples for Cahokia Lords: Preston Holder's 1955–1956 Excavations of Kunnemann Mound.* Memoirs of the Museum of Anthropology, no. 26. University of Michigan, Ann Arbor.

1994   *The Ascent of Chiefs: Cahokia and Mississippian Politics in Native North America.* University of Alabama Press, Tuscaloosa.

1997a Cahokian Political Economy. In *Cahokia: Domination and Ideology in the Mississippian World,* edited by T. R. Pauketat and T. E. Emerson, 30–51. University of Nebraska Press, Lincoln.

1997b The Special Garbage beneath Mound 51. *Cahokian* (spring 1997): 10–12.

1998   Refiguring the Archaeology of Greater Cahokia. *Journal of Archaeological Research* 6:45–89.

Pauketat, T. R., and T. E. Emerson, eds.

1997   *Cahokia: Domination and Ideology in the Mississippian World.* University of Nebraska Press, Lincoln.

Pauketat, T. R., and N. H. Lopinot

1997   Cahokian Population Dynamics. In *Cahokia: Domination and Ideology in the Mississippian World,* edited by T. R. Pauketat and T. E. Emerson, 103–23. University of Nebraska Press, Lincoln.

Pauketat, T. R., and M. A. Rees

1996   *Early Cahokia Project: 1994 Excavations at Mound 49, Cahokia (11–S–34–2).* Report submitted to Illinois Historic Preservation Agency, Springfield.

Payne, J. H.

1862   The Green-Corn Dance. *The Continental Monthly* 1:17–29.

Peck, J. M.

1837   *A Gazetteer of Illinois.* 2d ed. Grigg and Elliot, Philadelphia.

Peebles, C. S., and S. M. Kus

1977   Some Archaeological Correlates of Ranked Societies. *American Antiquity* 42:421–48.

Peet, R.

1993   Review of "The City as Text: The Politics of Landscape Interpretation in the Kandyan Kingdom," by J. S. Duncan. *Annals of the Association of American Geographers* 83:184–87.

Penicaut, A.

1988 [1723] *Fleur de Lys and Calumet Being the Penicaut Narrative of French Adventure in Louisiana.* Translated by R. G. McWilliams. University of Alabama Press, Tuscaloosa,

Penman, J. T.

1988   Neo-Boreal Climatic Influences on the Late Prehistoric Agricultural Groups in the Mississippi Valley. *Geoarchaeology* 3:139–45.

Perino, G.
   1957   Cahokia. *Central States Archaeological Journal* 3:84–88.
   1967   *The Cherry Valley Mounds and Banks Mound 3.* Memoir no. 1. Central States Archaeological Societies, Quincy, Ill.
   1971   The Mississippian Component at the Schild Site (No. 4), Greene County, Illinois. In *Mississippian Site Archaeology in Illinois: Site Reports from St. Louis and Chicago Areas.* Vol. 1. Bulletin no. 8. Illinois Archaeological Survey, Urbana, 1–148.

Phillips, P., J. A. Ford, and J. B. Griffin
   1951   *Archaeological Survey in the Lower Mississippi Alluvial Valley, 1940–1947.* Papers of the Peabody Museum of Archaeology and Ethnology, no. 25. Harvard University, Cambridge, Mass.

Polhemus, R. R.
   1987   *The Toqua Site—40Mr6: A Late Mississippian, Dallas Phase Town.* Publications in Anthropology, no. 44. Tennessee Valley Authority. Reports of Investigations, no. 41. Department of Anthropology, University of Tennessee Press, Knoxville.

Porter, J. W.
   1974   *Cahokia Archaeology as Viewed from the Mitchell Site: A Satellite Community at A.D. 1150–1200.* Ph.D. diss., Department of Anthropology, University of Wisconsin-Madison. University Microfilms, Ann Arbor, Mich.

Pozorski, T.
   1980   The Early Horizon Site of Huaca de los Reyes: Societal Implications. *American Antiquity* 45:100–110.

Pregill, P., and N. Volkman
   1993   *Landscapes in History: Design and Planning in the Western Tradition.* John Wiley and Sons, New York.

Prentice, G.
   1986   An Analysis of the Symbolism Expressed by the Birger Figurine. *American Antiquity* 51:239–66.

Price, J. E., and J. B. Griffin
   1979   *The Snodgrass Site of the Powers Phase of Southeast Missouri.* Reports of the Museum of Anthropology, no. 66. University of Michigan, Ann Arbor.

Pustmueller, A. E.
   1950   Personal Experiences. In *Cahokia Brought to Life: An Artifactual Story of America's Great Monument,* edited by R. E. Grimm, 13–14. The Greater St. Louis Archaeological Society, St. Louis, Mo.

Rapoport, A.
   1982   *The Meaning of the Built Environment.* SAGE Publications, Beverly Hills, Cal.

Rathje, W. A.
   1974   The Garbage Project: A New Way of Looking at the Problems of Archaeology. *Archaeology* 27:236–41.

Reed, N. A.
   1973   Monks and Other Mississippian Mounds. In *Explorations into Cahokia Archaeology,* edited by M. L. Fowler, 31–42. Rev. ed. Bulletin 7. Illinois Archaeological Survey, Urbana.

Reed, N. A., J. W. Bennett, and J. W. Porter
   1968   Solid Core Drilling of Monks Mound: Technique and Findings. *American Antiquity* 33:137–48.

Rees, R.
　　1980　Historical Links between Geography and Art. *Geographical Review* 70:60–78.
Reeves, D. M.
　　1936　Aerial Photography and Archaeology. *American Antiquity* 2:102–7.
Relph, E.
　　1976　*Place and Placelessness.* Pion, London.
　　1981　*Rational Landscapes and Humanistic Geography.* Croom Helm, London.
　　1989　Responsive Methods, Geographical Imagination and the Study of Land-scapes. In *Remaking Human Geography,* edited by A. Kobayashi and S. Mackenzie, 149–63. Unwin Hyman, Boston.
Renfrew, C.
　　1983　The Social Archaeology of Megalithic Monuments. *Scientific American* 249:152–63.
Renfrew, C., and J. F. Cherry, eds.
　　1986　*Peer Polity Interaction and Socio-Political Change.* Cambridge University Press, Cambridge.
Richardson, J. A.
　　1980　*Art: The Way It Is.* 2d ed. Prentice-Hall, Englewood Cliffs, N.J.
Riley, R.
　　1990　Bigger Than a Breadbox, Smaller Than the Cosmos: Twenty Questions About the Landscape Experience. In *Vision, Culture, and Landscape,* edited by P. Groth, 3–10. Department of Landscape Architecture, University of California, Berkeley.
Riley, T. J., and C. Said
　　1993　Fly Ash Analysis Supports Emergent Mississippian Agricultural Features at the Lunsford-Pulcher Site (11–S-40) in the American Bottom, Illinois. *Plains Anthropologist* 38:177–86.
Rindos, D., and S. Johannessen
　　1991　Human-Plant Interactions and Cultural Change in the American Bottom. In *Cahokia and the Hinterlands: Middle Mississippian Cultures of the Midwest,* edited by T. E. Emerson and R. Barry Lewis, 35–45. University of Illinois Press, Urbana.
Ringberg, J. E.
　　1996　*Ceramic Chronology and Mound Construction: A Temporal Sequence for Mound 48, Cahokia.* Master's thesis, Department of Anthropology, Northern Illinois University.
Roberts, B. K.
　　1987　Landscape Archaeology. In *Landscape and Culture: Geographical and Ar-chaeological Perspectives,* edited by J. M. Wagstaff, 77–95. Basil Blackwell, Oxford and New York.
Rolingson, M. A.
　　1996　Elements of Community Design at Cahokia. In *The Ancient Skies and Sky Watchers of Cahokia: Woodhenges, Eclipses, and Cahokian Cosmology,* edited by M. L. Fowler. *The Wisconsin Archeologist* 77:84–96.
Rossignol, J., and L. Wandsnider, eds.
　　1992　*Space, Time, and Archaeological Landscapes: Interdisciplinary Contributions to Archaeology.* Plenum Press, New York and London.
Rowe, J. H.
　　1953　Technical Aids in Anthropology: A Historical Survey. In *Anthropology To-day,* edited by A. L. Kroeber. University of Chicago Press, Chicago.

Rowntree, L. B.
   1996   The Cultural Landscape Concept in American Human Geography. In *Concepts in Human Geography,* edited by C. Earle, M. Kenzer, and K. Mathewson, 127–59. Rowman and Littlefield, Lanham, Md.

Rowntree, L. B., and M. W. Conkey
   1980   Symbolism and the Cultural Landscape. *Annals of the Association of American Geographers* 70:459–74.

Rubertone, P. E.
   1989   Landscape as Artifact: Comments on "The Archaeological Use of Landscape Treatment in Social, Economic, and Ideological Analysis." *Historical Archaeology* 23:50–54.

Ruesch, J., and W. Kees
   1956   *Nonverbal Communication: Notes on the Visual Perception of Human Relations.* University of California Press, Berkeley and Los Angeles.

Ruggles, D. F.
   1994   Vision and Power at the Qala Bani Hammad in Islamic North Africa. *Journal of Garden History* 14:28–41.

Ruggles, D. F., and E. Kryder-Reid
   1994   Introduction: Vision in the Garden. *Journal of Garden History* 14:1–2.

Sack, R. D.
   1980   *Conceptions of Space in Social Thought: A Geographic Perspective.* University of Minnesota Press, Minneapolis.

Salter, C. L.
   1978   Signatures and Settings: One Approach to Landscape in Literature. In *Dimensions of Human Geography: Essays in Some Familiar and Neglected Themes,* edited by K. W. Butzer, 69–83. Research Paper no. 186. Department of Geography, University of Chicago, Chicago.

Salzer, R. J.
   1975   Excavations at the Merrell Tract of the Cahokia Site: Summary Field Report, 1973. In *Cahokia Archaeology: Field Reports,* edited by M. L. Fowler, 1–8. Research Series, Papers in Anthropology, no. 3. Illinois State Museum, Springfield.

Sanders, W. T.
   1984   Pre-Industrial Demography and Social Evolution. In *On the Evolution of Complex Societies: Essays in Honor of Harry Hoijer, 1982,* edited by T. K. Earle, 7–40. Undena Publications, Malibu, Cal.

Santley, R. S., C. Yarborough, and B. A. Hall
   1987   Enclaves, Ethnicity, and the Archaeological Record at Matacapan. In *Ethnicity and Culture,* edited by R. Auger, M. F. Glass, S. MacEachern, and P. H. McCartney, 85–100. Proceedings of the Eighteenth Annual Chacmool Conference. Archaeological Association of the University of Calgary, Canada.

Sauer, C.
   1925   The Morphology of Landscape. *University of California Publications in Geography* 2:19–53.

Savulis, E. R.
   1992   Alternative Visions and Landscapes: Archaeology of the Shaker Social Order and Built Environment. In *Text-Aided Archaeology,* edited by B. J. Little, 195–203. CRC Press, Boca Raton, Fla., Ann Arbor, Mich., and London.

Scarry, C. M.
    1993 Agricultural Risk and the Development of Mississippian Chiefdoms: Pre-
          historic Moundville, a Case Study. In *Foraging and Farming in the Eastern
          Woodlands,* edited by C. M. Scarry, 157–81. University Press of Florida,
          Gainesville.
Schama, S.
    1989 *Citizens: A Chronicle of the French Revolution.* Alfred A. Knopf, New York.
Schnell, F. T., V. J. Knight, and G. S. Schnell
    1981 *Cemochechobee: Archaeology of a Mississippian Ceremonial Center on the
          Chattahoochee River.* University Press of Florida, Gainesville.
Scott, O. R.
    1979 Utilizing History to Establish Cultural and Physical Identity in the Land-
          scape. *Landscape Planning* 6:179–203.
Shapiro, G., and J. J. Miller
    1990 *The Seventeenth-Century Landscape of San Luis De Talimali: Three Scales of Analy-
          sis.* In *Earth Patterns: Essays in Landscape Archaeology,* edited by W. M. Kelso
          and R. Most, 89–101. University Press of Virginia, Charlottesville and London.
Sherratt, A.
    1990 The Genesis of Megaliths: Monumentality, Ethnicity, and Social Com-
          plexity in Neolithic North-West Europe. *World Archaeology* 22:147–67.
Sherrod, P. C., and M. A. Rolingson
    1987 *Surveyors of the Ancient Mississippi Valley: Modules and Alignments in Prehis-
          toric Mound Sites.* Research Series, no. 28, Arkansas Archaeological Survey,
          Fayetteville.
Silverberg, R.
    1968 *Mound Builders of Ancient America: The Archaeology of a Myth.* New York
          Graphic Society, Greenwich, Conn.
Simonds, J. O.
    1961 *Landscape and Architecture: The Shaping of Man's Natural Environment.* F. W.
          Dodge Corporation, New York.
Skele, M.
    1988 *The Great Knob: Interpretations of Monks Mound.* Studies in Illinois Archae-
          ology, no. 4. Illinois Historic Preservation Agency, Springfield.
Smith, B. D.
    1985 Mississippian Patterns of Subsistence and Settlement. In *Alabama and the
          Borderlands: From Prehistory to Statehood,* edited by R. R. Badger and L. A.
          Clayton, 64–79. University of Alabama Press, Tuscaloosa.
    1986 The Archaeology of the Southeastern United States: From Dalton to de
          Soto, 10,500 to 500 B.P. In *Advances in World Archaeology,* edited by F.
          Wendorf and A. E. Close, 1–92. Academic Press, Orlando, Fla.
    1992 Hopewellian Farmers of Eastern North America. In *Rivers of Change: Essays
          on Early Agriculture in Eastern North America,* 201–48. Smithsonian Institu-
          tion Press, Washington, D.C.
Smith, H. I.
    1902 The Great American Pyramid. *Harper's Monthly Magazine* 104:199–204.
Smith, H. M.
    1973 The Murdock Mound: Cahokia Site. In *Explorations into Cahokia Archaeol-
          ogy,* edited by M. L. Fowler, 49–88. Rev. ed. Bulletin 7. Illinois Archaeolog-
          ical Survey, Urbana.

Snyder, J. F.
    1917   The Great Cahokia Mound. *Illinois State Historical Society Journal*
           10:256–59.

Squire, E. G.
    1860   Ancient Monuments in the United States. *Harper's New Monthly Magazine*
           21:165–78.

Stilgoe, J. R.
    1982   *Common Landscape of America, 1580–1845*. Yale University Press, New
           Haven, Conn., and London.

Stoltman, J. B., ed.
    1991   *New Perspectives on Cahokia: Views from the Periphery*. Monographs in
           World Archaeology, no. 2. Prehistory Press, Madison, Wis.

Stout, C. B.
    1986   The Adams Site. In *Mississippian Towns of the Western Kentucky Border*,
           edited by R. B. Lewis, 9–105. Kentucky Heritage Council, Frankfort.

Stuart, G. E.
    1972   Who Were the Mound Builders? *National Geographic* 142:783–801.

Swanton, J. R.
    1928   The Interpretation of Aboriginal Mounds by Means of Creek Indian Cus-
           toms. *Annual Report of the Smithsonian Institution* (1927), 495–507.

    1929   *Myths and Tales of the Southeastern Indians*. Bulletin 88. Smithsonian Insti-
           tution, Bureau of American Ethnology. U.S. Government Printing Office,
           Washington, D.C.

    1931   *Source Material for the Social and Ceremonial Life of the Choctaw Indians*.
           Bulletin 103. Smithsonian Institution, Bureau of American Ethnology.
           U.S. Government Printing Office, Washington, D.C.

    1932   The Green Corn Dance. *Chronicles of Oklahoma* 10:170–95.

    1979 [1946]   *The Indians of the Southeastern United States*. Bulletin 137. Bureau of
           American Ethnology, Washington, D.C. Reprint, Smithsonian Institution
           Press, Washington, D.C.

Telford, W. M., J. P. Geldardt, R. E. Sheriff, and K. A. Keys
    1990   *Applied Geophysics*. 2d ed. Cambridge University Press, Cambridge.

Thomas, C.
    1891   *Report on the Mound Explorations of the Bureau of Ethnology*. Twelfth Annual
           Report of the Bureau of American Ethnology. U.S. Government Printing
           Office, Washington, D.C.

Titterington, P. F.
    1938   *The Cahokia Mound Group and Its Village Site Materials*. Privately pub-
           lished, St. Louis, Mo.

Tuan, Y. F.
    1972   *Topophilia: A Study of Environmental Perception, Attitudes, and Values*. De-
           partment of Geography, University of Minnesota, Minneapolis.

Tucker, S. J., comp.
    1942   *Indian Villages of the Illinois Country*. Vol. 2. Scientific Paper, pt. 1, Atlas.
           Illinois State Museum, Springfield.

Vander Leest, B. J.
    1980   *The Ramey Field, Cahokia Surface Collection: A Functional Analysis of Spatial
           Structure*. Ph.D. diss., Department of Anthropology, University of Wiscon-
           sin-Milwaukee. University Microfilms, Ann Arbor, Mich.

Varner, J. G., and J. J. Varner
    1951   *The Florida of the Inca.* University of Texas Press, Austin.

Wagner, P. L.
    1972   *Environments and Peoples.* Prentice-Hall, Englewood Cliffs, N.J.

Wagner, P. L., and M. W. Mikesell, eds.
    1962   *Readings in Cultural Geography.* University of Chicago Press, Chicago and London.

Wagstaff, J. M., ed.
    1987   *Landscape and Culture: Geographical and Archaeological Perspectives.* Basil Blackwell, Oxford.

Walthall, J. A., and E. D. Benchley
    1987   *The River L'Abbe Mission.* Studies in Illinois Archaeology, no. 2. Illinois Historic Preservation Agency, Springfield.

Ward, S.
    1967   *Electromagnetic Theory for Geophysical Applications.* Society for Exploration Geophysicists, Tulsa, Okla.

Waring, A. J., Jr.
    1968   The Southern Cult and Muskhogean Ceremonial. In *The Waring Papers,* edited by S. Williams, 30–69. Vol. 58. Papers of the Peabody Museum of Archaeology and Ethnology. Harvard University, Cambridge, Mass.

Waring, A. J., Jr., and P. Holder
    1945   A Prehistoric Ceremonial Complex in the Southeastern United States. *American Anthropologist* 47:1–34.

Watters, H. W., Jr., R. A. Dalan, G. R. Holley, and J. E. Ringberg
    1997   *Investigations at Mounds 59, 60, 94 and the West Borrow Pit Group, Cahokia Mounds State Historic Site.* Report submitted to Illinois Historic Preservation Agency, Springfield.

Webb, M. C.
    1989   Functional and Historical Parallelisms Between Mesoamerican and Mississippian Cultures. In *The Southeastern Ceremonial Complex: Artifacts and Analysis,* edited by P. Galloway, 279–93. University of Nebraska Press, Lincoln.

Wendland, W. M., and R. A. Bryson
    1974   Dating Climatic Episodes of the Holocene. *Quaternary Research* 4:9–24.

Wesler, K. W., and S. W. Neusius
    1987   *Archaeological Excavations at Wickliffe Mounds, 15BA4: Mound F, Mound A Addendum, and Mitigation for the Great River Road Project, 1985 and 1986.* Report no. 2. Wickliffe Mounds Research Center, Wickliffe, Ky.

Williams, K.
    1975   Preliminary Summation of Excavations at the East Lobes of Monks Mound. In *Cahokia Archaeology: Field Reports,* edited by M. L. Fowler, 21–24. Research Series, no. 3. Illinois State Museum, Springfield.

Williams, M.
    1989   *Americans and Their Forests: A Historical Geography.* Cambridge University Press, Cambridge.

Williams, R.
    1965   *The Long Revolution.* Penguin Books, Harmondsworth, England.

Williams, S., and J. P. Brain
    1983   *Excavations at the Lake George Site, Yazoo County, Mississippi, 1958–1960.* Papers of the Peabody Museum of Archaeology and Ethnology, no. 74. Harvard University, Cambridge, Mass.

Wilson, Peter J.
    1988   *The Domestication of the Human Species.* Yale University Press, New Haven,
           Conn., and London.

Wittry, W. L.
    1996   Discovering and Interpreting the Cahokia Woodhenges. In *The Ancient
           Skies and Sky Watchers of Cahokia: Woodhenges, Eclipses, and Cahokian Cos-
           mology,* edited by M. L. Fowler. *The Wisconsin Archeologist* 77:26–35.

Wittry, W. L., and J. O. Vogel
    1962   Illinois State Museum Projects. In vol. 1 of *Annual Report: American Bot-
           toms Archaeology, October 1961 to June 1962,* edited by M.L. Fowler, 15–30.
           Illinois Archaeological Survey, Urbana.

Witty, C. O.
    1993   The Fingerhut (11S34/7) Cemetery Three Decades Later. In *Highways to
           the Past: Essays in Illinois Archaeology in Honor of Charles J. Bareis,* edited by
           T. E. Emerson, D. McElrath, and A. J. Fortier. *Illinois Archaeology* 5:425–33.
           Illinois Archaeological Survey, Urbana.

Woods, W. I.
    1977   The Quantitative Analysis of Soil Phosphate. *American Antiquity*
           42:248–52.
    1982   Analysis of Soils from the Carrier Mills Archaeological District. In *The
           Carrier Mills Archaeological Project: Human Adaptations in the Saline Valley,
           Illinois.* Center for Archaeological Investigations, Southern Illinois Uni-
           versity at Carbondale.
    1984   Soil Chemical Investigations in Illinois Archaeology: Two Example Studies. In
           Archaeological Chemistry—III, Advances in Chemistry Series No. 205, edited by J.
           B. Lambert, 67–77. American Chemical Society, Washington, D.C.
    1985   *Archaeological Testing at the Cahokia Mounds Interpretative Center Tract—
           Location II, St. Clair County, Illinois.* Report submitted to Illinois Historic
           Preservation Agency, Springfield.
    1987   Maize and the Late Prehistoric: A Characterization of Settlement Location
           Strategies. In *Emergent Horticultural Economies of the Eastern Woodlands,*
           edited by W. F. Keegan, 273–92. Occasional Papers, no. 7. Center for
           Archaeological Investigations, Southern Illinois University at Carbondale.
    1993a ICT-II Phase II Testing. In *The Archaeology of the Cahokia Mounds ICT-II:
           Testing and Lithics.* Illinois Cultural Resources Study no. 9. Illinois Historic
           Preservation Agency, Springfield.
    1993b A Study of Prehistoric Settlement-Subsistence Relationships in Southwest-
           ern Illinois. In *Proceedings of the First International Conference on Pedo-
           Archaeology,* edited by J. E. Foss, M. E. Timpson, and M. W. Morris,
           175–84. Special Publication, no. 93–03. Agricultural Experiment Station,
           University of Tennessee, Knoxville.
    1995   *Comments on the Black Earths of Amazonia.* Papers and Proceedings of the
           Applied Geography Conferences. Applied Geography Conferences, Den-
           ton, Tex.

Woods, W. I., and G. R. Holley
    1991   Upland Mississippian Settlement in the American Bottom Region. In *Ca-
           hokia and the Hinterlands: Middle Mississippian Cultures of the Midwest,*
           edited by T. E. Emerson and R. Barry Lewis, 46–60. University of Illinois
           Press, Urbana.

Worthen, A. H.
    1866 *Geology of Illinois.* Illinois Geological Survey no. 1. University of Illinois, Urbana.
Yerkes, R. W.
    1989 Mississippian Craft Specialization in the American Bottom. *Southeastern Archaeology* 8:93–196.
Zube, E. H.
    1970 Foreword to *Landscapes: Selected Writings of J. B. Jackson,* edited by E. H. Zube. University of Massachusetts Press, Amherst, Mass.

BIOGRAPHICAL

SKETCHES

Dr. Rinita A. Dalan is an assistant professor of anthropology and earth science at Minnesota State University Moorhead. She is the author of numerous articles on the application of geophysical techniques to archaeological properties. Her research interests focus on geophysical prospection and soil magnetic methods as they apply to landscape research and human/environment interactions.

Dr. George R. Holley is an adjunct assistant professor of anthropology and earth science at Minnesota State University Moorhead. He has conducted archaeological research in the United States (Southeast, Southwest, and Midwest) and Mesoamerica and is the author or coauthor of more than twenty publications. He is currently involved in summarizing the significance of the long-scale mitigation project associated with the construction of MidAmerica Airport near the Cahokia site. His research interests include the analysis of ceramics and settlement patterns.

Associate Professor John A. Koepke is the head of the Department of Landscape Architecture at the University of Minnesota. His scholarship embraces design research involving cultural and ecological relationships, which often deal with the Native American community, thus maintaining a connection to his Ojibwa heritage. His work with archaeological properties has focused on spatial analysis and three-dimensional visualization of ancient sites. As a registered landscape architect in the state of Minnesota, he has many years of diverse professional experience in both private practice and academia.

Harold W. Watters, Jr., is associated with the mine subsidence mapping project conducted jointly by the Department of Geography of Southern Illinois University Edwardsville and the Abandoned Mines Reclamation Division of the Office of Mines and Minerals, Illinois Department of Natural Resources. He has conducted topographic surveys and mapped archaeological sites in southern Illinois, Belize, and Greece and has worked extensively at the Cahokia site. His research interests include historical cartography and the utilization of spatial and three-dimensional computer modeling techniques in archaeological contexts.

Dr. William I. Woods is a professor in the Department of Geography and the director of the Office of Contract Archaeology at Southern Illinois University Edwardsville. All three of his degrees are from the University of Wisconsin-Milwaukee. Since 1970 he has conducted field investigations in the eastern United States, Latin America, and Europe, and he is the author or coauthor of over fifty publications. His research interests focus on prehistoric settlement-subsistence systems, soils and sediments, and paleolandscapes.

INDEX